LEGENDARY LOCALS

OF

PLYMOUTH

MICHIGAN

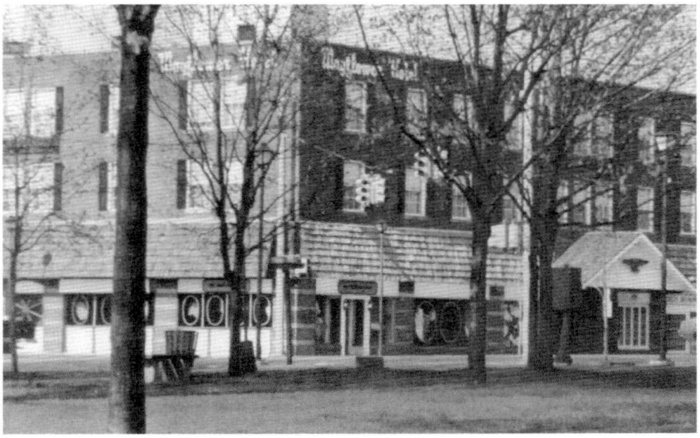

I0806123

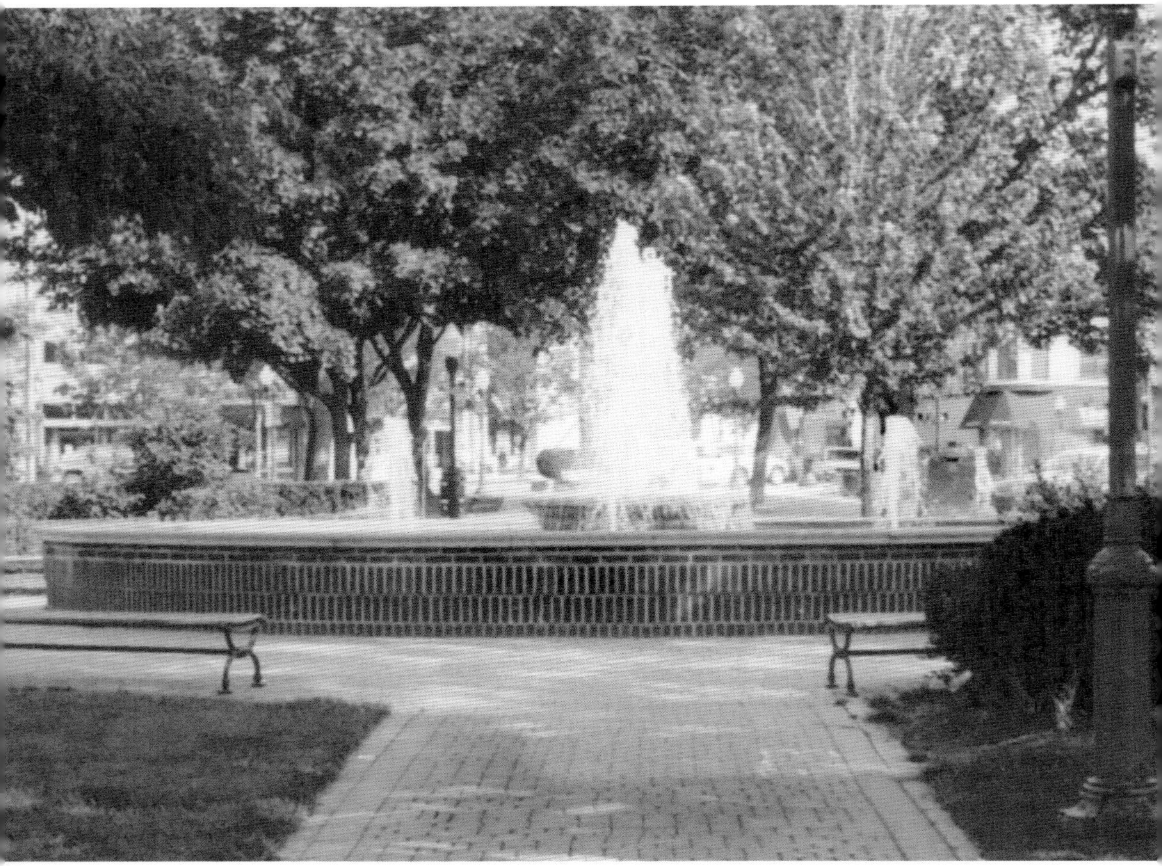

Page 1: **The Mayflower Hotel, Late 1970s.**
The Mayflower Hotel, which stood on the corner of Main Street and Ann Arbor Trail, had for years quite a presence in the community. Its restaurant offered great dining and hosted several celebrities, including Gordie Howe, Diana Ross, and former president George H.W. Bush. The main part of the hotel was demolished in the 1990s, and today the site houses condos, businesses, and a Panera Bread. (Photograph courtesy of Plymouth Historical Museum.)

Page 2: **Kellogg Park Fountain.**
In the heart of downtown Plymouth is Kellogg Park. This beautiful park is the center of much activity for the small city. The fountain is a popular attraction for both young and old, and serves as a charming focal point. Kellogg Park hosts Art in the Park, the International Ice Festival, Music in the Park, and the Fall Festival. (Photograph courtesy of author.)

LEGENDARY LOCALS

OF

PLYMOUTH

MICHIGAN

LEIS DAUZET-MILLER

LEGENDARY LOCALS

ISBN 978-1-4671-0037-3

Legendary Locals is an imprint of Arcadia Publishing
Charleston, South Carolina

Printed in the United States of America

Library of Congress Control Number: 2012940294

For all general information, please contact Arcadia Publishing:
Telephone 843-853-2070
Fax 843-853-0044
E-mail sales@arcadiapublishing.com
For customer service and orders:
Toll-Free 1-888-313-2665

Visit us on the Internet at www.arcadiapublishing.com

Dedication
This book is dedicated to parents and teachers who instill in children a joy and curiosity for learning.

On the Cover: From left to right:
(TOP ROW) Charles Bennett, founder, Daisy Air Rifle (Courtesy of Plymouth Historical Museum, page 29); Margaret Dunning, philanthropist (Courtesy of Plymouth Historical Museum, page 40); Russell Isbister, school superintendent (Courtesy of Plymouth Historical Museum, page 68); Lewis Hanchett Bennett, local business owner (Courtesy of Plymouth Historical Museum, page 29); Margaret Wilson, owner, Penn Theatre (Courtesy of Plymouth Historical Museum, page 98).
(MIDDLE ROW) Phoebe Patterson, judge (Courtesy of Plymouth Historical Museum, page 38); Lewis Cass Hough, original team member, Daisy Air Rifle (Courtesy of Plymouth Historical Museum, page 24); Helen Farrand, teacher (Courtesy of Plymouth Historical Museum, page 61); Ruth Huston Whipple, city commissioner and mayor (Courtesy of Plymouth Historical Museum, page 39); George Henry Wilcox, farmer and business owner (Courtesy of Plymouth Historical Museum, page 22).
(BOTTOM ROW) Sidney Davis Strong, village manager (Courtesy of Plymouth Historical Museum, page 17); Debra Madonna, occupational therapist and educator (Courtesy of Miracle League of Plymouth, page 44); Anna Smith, educator (Courtesy of Plymouth Historical Museum, page 87); Ebenezer Penniman, settler and founder (Courtesy of Plymouth Historical Museum, page 13); Harry Lush, founder, Penn Theatre (Courtesy of Plymouth Historical Museum, page 96).

CONTENTS

ACKNOWLEDGMENTS

I would like to thank Arcadia Publishing for allowing me the opportunity to give back a little something to the community I call home. I will be forever grateful. When I started volunteering as a docent at the Plymouth Historical Society and Museum, I never imagined that I would receive such an opportunity as this. Every time I work at the museum, I am inspired and I walk out thinking how fortunate we are to have such a treasure and a place to record our history. It is true that you get more out of volunteering than you give. A big thank-you goes to the museum for supporting me in this endeavor. Without their faith and trust in me, I'm not sure I would have pursued the chance further.

A personal thank-you goes to Liz Kerstens, executive director of the Plymouth Museum, and Heidi Nielsen, archivist for the museum, for their patience, direction, and time spent with me while putting this book together. I thank you for the privilege. A big thank-you goes to Catherine Hrbal, intern at the museum, whose knowledge of computers and scanning proved priceless; also to intern Paige Wojcik, for pulling information out so diligently and always with a smile. All of you, with your patience and steadfast ways, helped me navigate through this project. This has been quite a journey. It has been at times hard, fun, interesting, and educational, both personally and professionally. I gratefully acknowledge past historians and current recorders of history, whose efforts and contributions cannot go unmentioned. To my husband, Greg, and children, Ava and Nicklas, and to family and friends, I thank you for your love, support, and patience with me throughout this project. I dedicate this book to you.

INTRODUCTION

When spending any amount of time in a small town, one can quickly become enchanted by its history and imagine how things might have been for those who came before. Almost everywhere you go in Plymouth, you encounter history. With its big, old houses on tree-lined streets and buildings housing businesses founded in Plymouth and embedded with old date markers as far back as 1825, it is easy to let your imagination go. Driving beyond the downtown area, you will encounter old schoolhouses, past their original use and now visited by schoolchildren as part of their educational curriculum. Fields still open and used for farming, and a cemetery rich with history and filled with beautiful old grave markers and statues, lend Plymouth an intoxicating charm. It is a great place to learn, love, and live.

The community of Plymouth encompasses the city of Plymouth, the township of Plymouth, Salem and Superior townships, and has working ties with Canton township. The population of the city and township of Plymouth is about 37,000, and the entities cover 18.27 square miles. Plymouth township was settled in 1824, and the city of Plymouth was settled in 1825. They have long histories and offer stories of courage, strength, resilience, and determination. The founders, desiring a name that held relevance and importance, chose Plymouth in honor of the settlers who landed at Plymouth Rock. Plymouth quickly became known for its railroad tracks, which can take a person in all four directions. The railroad business brought industry and helped businesses like Daisy Manufacturing and Markham Air Rifle reach out across the country. Today, trains still run through Plymouth, and citizens and visitors to the area can take in the waiting of a train to pass, as part of the experience that is Plymouth. Henry Ford also left a mark in Plymouth when, during World War II, he made jobs available at the Phoenix Mill Plant, located on Northville Road, to women who needed to support their families or themselves. He was also instrumental in providing a beautiful parkway from Dearborn to Northville. Hines Park is a beautiful, natural setting that provides baseball and soccer fields and picnic areas with tables and barbeque grills. Lakes for canoeing and fishing, and the occasional rest stop, complete the setting. Plymouth boasts several smaller parks, including a water park for children to enjoy in the summer months. Kellogg Park, known in the early days as the Village Green, sits in the center of downtown Plymouth and serves as a hub for civic activity. Sitting in the park, you can watch people and traffic pass by and enjoy an ice cream or a coffee from a nearby shop. Kellogg Park is truly a gem, offering the community a beautiful fountain, a grassy area, and benches. The setting is ideal for festivals, such as Art in the Park, the Summer Concert Series, the Green Street Fair, the Fall Festival, and the Chili Cook-Off. In the winter months, it is a place for ice-carvers during the ever-popular and growing International Ice Festival.

North and east of town is another special place, Old Village. This little community within a community has several businesses such as restaurants, a brewery, an art gallery, and some retail. It also has large, old homes, some of which have been turned into apartments, thus offering a lovely option for both young and old looking for a downtown-living experience. Old Village is also where George Starkweather, the first white child born in Plymouth, was raised, lived, and worked. His home still stands, on the corner of Starkweather and Liberty Streets. Starkweather grew up to be a community and state leader.

Founders and leaders of Plymouth have certainly worked hard to provide its inhabitants with a lovely community, one that thrives with business and the spirit of competition. Today, the community is a nice blend of old and new and, while not without its challenges, continues to press forward.

Throughout Plymouth's long history, women have been instrumental in its success. The community has benefited from female leaders in legislative and judicial circles, local politics, education, philanthropy, and the arts. Reading of their determination and dedication, you may be inspired to do more for your community. Among these amazing women are Phoebe Patterson, one of the first women in Michigan to serve as a justice of the peace and, more currently, Debra Madonna, who works tirelessly for education and children with disabilities.

Education in Plymouth is very important. The Plymouth-Canton Community School district is the third-largest in the state of Michigan. It offers many different program options for students. With sixteen elementary schools, five middle schools, three high schools, an early special education intervention program, an extended-day program, an adult education center, and a continuing education department for recreational and hobby-like classes, it is a big operation. Dedicated teachers and staff make it all possible on a daily basis. For the district, offering progressive and innovative programs while keeping class sizes small and manageable are the keys to success. There are also several private school options available for parents and students. With so many choices and opportunities available, it would seem that one would have to work really hard to fail. In the neighboring community of Livonia is Schoolcraft Community College, which offers a slightly reduced tuition rate for those residing in the community and works closely with the school district in many ways. Schoolcraft College has seen a lot of growth in its programming and recently celebrated its 50th birthday.

Yes, the community of Plymouth is a special one. With beautiful homes and neighborhoods, shops, dining, education, recreation, the arts, and volunteer opportunities, it offers quite a bit in a relatively small package. A combination of city with a little bit of country, it offers visitors gracious lodging in the downtown area and just outside of town. If you ever get the opportunity to visit Plymouth, you are advised to do so. You will not be disappointed.

CHAPTER ONE

Founders and Leaders of Plymouth

Founders and leaders of any area are those who bravely set out to explore and establish a place where they can grow and live their lives. They also take the lead in establishing an area so that others will follow with more opportunities. When William Starkweather set out to make his mark in the world, he did so solely on faith and a trust in himself that it would work. How brave he was. Modern readers can only imagine his trepidation from time to time, but there was little room for self-doubt. There was work to be done, and the days were long and full. Leaders establish permanence and a sense of stability, and it was William Starkweather's brothers George and Samuel who urged the next famous citizen of Plymouth to embark on a journey.

Ebenezer Penniman, on the advice of the Starkweather brothers, set out to make a home for himself and his new wife. In his time spent in Plymouth, he did so much more, and his family that followed also made an impression upon the community. The Penniman name appears throughout the town, in many facets. In the years since, the area has had several prominent leaders, offering their own history, connection, and reasons for wanting to make the community stronger and better.

In Sidney Davis Strong, there was an individual who was obviously dedicated to quality of life. He worked hard to realize many major improvements in the community and exhibited foresight and imagination in planning the direction of the future of Plymouth.

Sanford Burr, whose family can be traced to the 1800s in Plymouth, also contributes greatly to the town with his time and memories, both of which are invaluable.

The founders and first leaders of Plymouth were certainly dedicated and driven. Guiding, planning, and working the area, they succeeded in making better lives for those that would follow. Through the years, that drive and purpose has affected many, and the area has become better for it. Vision and purpose in one life can affect many lives, and today's Plymouth citizens are all proof of that.

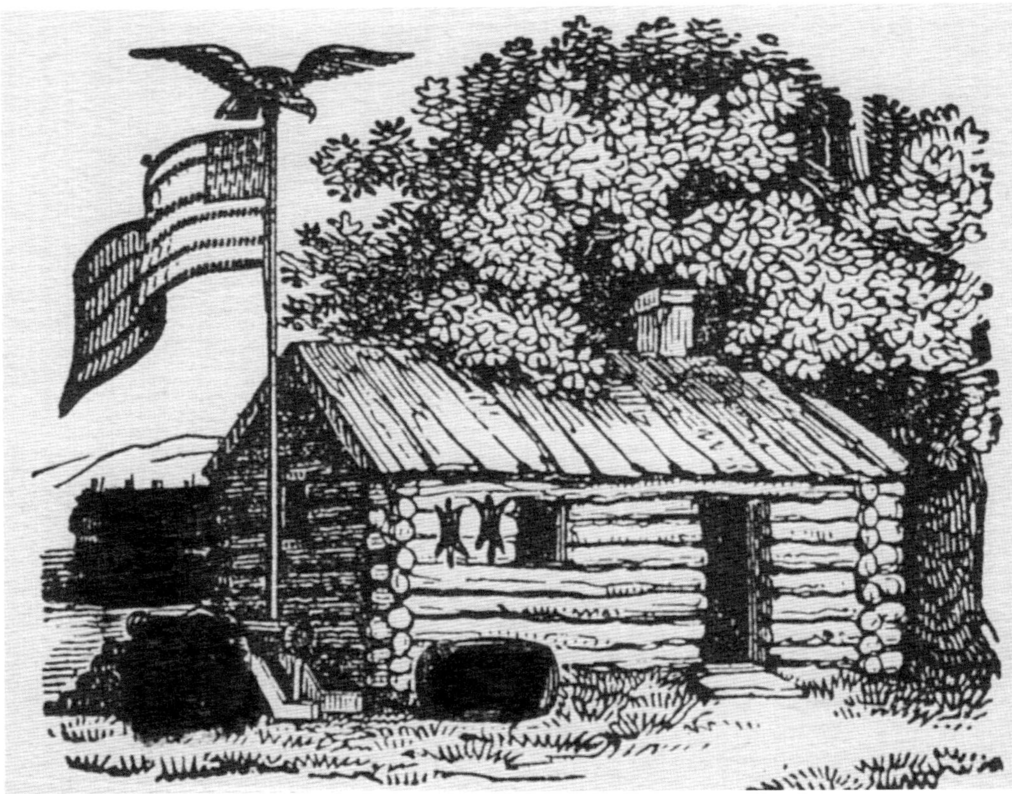

William and Keziah Starkweather.
William and Keziah Starkweather were the first couple recorded to build a home in Plymouth, and the home still stands, on the corner of Starkweather and Liberty Streets in Old Village. William and Keziah were also the first whites to have a child born in Plymouth—a son, George. William lived from 1796 to 1844. There is very little information about Keziah. These pencil etchings were most likely used in a community directory or atlas. The above image is an etching of the first Starkweather home, a log cabin. (Images courtesy of Plymouth Historical Museum.)

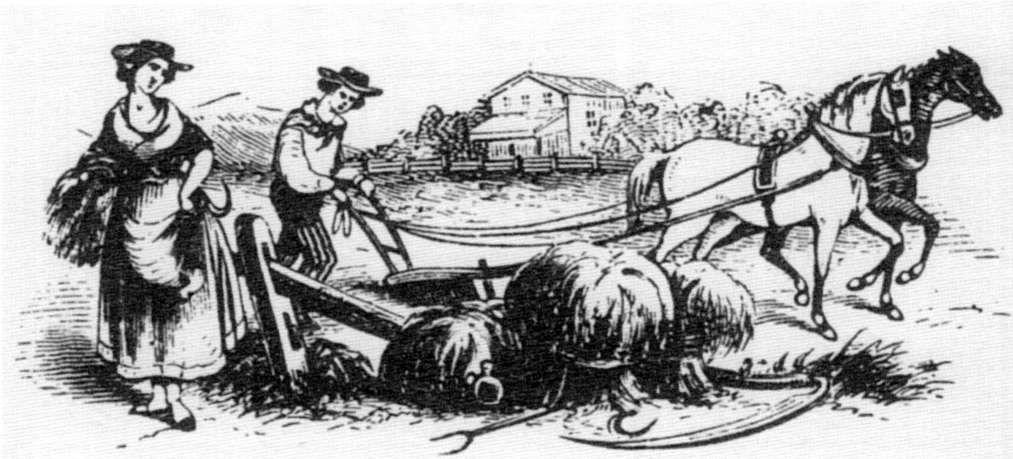

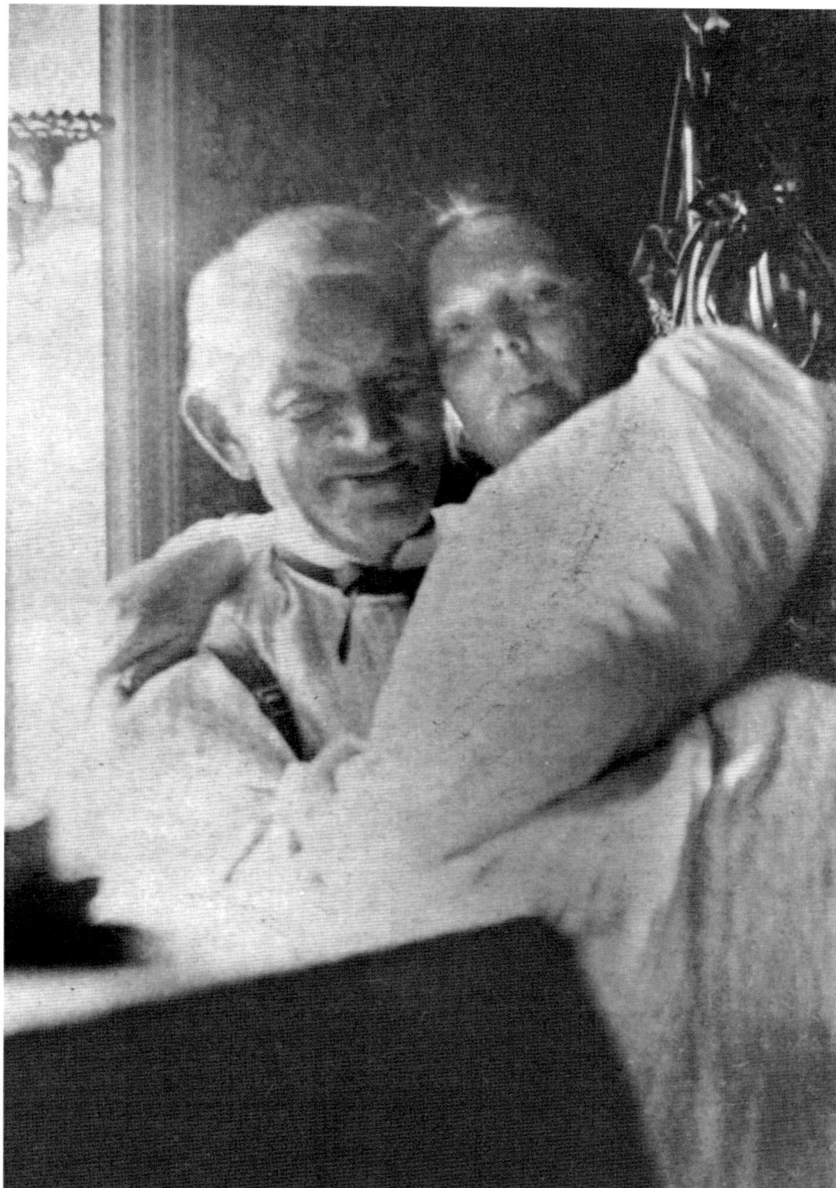

George and Amelia Starkweather, 1901.
George Starkweather was the first white child born in Plymouth. In 1865, George married a girl 18 years his junior, named Amelia. They had two daughters, Mary and Blanche. George became a very successful farmer, businessman, and politician. He owned a general store across the street from Kellogg Park, but he later moved it to Old Village at what is now Starkweather and Liberty Streets. He served as a Michigan legislator in 1854 and as president of Plymouth Village in 1898. George eventually became a prominent lawyer, writing more wills than any other attorney in the county. At the age of 79, George was struck by a trolley car. He survived, and lived another three years, passing away in 1908. (Photograph courtesy of Plymouth Historical Museum.)

The Starkweathers.
Driving through Plymouth, one comes across several streets named in honor of Starkweather family members. Amelia Street is named after George Starkweather's wife, Blanche Street after his daughter, and Rose Street after another member of the family. Starkweather Street, originally known as Oak Street, was renamed by the village council in 1908 shortly after George Starkweather's death. There are many streets in Plymouth named after founding members and leaders, including Roe Street, Penniman Avenue, Wilcox Road, Holbrook Street, and Hamilton Street, to name just a few. (Photographs courtesy of author.)

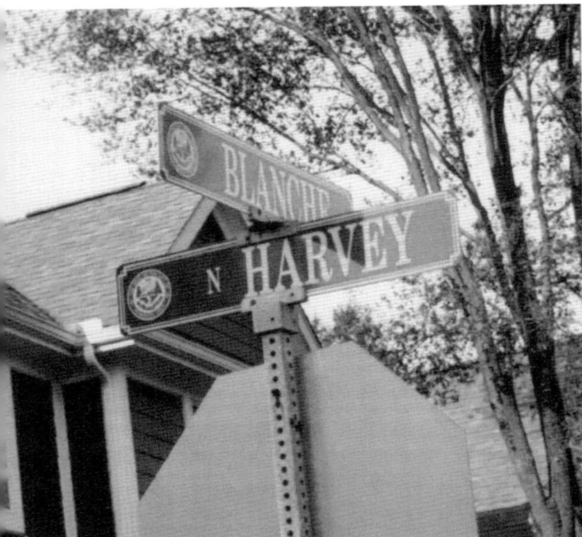

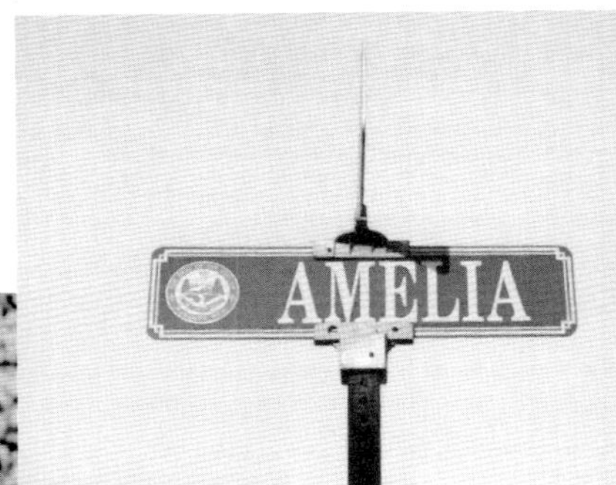

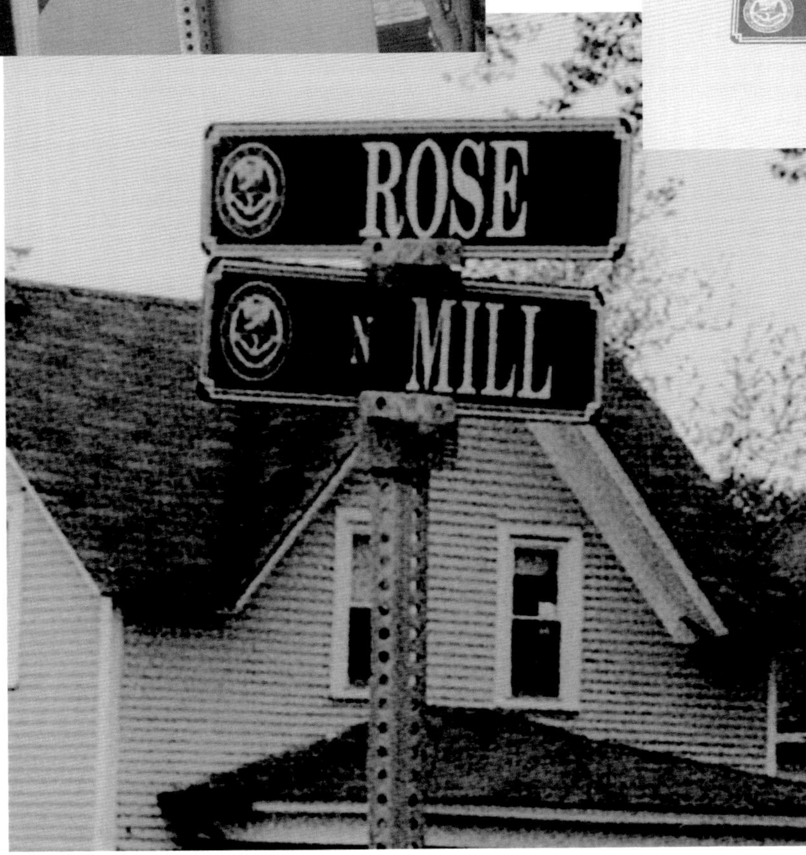

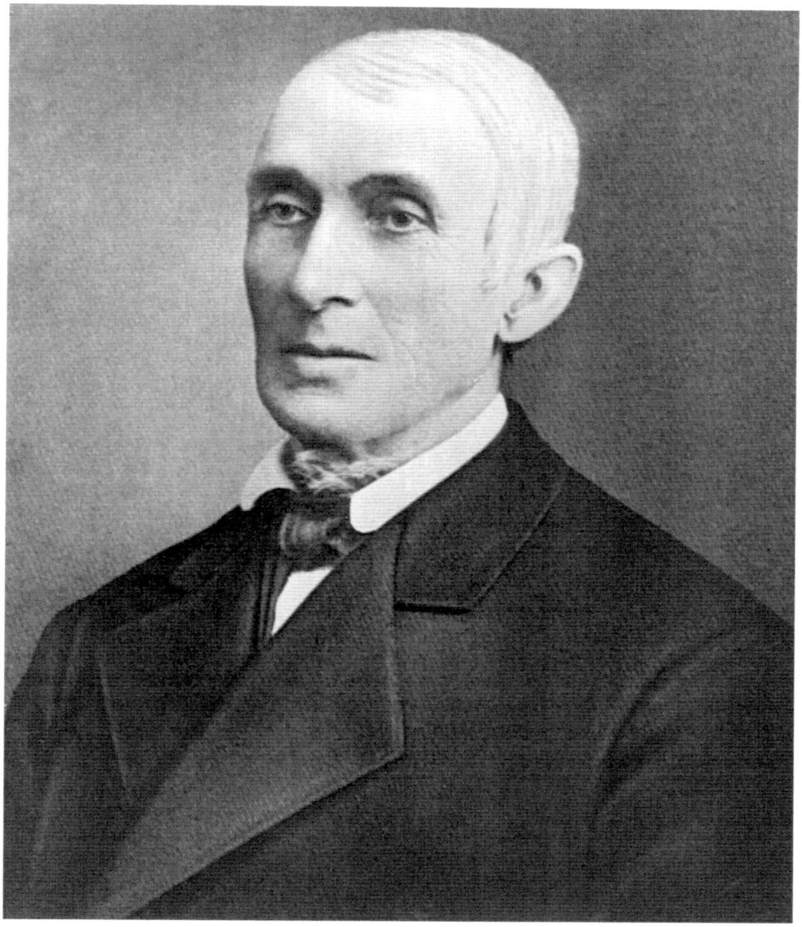

Ebenezer Penniman.
Ebenezer Penniman (January 11, 1804–April 12, 1890) was raised in Lansingburg, New York, and Cooperstown, New York. In his teens, he set out to learn a trade and chose printing. He studied in Keene, New Hampshire, and then moved back to New York in hopes of securing a printing position. The job market was not as good as he had hoped, so he set out for Vermont. There, he met and married his wife. Hearing about Plymouth, Michigan, from his neighbors back home, George and Samuel Starkweather—because their brother William had settled there earlier—Penniman and his wife decided to travel there. So, at the age of 31, in 1835, that is what they did. Today, he, along with William Starkweather, is considered to be one of the area's first settlers. Penniman quickly purchased a sizable parcel of land and began farming. In New York, he had learned enough about the art of trading to eventually establish what became the first bank in Plymouth. Ebenezer was the first president of the National Bank of Plymouth and served in this position until the age of 80, in 1885. It is rumored that, at Christmas, Penniman would pass out quarters at the bank to every child who came in and wished him a Merry Christmas.

Penniman erected a seminary upon his arrival, and for years it stood on Church Street in Plymouth. In 1853, he generously donated the building and the land surrounding it to the school district. Central Middle School stands at that location today.

Penniman was a supervisor of Plymouth township from 1842 to 1844 and again in 1850. He was elected to Congress and served from 1851 to 1853. (Photograph courtesy of Plymouth Historical Museum.)

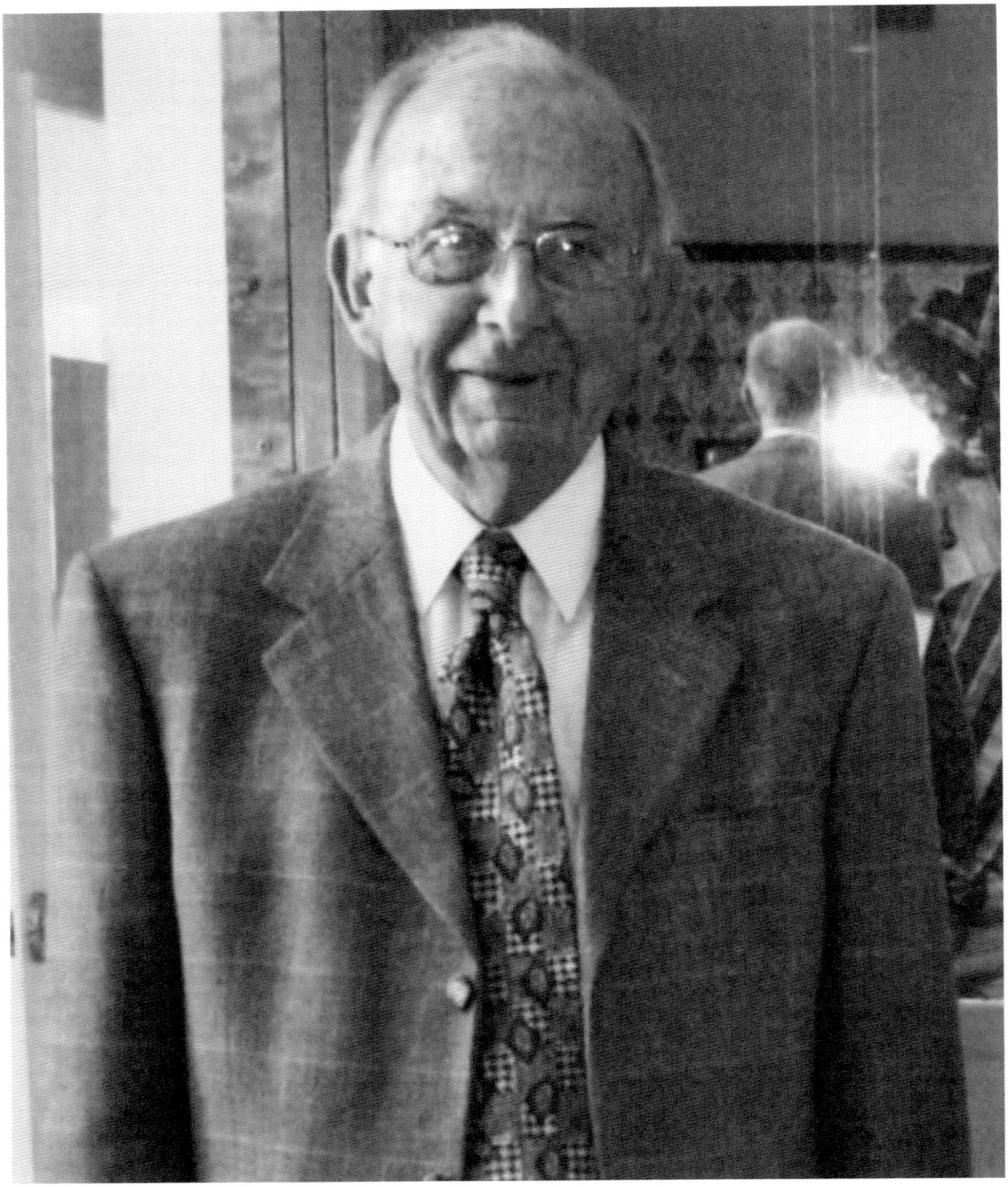

Sanford Burr.
The Burr family has long been associated with Plymouth. They are descended from the Bennett and Lyndon families, both of which were early settlers to the area. In the 1800s, Caleb Lyndon walked from Monroe County, New York, to Plymouth, Michigan. His goal was to seek out parcels of land for the family. In 1826, he purchased 320 acres. Caleb then walked back to New York, dying soon after. His son, Samuel, came to the area in 1833 to look after the property his father had purchased. Samuel farmed the property, raised his family, and buried two wives while living in Plymouth. Sanford Burr and his sister, Margaret, are descended from Samuel's third wife. Sanford, shown here, was born in 1926. (Photograph courtesy of Plymouth Historical Museum.)

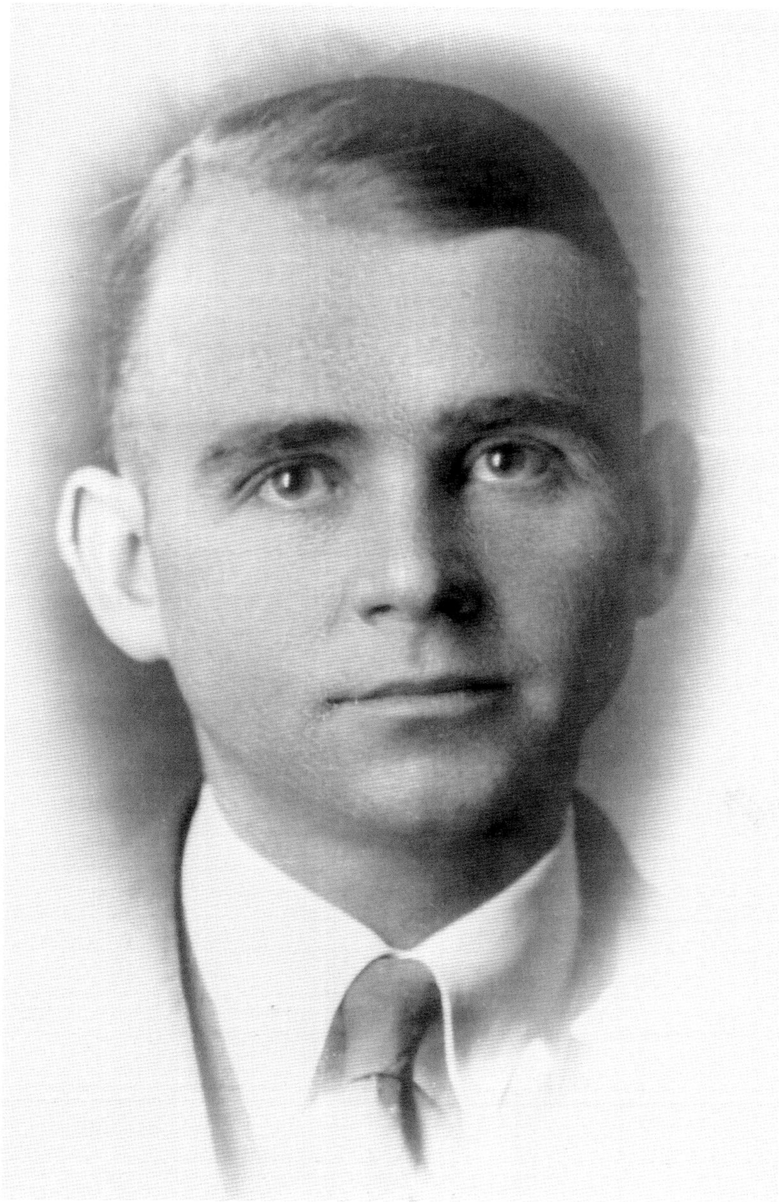

George Burr, 1937.
George Burr, Sanford and Margaret's father, worked, lived, and raised his family in Plymouth. George worked many years for the Wayne County Road Commission, served on the Plymouth-Canton School Board for 16 years, was president of the Plymouth Kiwanis Club, and was an active member of the Historical Society of Michigan. While working for the road commission, Burr rescued a coworker, a Mr. Benjamin, from a gas explosion. George sustained serious burns; his children remember having limited visits with him while he recuperated. He eventually made a full recovery and went back to work, having come out stronger and more determined to get things done. (Photograph courtesy of Plymouth Historical Museum.)

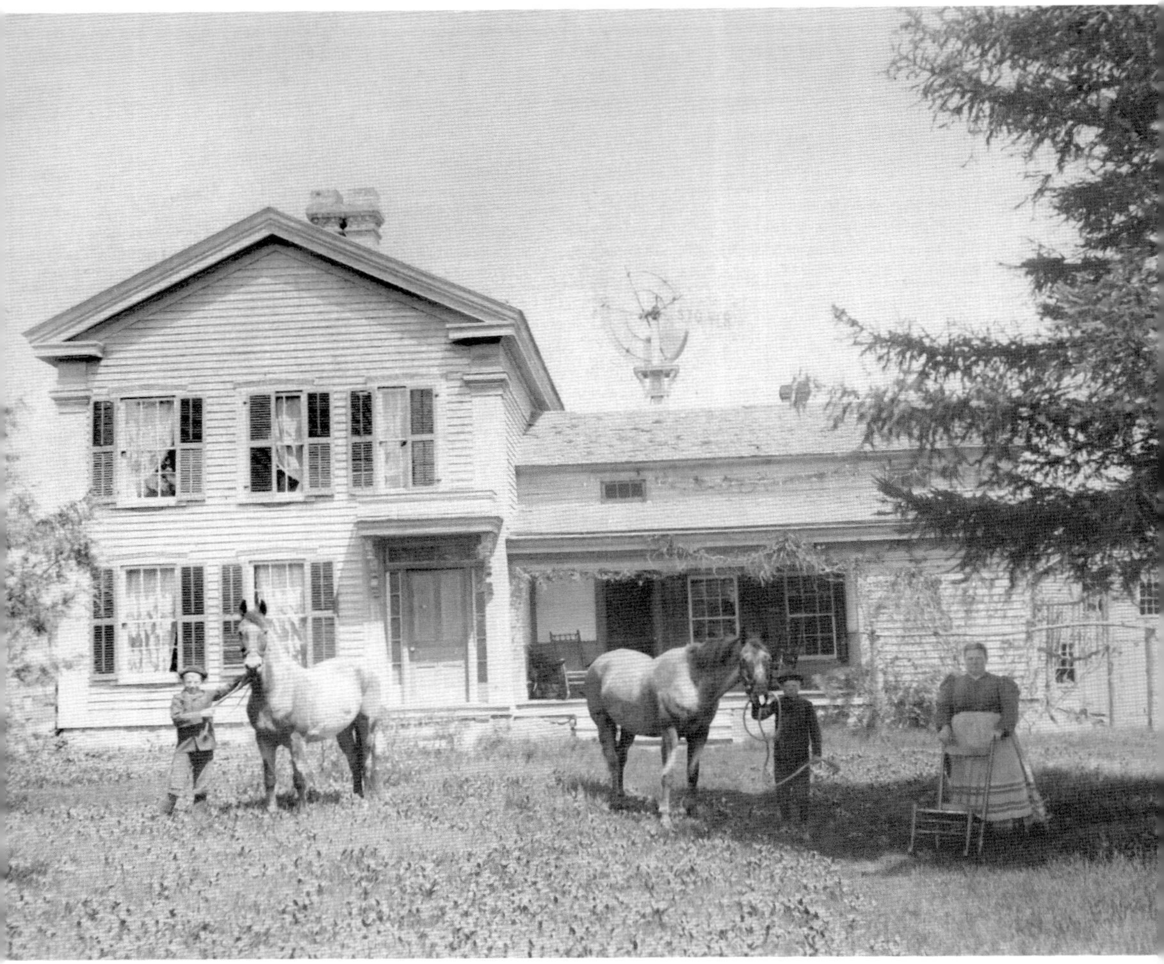

Burr Farmhouse, 42350 East Ann Arbor Trail, Early 1900s.
In 2007, Sanford Burr was recognized as volunteer of the year by the historical society. In 2008, Plymouth mayor Phil Purcell declared July 10 the official commemoration day of Sanford for his lifelong contributions to the area. In 1951, Sanford married Ruth. They had two sons, both of whom now live in Coldwater, Michigan, and are very active in the community, particularly with the Tibbits Opera House. Ruth Burr was a teacher at West Middle School. She passed away on November 11, 2011. Today, Sanford and his sister, Margaret, carry on the family tradition and stay active in the community, especially with the Plymouth Historical Society. The Sanford Burr Meeting Room in the Plymouth Historical Museum honors this great contributor to the community. The house and land were once owned by Ambrose Burr. (Photograph courtesy of Plymouth Historical Museum.)

Sidney Davis Strong.
Sidney Davis Strong (seated in truck) earned a bachelor of arts degree from Kalamazoo College and then a bachelor's in engineering from the University of Michigan. In 1909, he married Alice Vincent, and they had five children together—Alan, Elizabeth, Jean, Richard, and Edward. In 1920, Sidney became only the second city manager for the village of Plymouth. During his time as manager, he oversaw creation of a new water pump, reservoir, lights, and sanitary sewers, and he remodeled the village hall. In 1924, he designed the first official village seal, and he pushed to get some local streets paved. Sidney is pictured here being the first man to drive Plymouth's brand-new fire truck in 1925. The other two men are unidentified. (Photograph courtesy of Plymouth Historical Museum.)

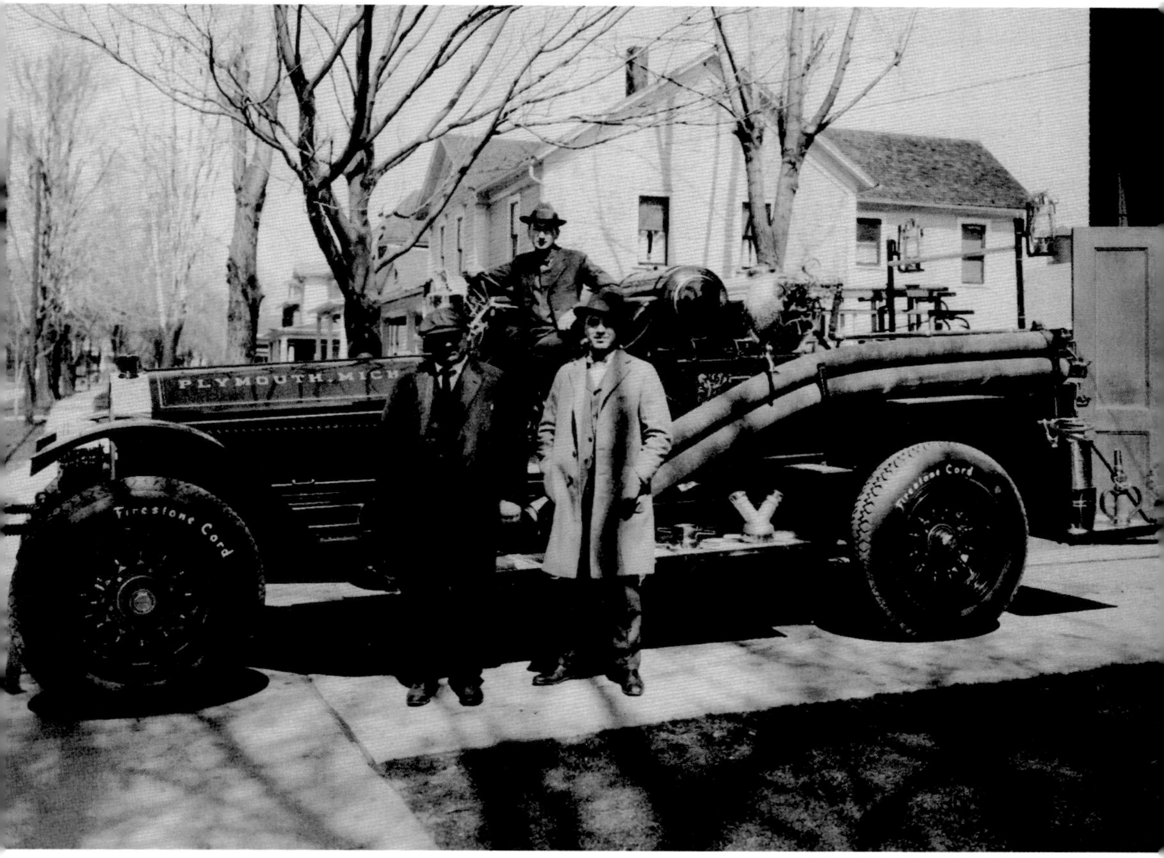

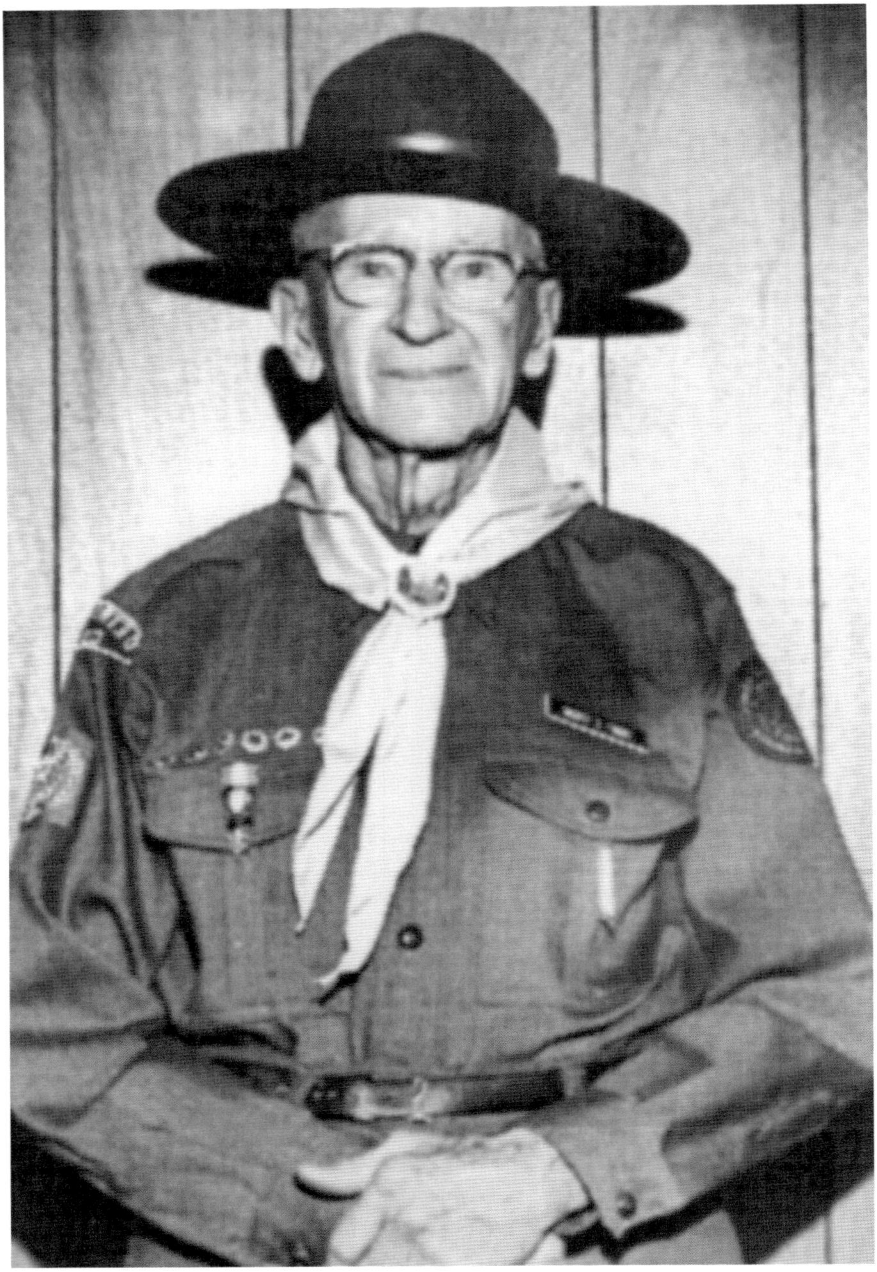

Sidney Davis Strong in Scout Uniform.
In 1927, after a seven-year run, Strong decided to resign as city manager, stating simply, "Too much politics." He then went into private practice. In 1938, he served on the city planning commission and board of review. In 1948, he became a member of the Plymouth Historical Society. He retired from his profession in 1967 at the age of 83. He is also responsible for introducing the Boy Scouts of America to Plymouth. Upon his retirement and before his death, he celebrated 50 years of Scouting. Strong was born in 1884 and died in 1969 at the age of 85. (Photograph courtesy of Plymouth Historical Museum.)

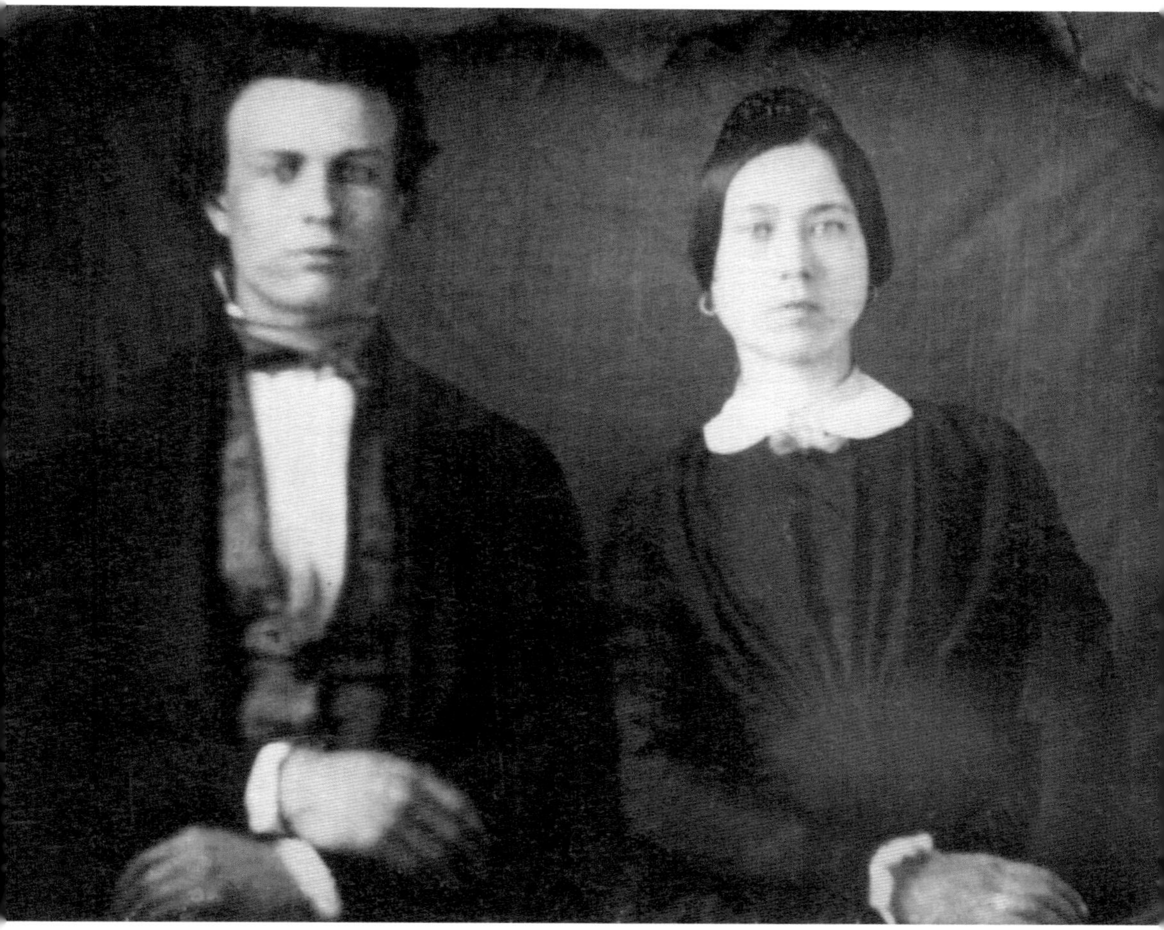

Orson Polley.
An early settler of Plymouth, Orson Polley held the important job of blacksmith. His business stood at the current site of Plymouth City Hall, and where his home stood is now the location of the Plymouth Museum. The skills of a blacksmith were vital to any community just establishing itself. People relied on the blacksmith to build, fix, or repair anything made from iron. A blacksmith would have made nails for building, tools for working, door handles, pans, hinges, and gates. Polley's house was just across the street from his business, as was typical of blacksmiths, being often called upon at all times of the day and night. The business would not have been attached to the residence because of the risk of fire. In many towns, blacksmiths held positions of authority because they were deemed smart, skilled, and good at business. Polley is pictured here with his wife, Margaret. (Photograph courtesy of Plymouth Historical Museum.)

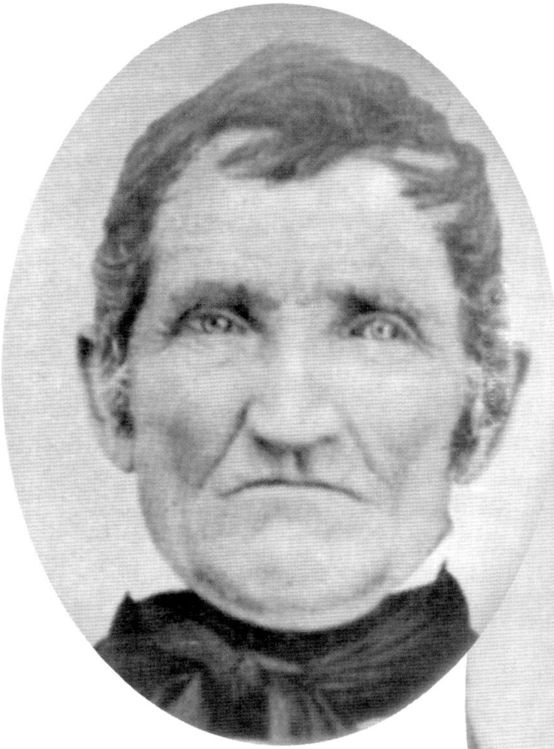

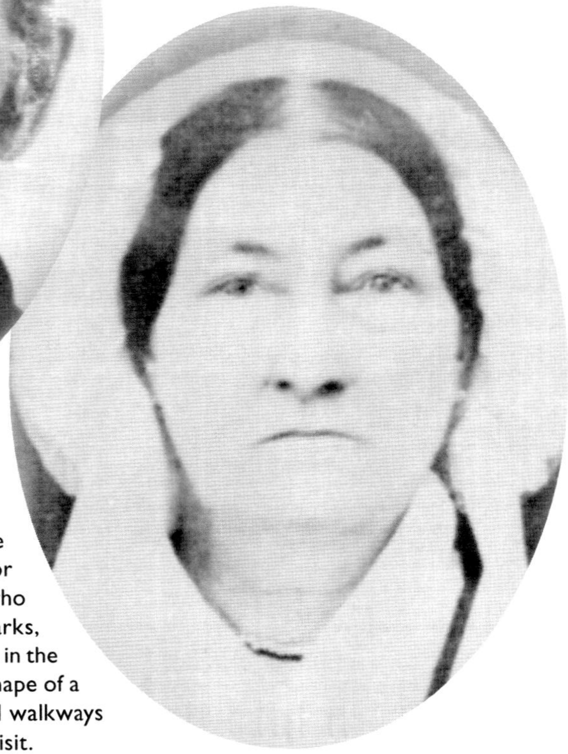

John Kellogg.
John Kellogg settled in Plymouth in 1834. He purchased land at $1.25 an acre, which today makes up the city of Plymouth. In 1835, he started mapping the area and laid out plans for business and residential lots, selling to those who were interested. He also donated land for parks, churches, and schools. Today, Kellogg Park sits in the center of town in his honor. Laid out in the shape of a triangle, Kellogg Park has beautiful tree-lined walkways and a fountain, which young and old love to visit.

Kellogg Park, for years called the Village Green, has always been a center of activity for the city. During the Civil War, soldiers would meet on the green and start their long journeys to battle. John, a soldier in the War of 1812, also built and ran a hotel for years, which sat on the corner of Main Street and Ann Arbor Trail. He is pictured here around 1865 with his wife, Eleanor (Faurot) Kellogg. (Photographs courtesy of Plymouth Historical Museum.)

CHAPTER TWO

Business Owners

Next to owning a home, having one's own business is, for many people, part of the American dream. Through hard work, perseverance, and a vision, a citizen can create the company he or she always wanted. The men featured in this chapter are no exception, but instead are the rule to follow. Men like the Houghs, Bennetts, and William Markham employed people from the city and beyond, making Plymouth a town to note. These men also made their fortunes and marks upon the world. Providing jobs for people, on a small scale or large, is a mighty responsibility. To be the owner of a company, one has to be tough, fair, democratic, sympathetic, a teacher, a leader, a janitor, a banker, a lawyer, a judge, a good listener, and an effective communicator. It is a tall order, but men like the Schraders of Plymouth have been successful in business for many decades. Originally furniture salesmen, the Schrader brothers changed careers and started the Schrader Funeral Home. The funeral home has been a consistent presence in the community, helping numerous families during difficult times with style, grace, and professionalism.

Entrepreneurs are driven and have dreams of what they want their products to be, how these products are to be represented, and what they will do to improve the lives of those around them. Harold Guenther, another successful entrepreneur, started CD Sparling. The company is devoted to a quality of life and a sense of independence, providing products for the aging and those with physical challenges. The CD Sparling Company has been a constant in the community of Plymouth for a number of years.

Throughout its history, Plymouth has seen the ebb and flow of trends and eras, but the entrepreneurial spirit is always strong and welcomed. In this chapter, readers will learn about Ralph Lorenz, a lifelong resident and business owner who for years operated the grand Mayflower Hotel, welcoming guests from other states and other countries to his establishment. They will also learn a little about George Wilcox, whose family name is synonymous with Plymouth, and Dr. Peck, who delivered many of Plymouth's residents. If readers are considering starting their own businesses or have only dreamed about it, the hope is that the stories in the following pages will offer inspiration.

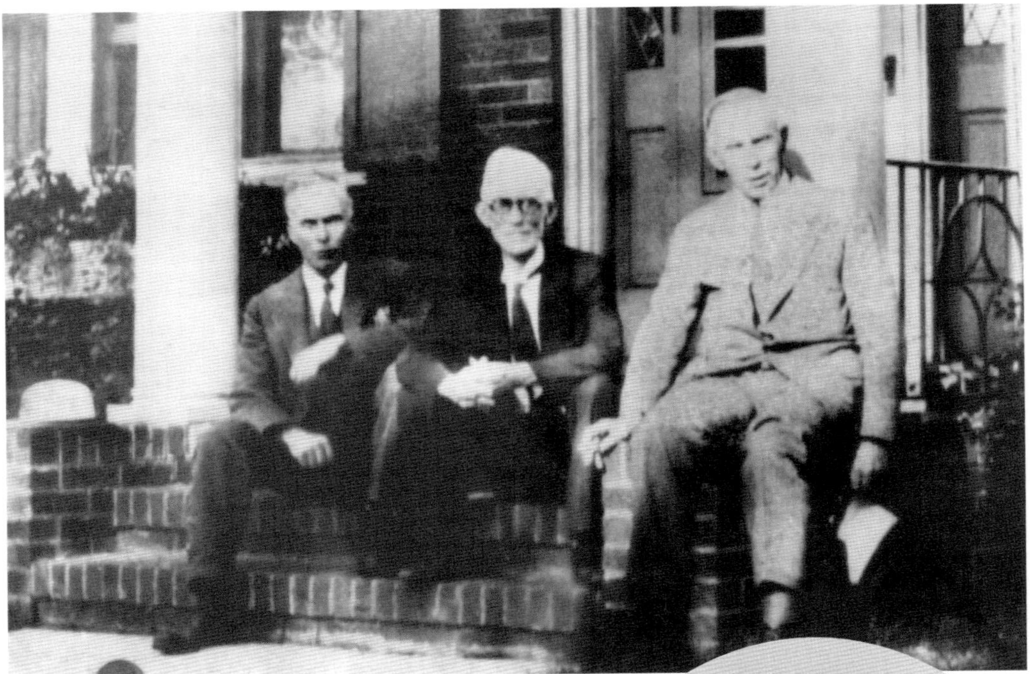

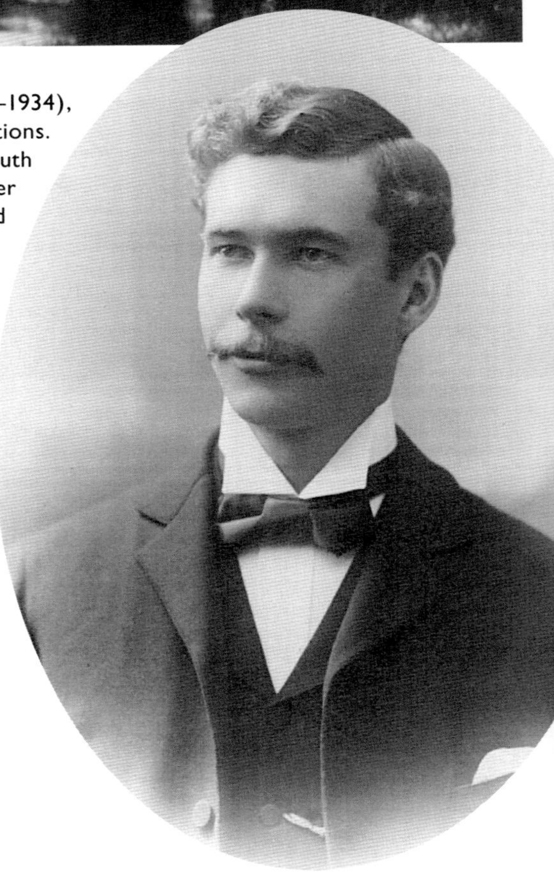

George Henry Wilcox III.
The family of George Henry Wilcox III (1873–1934), pictured at right, can be traced back 10 generations. David Bailey Wilcox, George's father, lived in Plymouth but owned a drugstore in Holly, Michigan. He later opened a hardware store in Detroit. In 1879, David Bailey purchased a flour mill in Plymouth. He worked there until his death in 1902. He married Elizabeth Ovenshire and together they had four children—Clinton, Mary, John, and George. George went on to run the mill and eventually married Harriet Kelsey Hill in 1909. They raised three children in the area—Julie, Katherine, and Jack. For years, the Wilcox family lived in the Markham house near Kellogg Park in downtown Plymouth. In 1926, George sold land to the Woodward Theater Company. It is where the Penn Theater now stands. Pictured above in the 1950s are George Henry Wilcox II (left), Clinton Wilcox (center), and John C. Wilcox. (Photographs courtesy of Plymouth Historical Museum.)

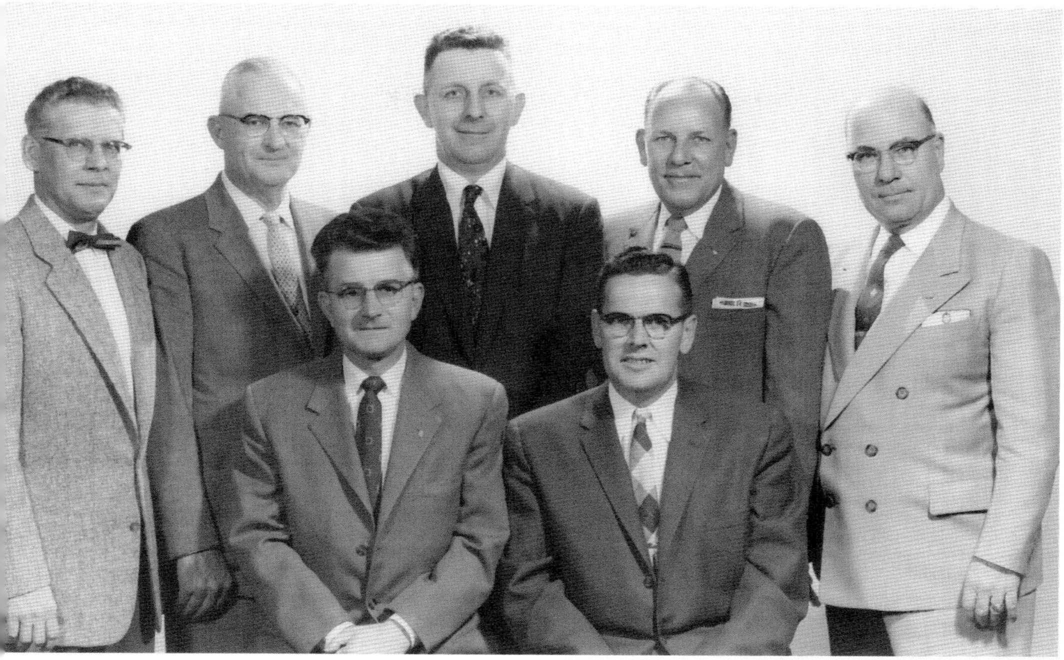

Harold Guenther.
Harold Guenther was the owner and founder of CD Sparling. Founded in 1949, the CD Sparling Company has been around for almost 65 years. The company makes equipment for showers and tubs that make it safer for older loved ones to live independently. CD Sparling works with nursing homes, retirement villages, and hospitals. Along with his business, Guenther served two terms on the city commission, from 1954 to 1961 and then again from 1969 to 1975. He also served as mayor of Plymouth from 1959 to 1961 and was chairman of the city's parking commission. He is pictured here (seated, left) while serving on the city commission in the 1960s. (Photograph courtesy of Plymouth Historical Museum.)

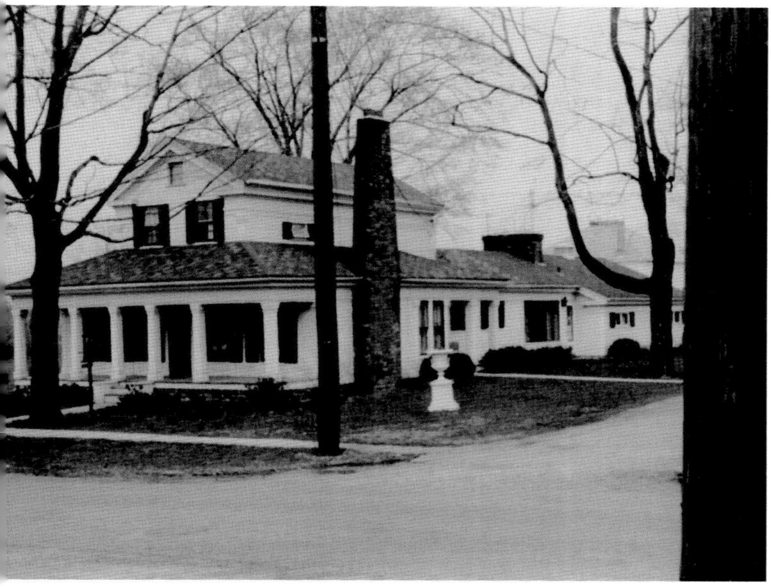

Guenther Home.
Harold Guenther and his wife, Geneva, lived in the old Wilcox house at 1142 Holbrook, pictured here, for 50 years. Geneva remained there until her death in 2005. (Photograph courtesy of Plymouth Historical Museum.)

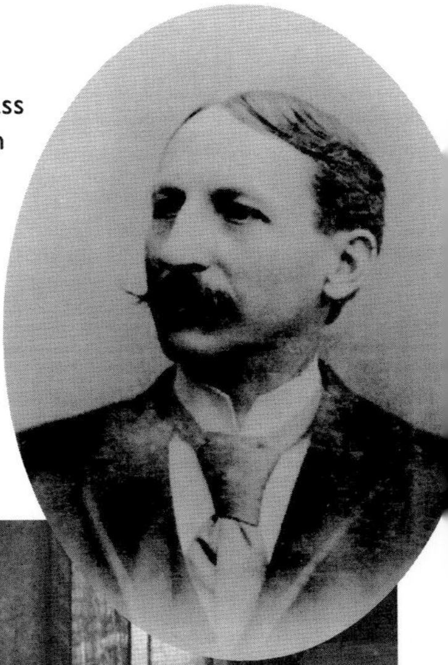

Lewis Cass Hough.
Lewis Cass Hough, father of Edward C. Hough and grandfather of Cass Hough, was considered part of the original Daisy team. Hough invested in what was known as Plymouth Iron Windmill, which later became Daisy Air Rifle. Hough instilled a strong work ethic and civic responsibility in his family. Daisy Manufacturing grew to become a big business in the area and employed many people. The Daisy Air Rifle has enjoyed great success; to date, it is the most popular BB gun in the world, selling over nine million units since its introduction to the market in the late 1940s. (Photograph courtesy of Plymouth Historical Museum.)

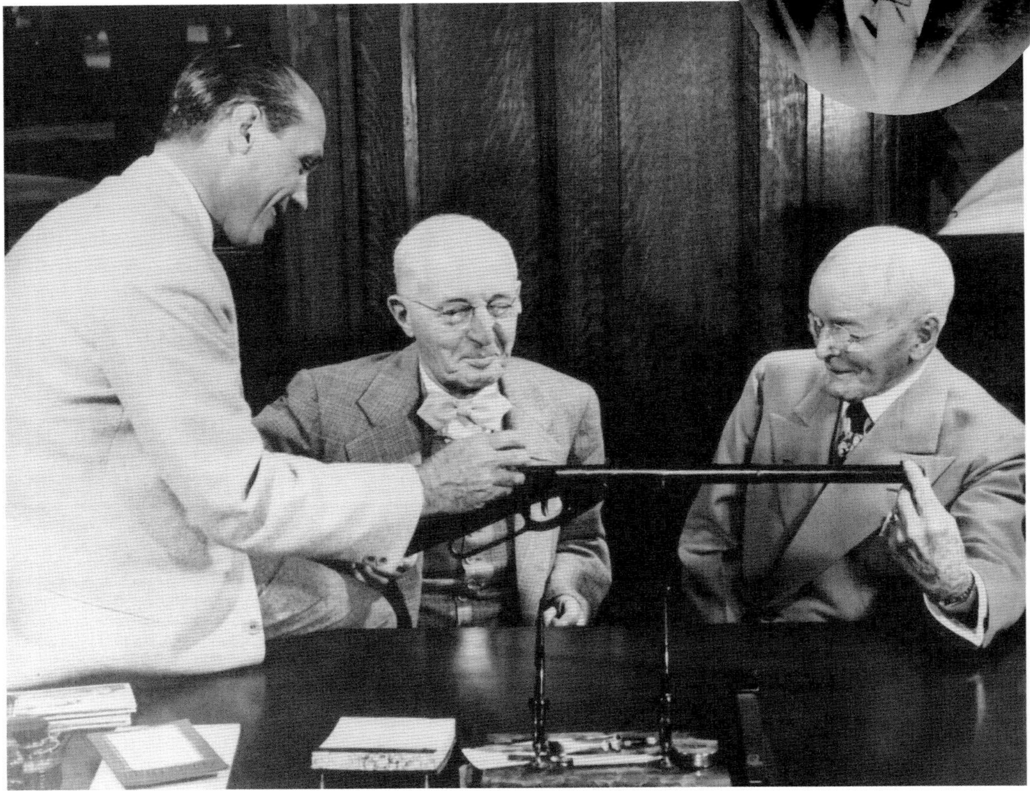

Edward C. Hough.
Edward C. Hough helped to put Plymouth on the map when he introduced millions of young boys to the Daisy Air Rifle, a toy now celebrated each Christmas in the movie *A Christmas Story*. Hough began working for Daisy upon graduation from high school. In 1902, he was appointed treasurer, and 13 years later became vice president. Like his friend Charles Bennett, Hough learned hard work and the skill of owning a business from his father, Lewis Cass Hough. Shown here in 1956 are Cass Hough (left), Edward C. Hough (center), and Charles Bennett at the Daisy offices. In business for many years together, these three gentlemen made a great team and were considered industry giants. (Photograph courtesy of Plymouth Historical Museum.)

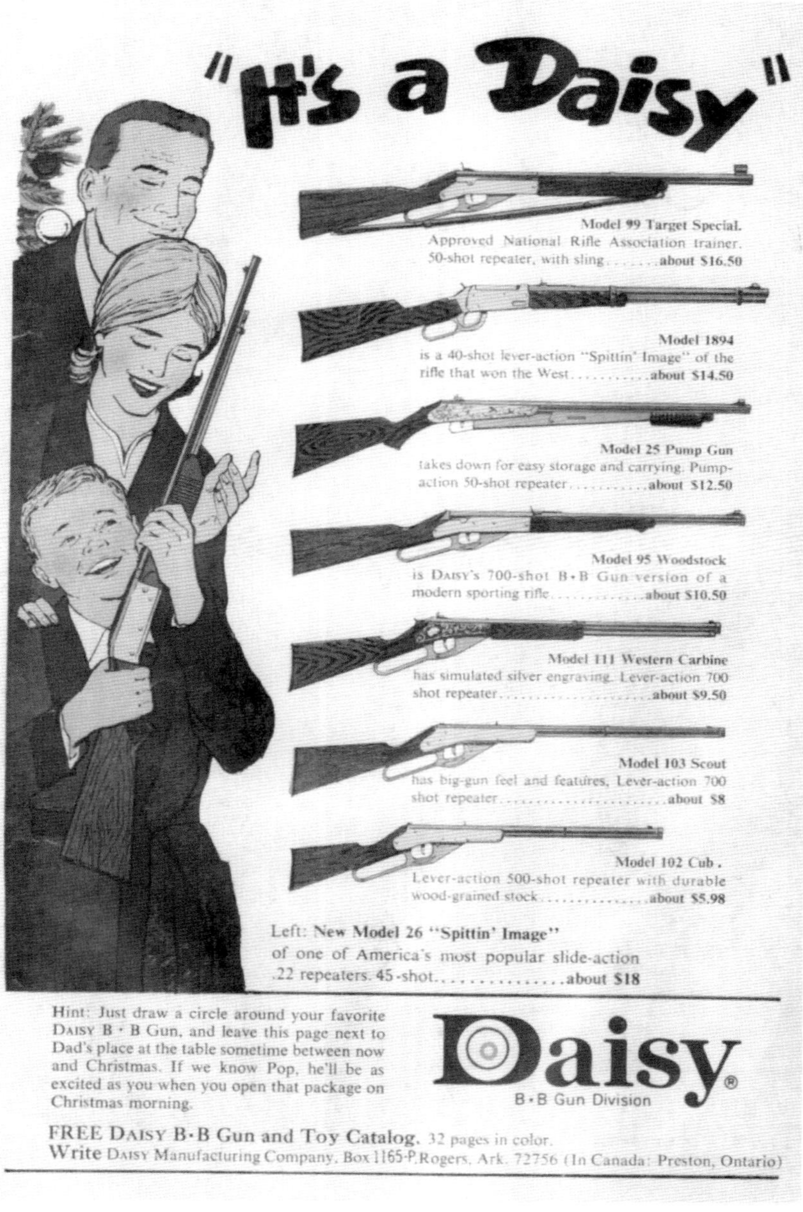

Daisy BB Gun Advertisement from an Archie comic book, 1956.
In 1956, Charles Bennett, president and founder of Daisy, died, and Ed Hough was named president of the company. He remained with the company until his death in 1959. A civic leader and philanthropist, Hough established the Hough Kimball Foundation and donated greatly to the local library. The foundation made available a number of grants and helped support many civic purposes and activities. He was also a member of the Plymouth Rotary Club, founded in 1924. A friend of Henry Ford, Hough also donated a number of historical items throughout his life to Greenfield Village in Dearborn, Michigan. Cass Hough moved the company forward with advertising, using celebrities to target the product's market audience. (Courtesy of Plymouth Historical Museum.)

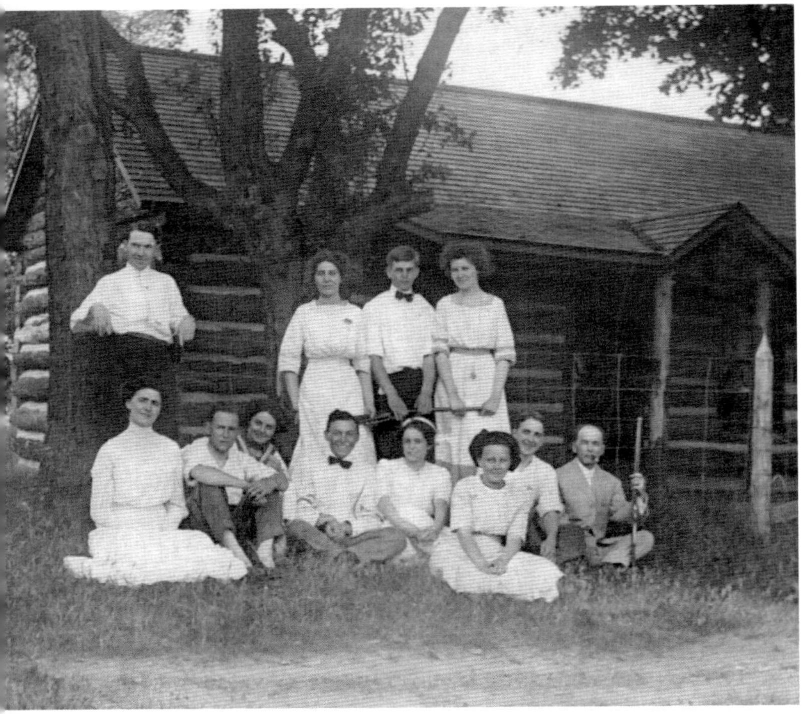

Hough Family Log Cabin, 1910.
The Hough log cabin, which once stood on the corner of Warren and Haggerty Roads, was rebuilt in 1904 by second-generation Houghs to honor the memory of their earlier family members. The original burned down in 1835. Ira Marshall Hough, the builder of the original log cabin, was the grandfather of Edward C. Hough. Where the log cabin once stood is now home to industrial buildings and businesses, on the border of Plymouth and Canton. (Photograph courtesy of Plymouth Historical Museum.)

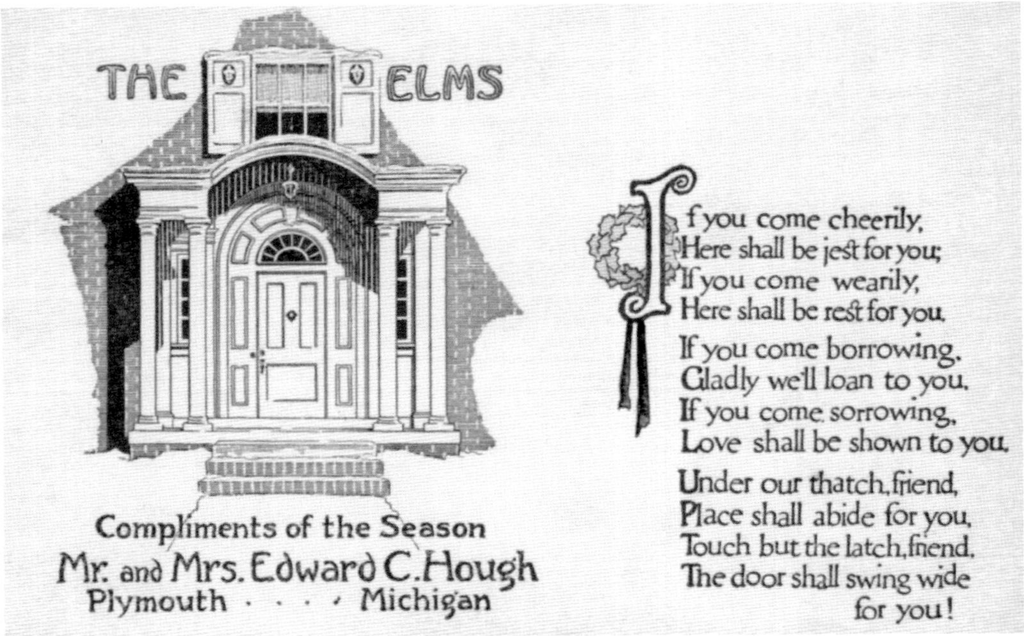

Christmas Greeting from Edward and Louise Hough, 1912.
Edward C. Hough married Louise Sheffield in October 1896, and the couple had three children—Cass, Corette, and Marie. Louise died in 1943. Edward was born in 1872 and died in 1959 at the age of 87. (Card courtesy of Plymouth Historical Museum.)

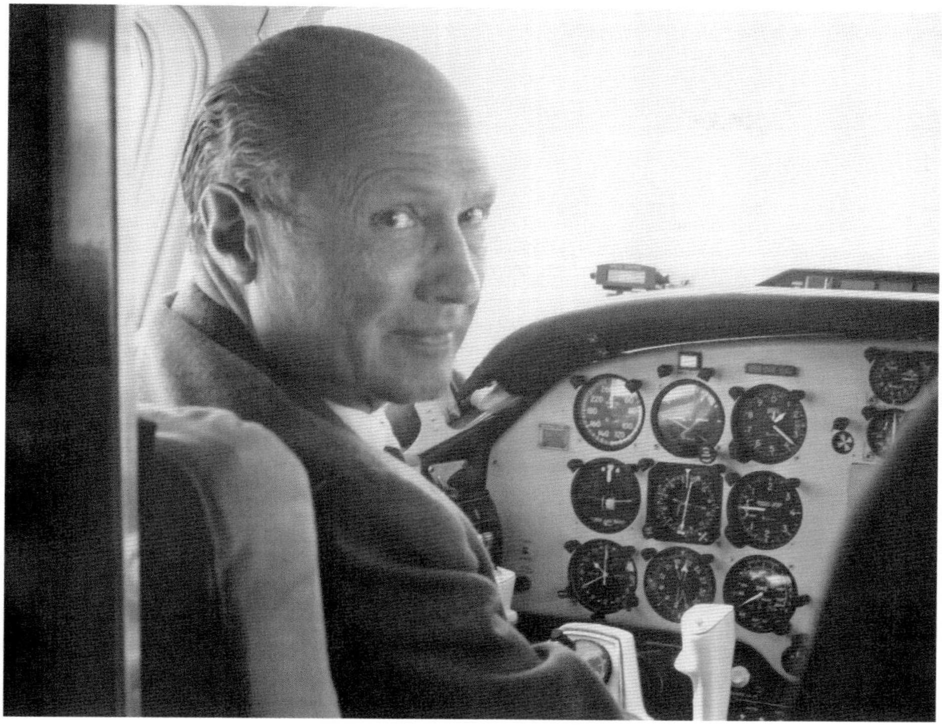

Cass S. Hough.
Cass S. Hough (October 4, 1904–September 1990), son of Edward C. Hough, succeeded his father in 1959 as president of Daisy Air Rifle. In 1975, he became president of Victor Recreation Products, when Daisy was sold to that company. He retired one year later, when Victor was acquired by Kiddie, Inc., a company based in New Jersey. Cass was with the Daisy Company for 50 years. He attended college at the University of Michigan and, shortly after graduating, was offered a position as a teacher of astronomy. He taught for one year, and in 1926 joined his father at Daisy. Between 1934 and 1940, the marketing strategies and techniques began to change at Daisy, largely due to Cass. He realized the value of working with famous personalities to promote a product. In 1957, Cass decided to move the Daisy Company to Roger's City, Arkansas. During his time in Plymouth, Cass served on the city commission and was mayor in the 1950s. An avid pilot, Cass is pictured here in the 1980s in the cockpit of an airplane. (Photograph courtesy of Plymouth Historical Museum.)

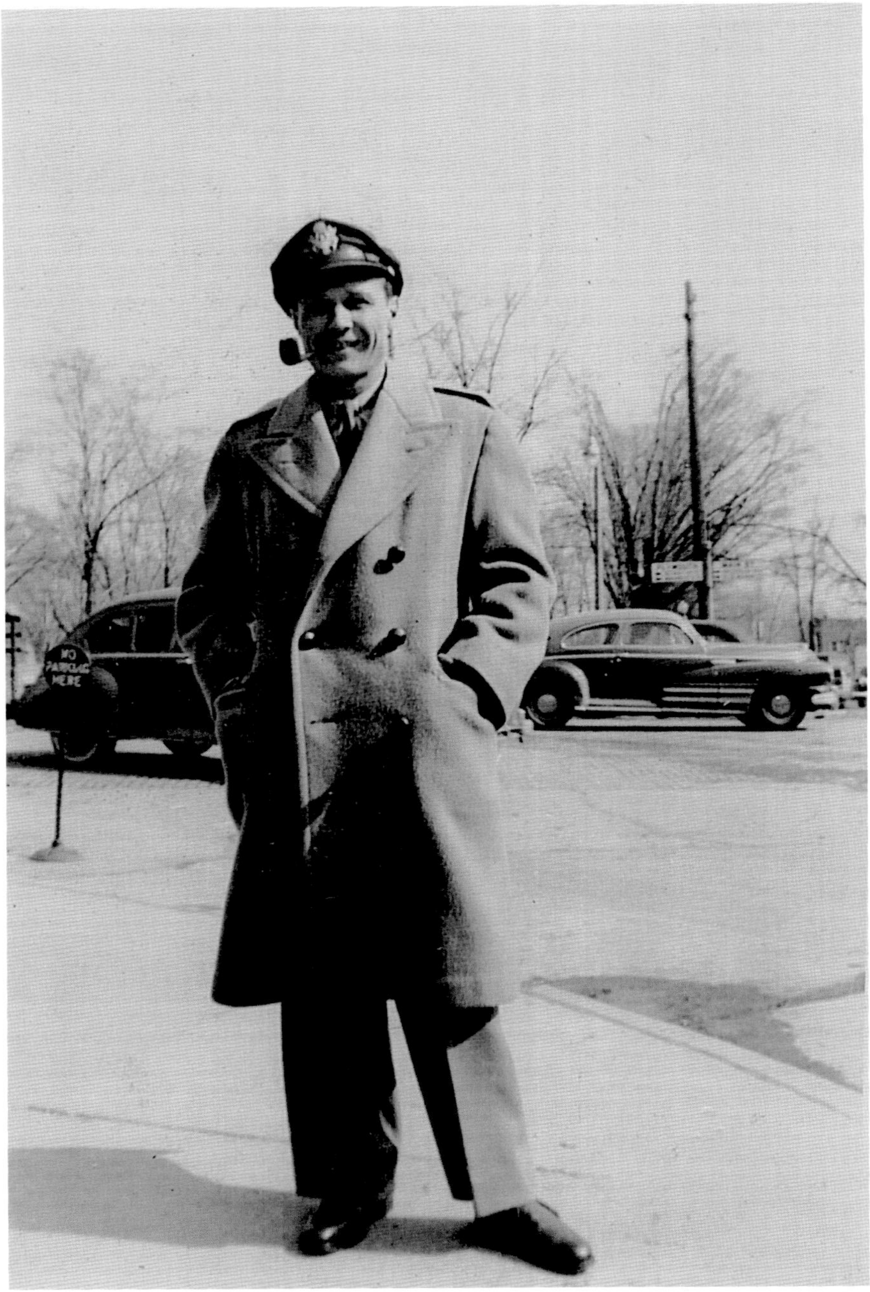

Lt. Col. Cass S. Hough, March 12, 1943.
Along with his role as businessman, Cass S. Hough served in World War II as a pilot. He set a world record for flight in the 1940s, successfully traveling faster than the speed of sound. The test flight provided invaluable technical information that helped in the war effort. He was awarded the Distinguished Flying Cross for his achievement by the War Department. (Photograph courtesy of Plymouth Historical Museum.)

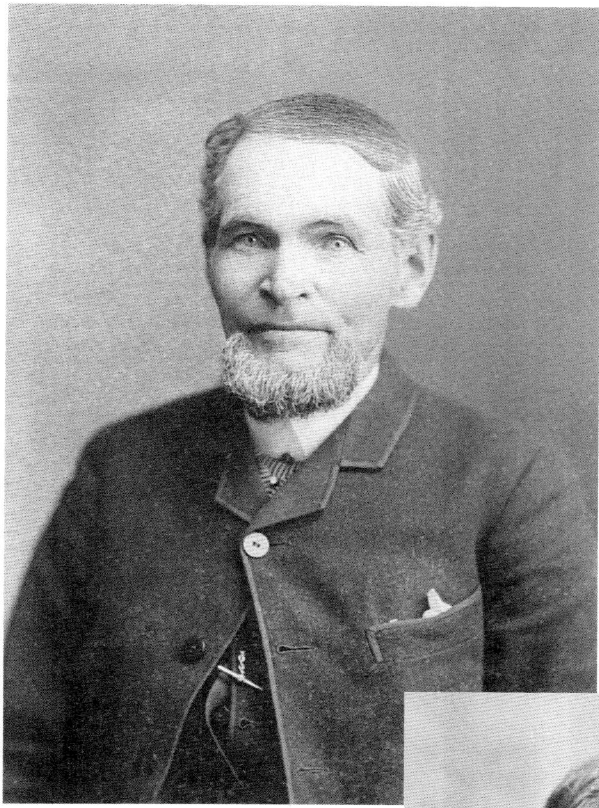

Charles and Lewis Bennett. Charles Bennett (below), son of Lewis Hanchett (left) and Caroline Bennett, was born in Plymouth on June 27, 1863. He was destined to run a business, working for his father at a young age in the Fanning Mill Factory, which was located at Main and Union Streets in downtown Plymouth during the 1860s. The Fanning Mill is considered to be the first factory in Plymouth. Bennett later became a founding member of Daisy Air Rifle, which at one time was known as Plymouth Iron Windmill. He traveled the world promoting Daisy and its products and setting up distribution. Known as the "salesman," he was well liked and respected. In 1912, Bennett became president of Daisy and was with the company for 44 years. (Photographs courtesy of Plymouth Historical Museum.)

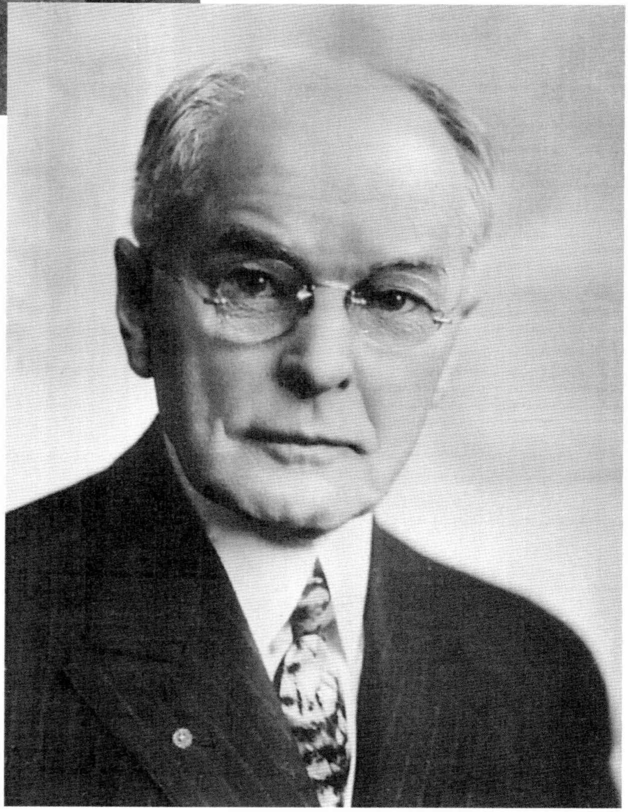

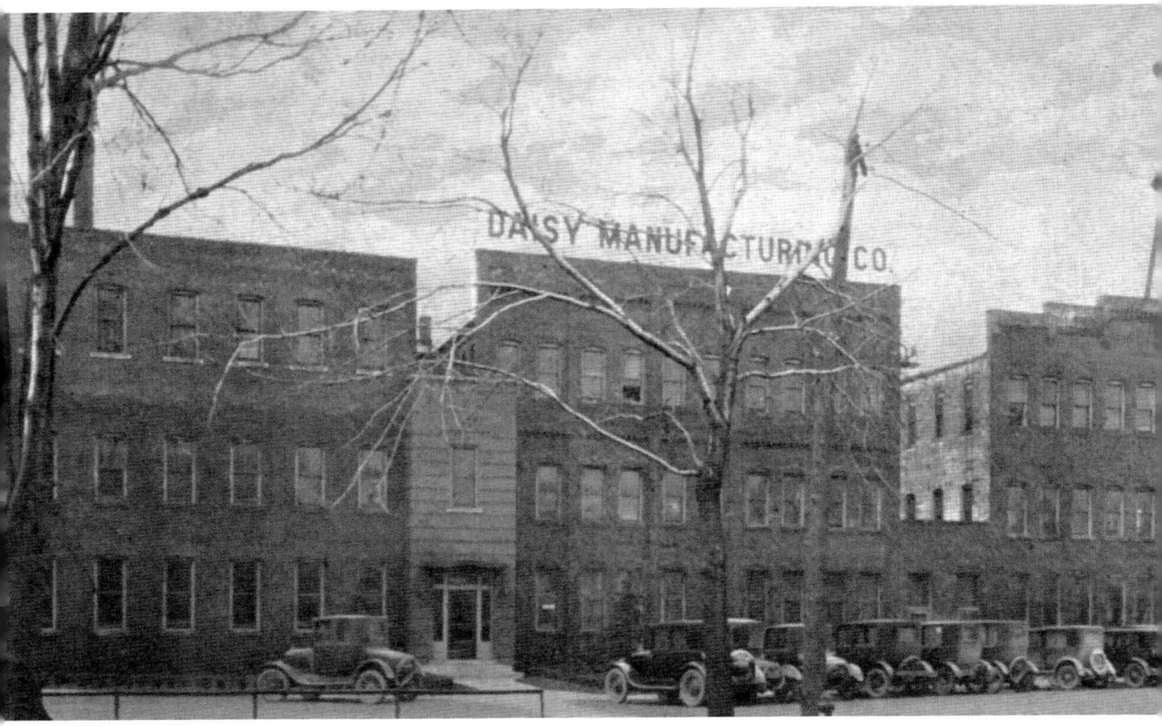

Daisy Plant, 1920s.
Charles Bennett was one of the original 12 investors in Ford Motor Company. Henry Ford, struggling to get his company started, met Charles on a chance encounter while the two were buying suits. After their discussion, Bennett decided to invest $5,000 in Ford Motor. By 1905, when he sold his shares, that investment had netted him $40,000. Some thought he made a mistake in selling his shares of Ford stock, but he claimed he did not regret his decision, as he went on to a very profitable career with the Daisy Air Rifle Company, which he helped found and for which he later served as president. He married Carrie L. Peck on June 24, 1891. They lived for many years at 134 North Main Street in downtown Plymouth. Bennett died in Plymouth at the age of 93 on September 17, 1956. (Postcard courtesy of Plymouth Historical Museum.)

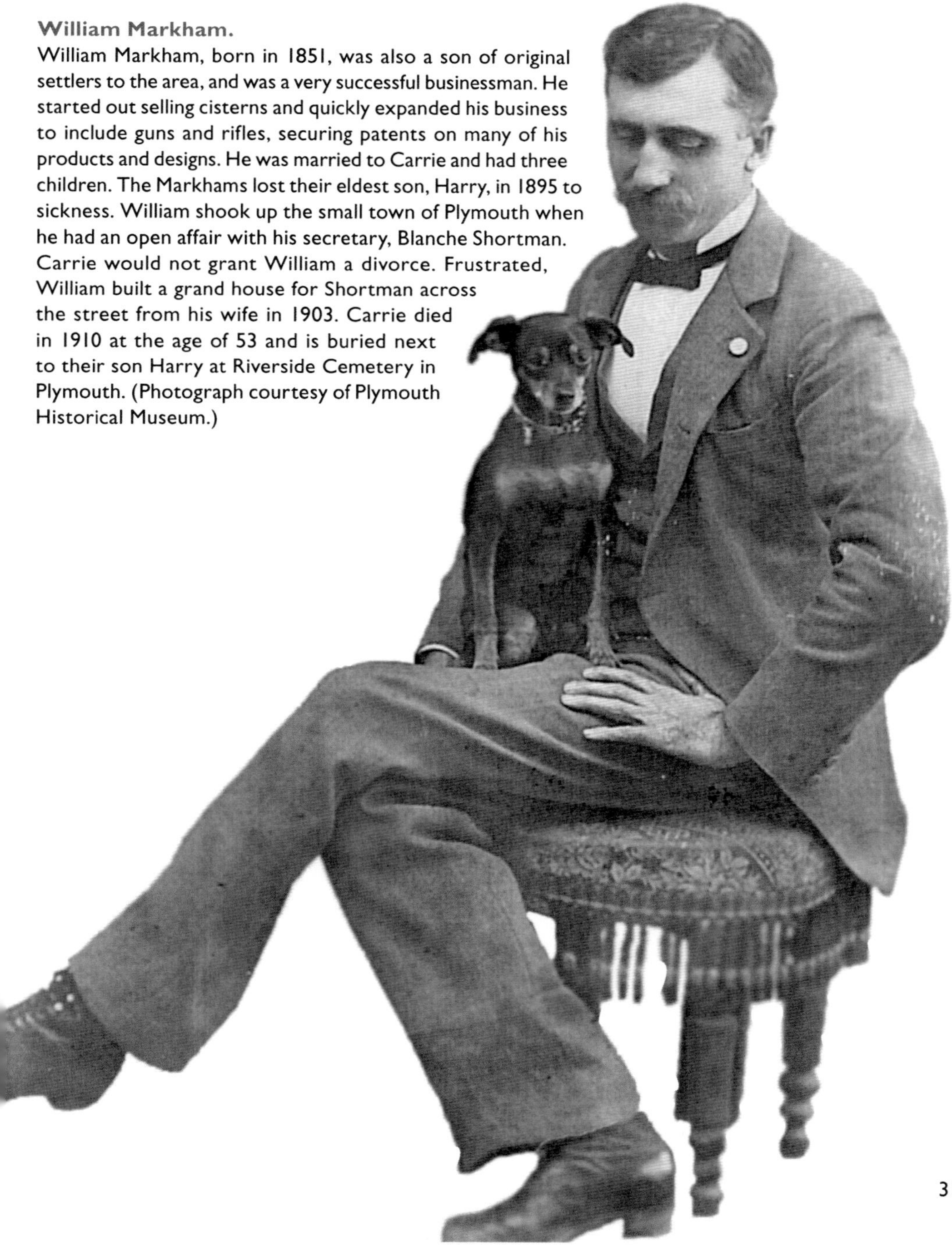

William Markham.
William Markham, born in 1851, was also a son of original settlers to the area, and was a very successful businessman. He started out selling cisterns and quickly expanded his business to include guns and rifles, securing patents on many of his products and designs. He was married to Carrie and had three children. The Markhams lost their eldest son, Harry, in 1895 to sickness. William shook up the small town of Plymouth when he had an open affair with his secretary, Blanche Shortman. Carrie would not grant William a divorce. Frustrated, William built a grand house for Shortman across the street from his wife in 1903. Carrie died in 1910 at the age of 53 and is buried next to their son Harry at Riverside Cemetery in Plymouth. (Photograph courtesy of Plymouth Historical Museum.)

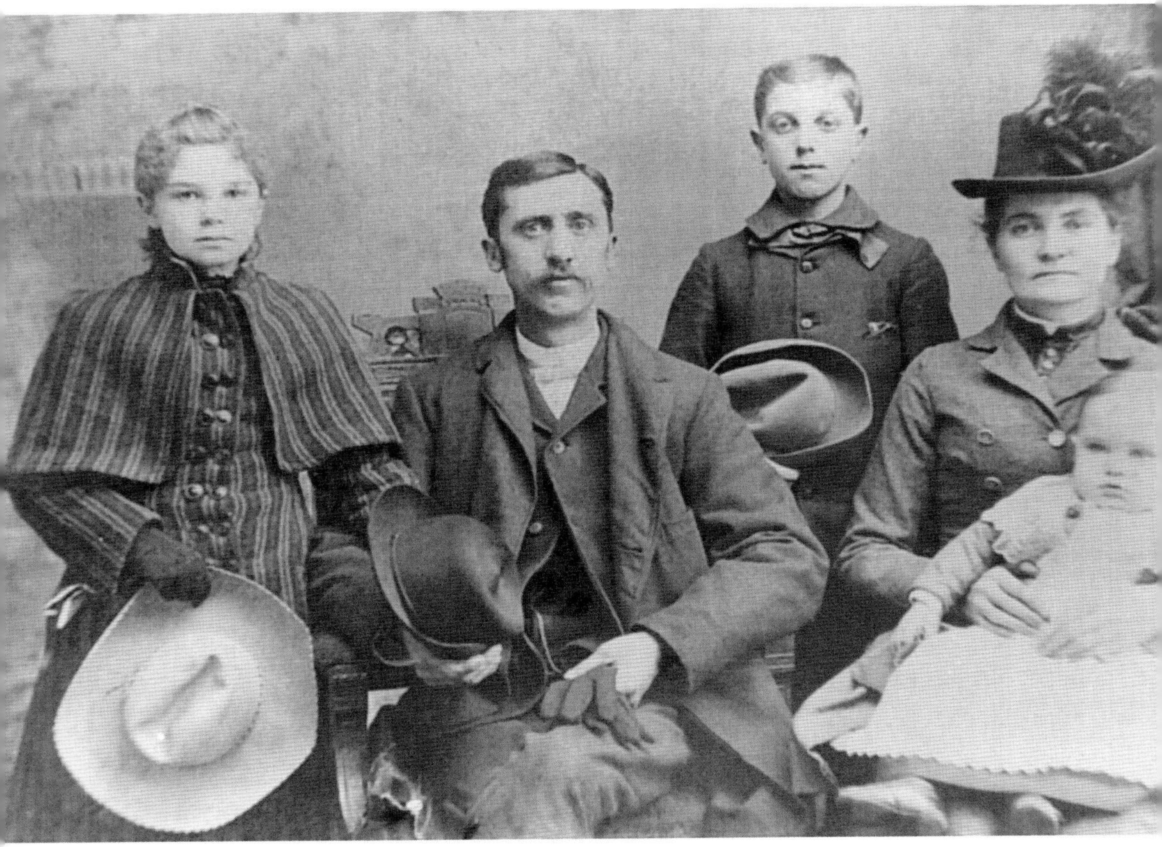

Markham Family, Late 1800s.
William Markham and Blanche Shortman, free to marry in 1910, did so, but the community stayed loyal to the first Mrs. Markham. William and Blanche moved to California in 1911. There, Markham bought a great deal of land, which is now known as Hollywood. In 1916, he sold what was left of his controlling interest in Markham Air Rifle. He died on April 30, 1930, at the age of 79 in Glendale, California. Upon his death, his fortune was estimated at over $1 million. Blanche died in 1937 at the age of 67. The remainder of Markham's fortune was left to his friend and attorney Harlan G. Palmer and the Palmer children. (Photograph courtesy of Plymouth Historical Museum.)

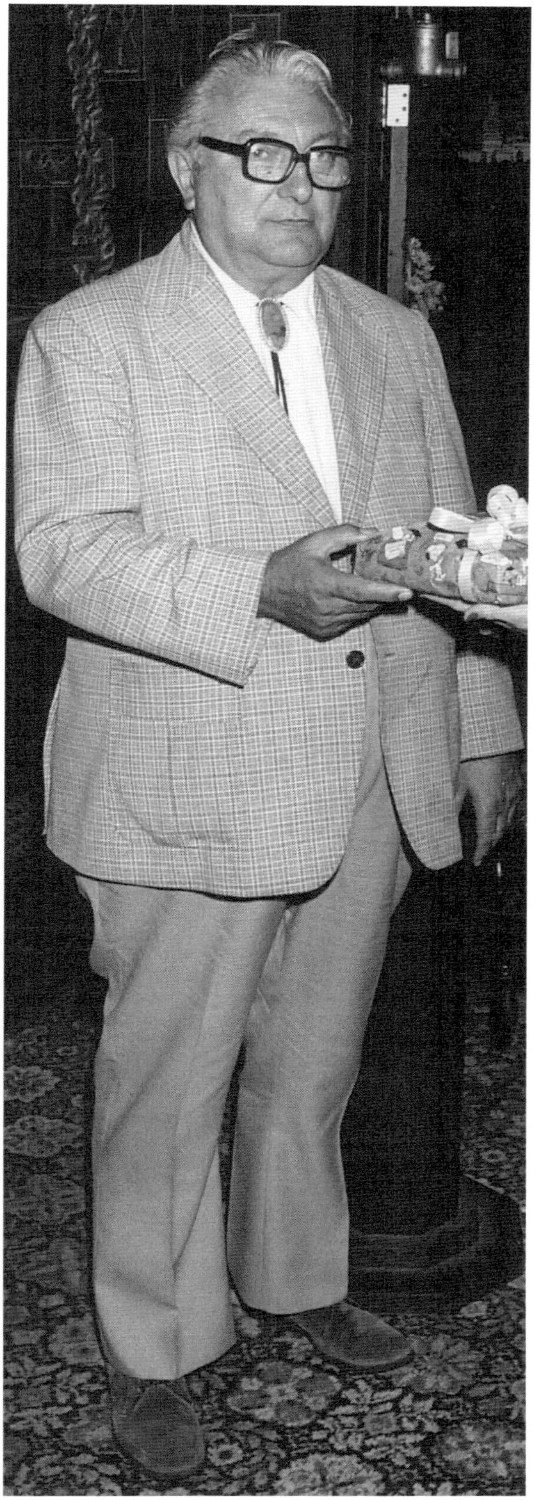

Ralph Lorenz.
Growing up in Plymouth, Ralph Lorenz started working at a young age. As a boy, he worked at the Penniman Allen Theater running the projector and then later as an usher. He also set up pins in the bowling alley next door to the theater. He went on to own the First National Bank of Plymouth complex and also eventually opened the Mayflower Hotel. The hotel officially opened its doors on November 11, 1927, with over 200 residents and guests in attendance. The cost of the dinner was $1.25 and consisted of oysters poulette and prime rib. The Mayflower was originally intended to have five stories, but ended up with only three. It had 50 rooms, terrazzo floors, top-of-the-line kitchen equipment, and was beautifully decorated with furniture brought in from Grand Rapids, Michigan, to fill its guest rooms. The Mayflower Hotel was also one of the first hotels in the state to offer air-conditioning and free television. The hotel, which stood on the corner of Ann Arbor Trail and Main Street, is gone. However, a portion of the building remains where beautiful banquets and weddings are still held. Where the main part of the hotel once stood are now offices, condos, and a Panera Bread. Lorenz is pictured at work in the 1970s. (Photograph courtesy of Plymouth Historical Museum.)

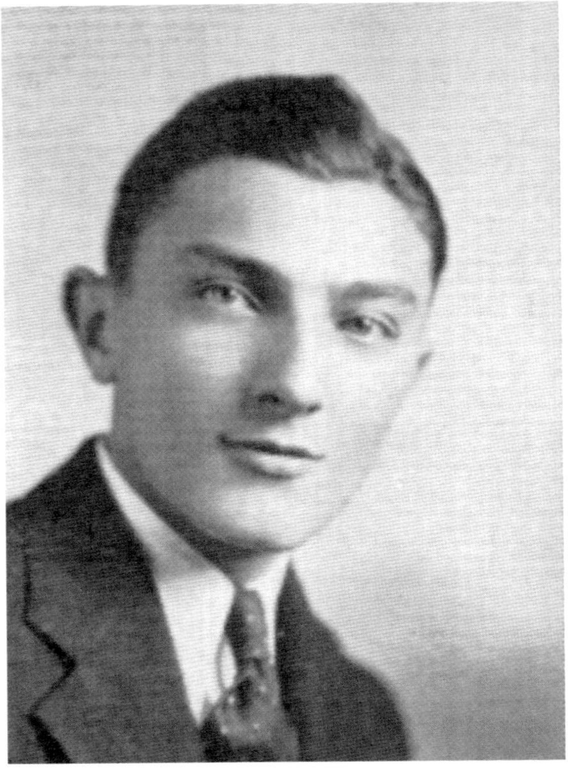

Ralph Lorenz, 1930.
Ralph is shown here in his senior high school picture in 1930. (Photograph courtesy of Plymouth Historical Museum.)

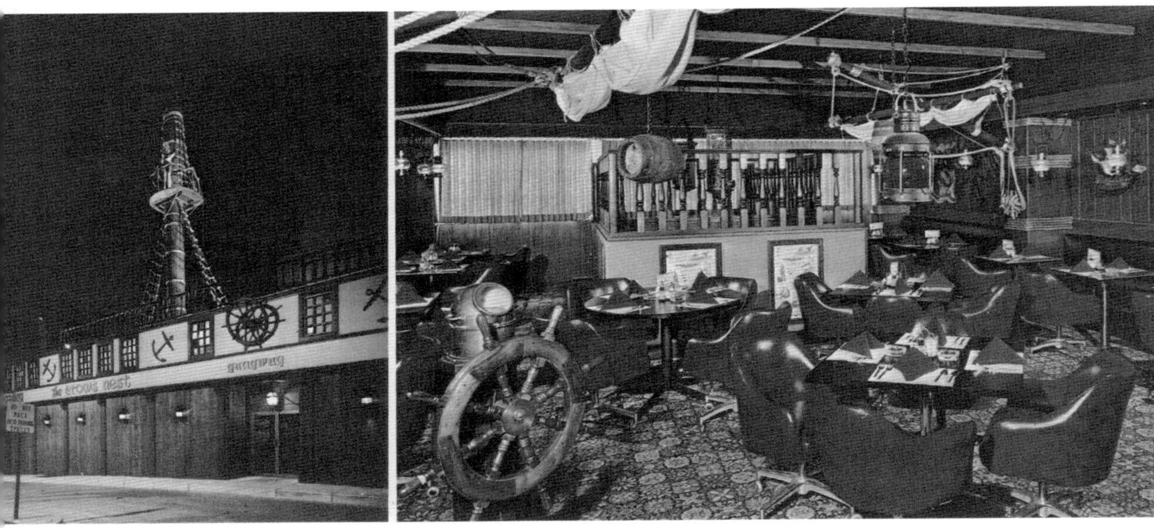

Crow's Nest and Bar from Mayflower Hotel, 1975.
The Mayflower Hotel offered beautiful accommodations and services and was considered ahead of its time. The crow's nest, complete with mermaid, stood as a sign for the famous restaurant and bar inside the hotel. The Crow's Nest Restaurant, which was a popular dining spot, was added to the hotel in 1973. The hotel and restaurant hosted several celebrities, such as Woody Hayes, Ricky Nelson, and Jim Lovell. (Postcard courtesy of Plymouth Historical Museum.)

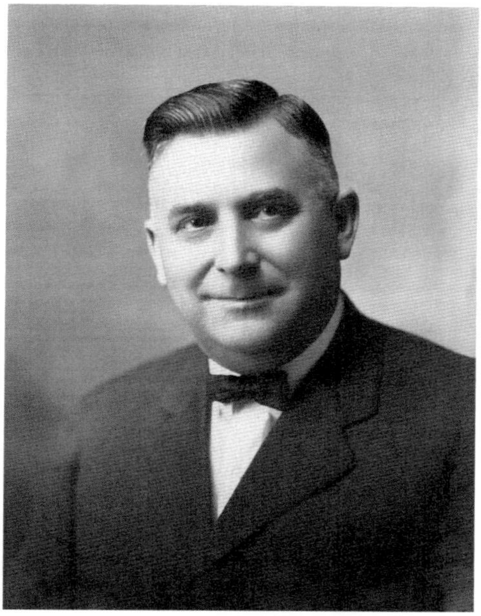

Fred D. Schrader.
Schrader's Funeral Home was started in 1904 by Fred D. Schrader and his brother, Nelson. The two brothers also owned a furniture business on Penniman Avenue. Nelson decided to move to Northville in 1908 and opened up a branch of the funeral home there. (Photograph courtesy of Plymouth Historical Museum.)

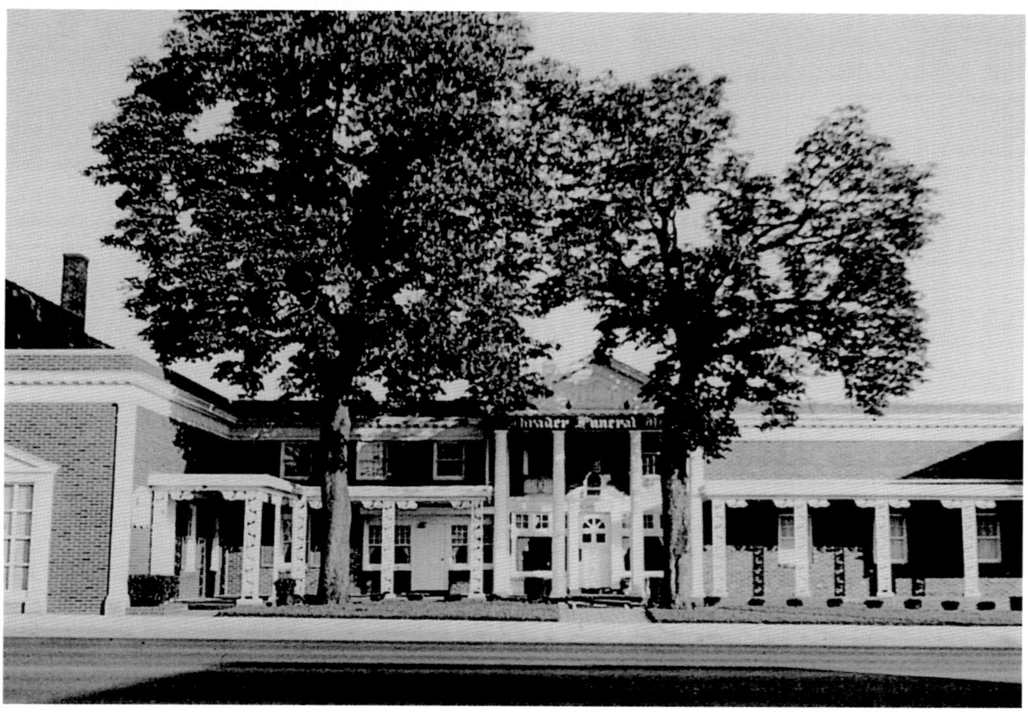

Schrader's Funeral Home, Late 1970s.
In 1908, Fred purchased the home of his brother-in-law, Dr. A. Patterson, and moved the funeral business there. The home, located at 280 South Main Street, is where Schrader's Funeral Home still operates as a family business. Providing years of comfort and service to the community, Fred D. Schrader, born in 1875, died in 1945. (Photograph courtesy of Plymouth Historical Museum.)

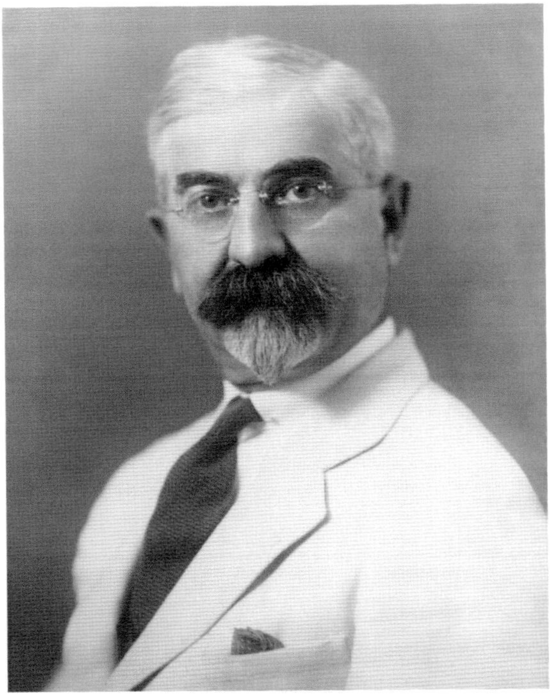

Dr. Luther Peck.
Dr. Peck was a family doctor in Plymouth for just over half a century. His home and office were located in downtown Plymouth, and Dr. Peck knew a great deal of the families in the area and delivered many of them into the world. Peck was remembered by those who knew him as quite a character. Below, Dr. Peck is pictured in his automobile, with Rose Hillmer Holstein, granddaughter to Amelia Davis Starkweather, seated in the front. A Miss O'Toole (left) and Mrs. Starkweather are in the backseat. Born in 1880, Dr. Peck died in 1963 at the age of 83. (Photographs courtesy of Plymouth Historical Museum.)

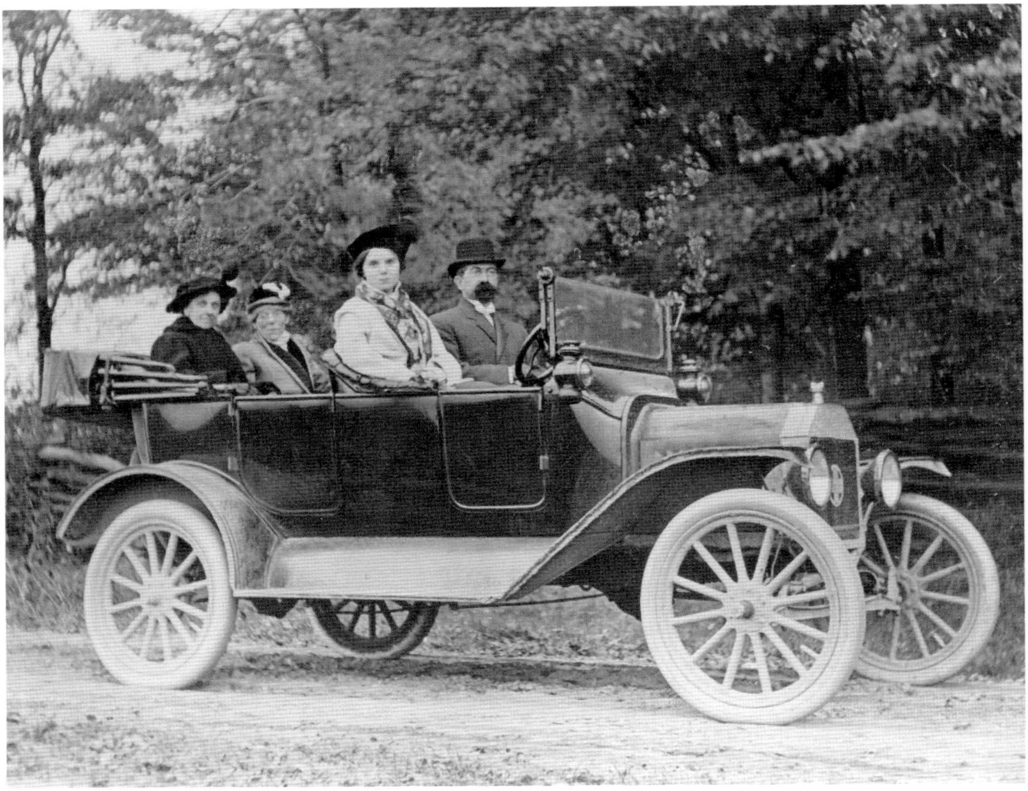

CHAPTER THREE

Women of Plymouth

Virginia Woolf once wrote, "For most of history, Anonymous was a woman." Not so in this chapter. This is an exciting chapter, because women have been instrumental in the progress of Plymouth from the beginning. Here, the reader will learn about women, past and present, who have made a positive impact on the small community. Today, the most common concern for women is striking a balance between home, work, and time for one's self. The women on the following pages undoubtedly experienced the same struggle. Days go by quickly, years go by faster, and there is always something to do or someone who needs attention. The good news is, most people make it work somehow.

This chapter introduces seven different women who span many different decades, each decade bringing about its own expectations and challenges. For example, Phoebe Patterson, one of the first leading ladies of Plymouth, helped to institute change for women and their futures. Ruth Huston Whipple paved the way for later women, raising a family and helping young students learn the skill of debate. Yes, women have been pivotal since time began in all aspects of bringing and sustaining a community to its full value. Women like Bessie Dunning and her daughter Margaret, whose philanthropic calling helped Plymouth obtain beautiful dwellings and opportunities for residents to visit, read, and learn more about its past. In the fields of arts and education, there are Debra Madonna, Joanne Winkleman Hulce, and Nan Washburn, all three of whom are smart, humble, gracious, and lovely in their own right. This chapter was an honor to put together, and readers should find these women's stories interesting. The running theme through this chapter is humility. All seven of these women either wrote or mentioned that, without the help and support of others, their work could not have been done. Their interests, while somewhat varied, all have a maternal aspect. Each woman gives of herself to help others live better, experience more, learn more, and simply be better for the opportunity.

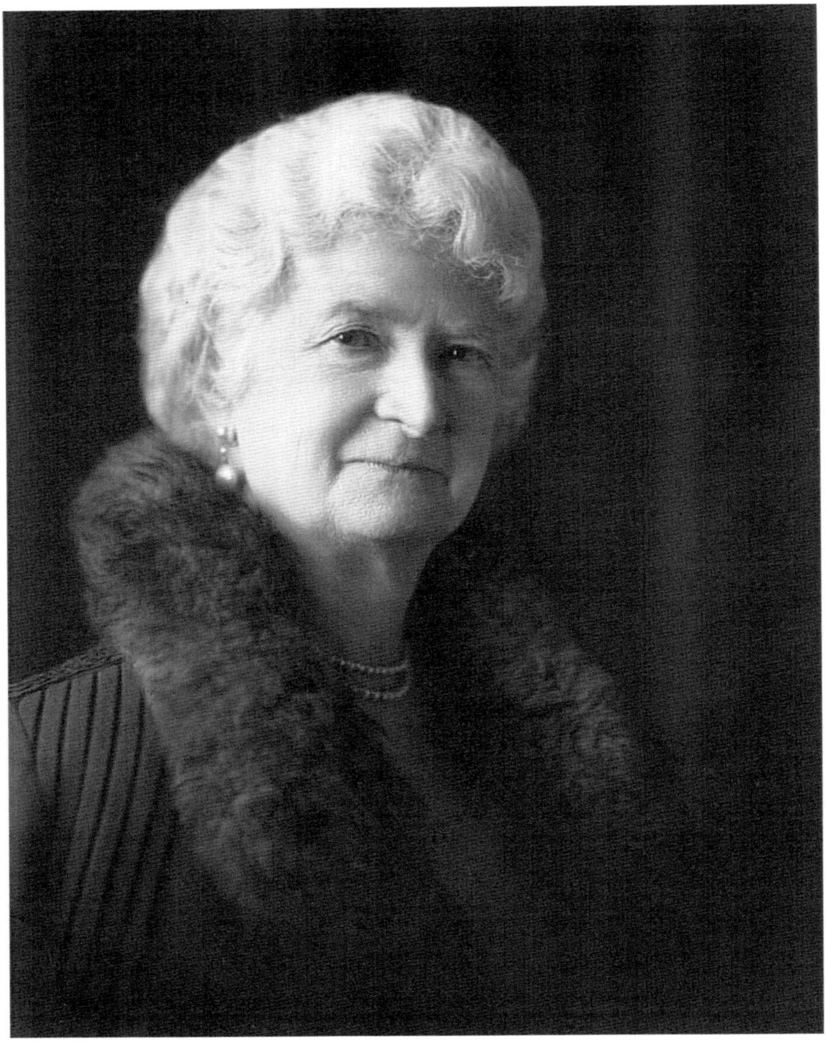

Phoebe Patterson.
Phoebe Patterson, born in 1857, was the first woman in the state of Michigan to be a justice of the peace. A leader in the community, Patterson worked tirelessly for the League of Women Voters and in the Women's Christian Temperance Union. She was also very active in the Business and Professional Woman's Club.

In December 1920, Patterson was asked to appear before Judge Henry A. Mandell. The case filed against her was from a Mr. Leibnitz, who stated that she could not and should not be a justice of the peace because she was a married woman. The case, argued by Leibnitz's attorney, James Pound, was quickly brought to an end by Judge Mandell, who stated, "A woman's services, thoughts and actions are not the property of her husband."

Patterson, controversial, hardworking, and committed to women and their freedoms, was proud to stand by her friends when the first election in which women were allowed to vote in Plymouth took place on March 10, 1919. It was to elect the village commissioners. Patterson lived a full life and died in 1931 at the age of 74. She is buried at Riverside Cemetery in Plymouth. (Photograph courtesy of Plymouth Historical Museum.)

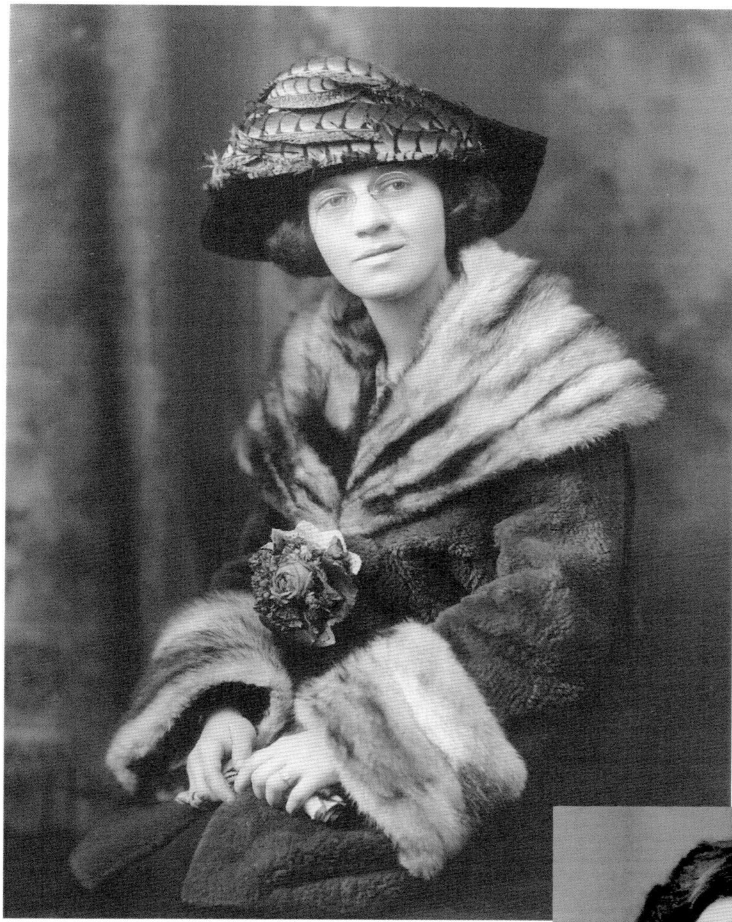

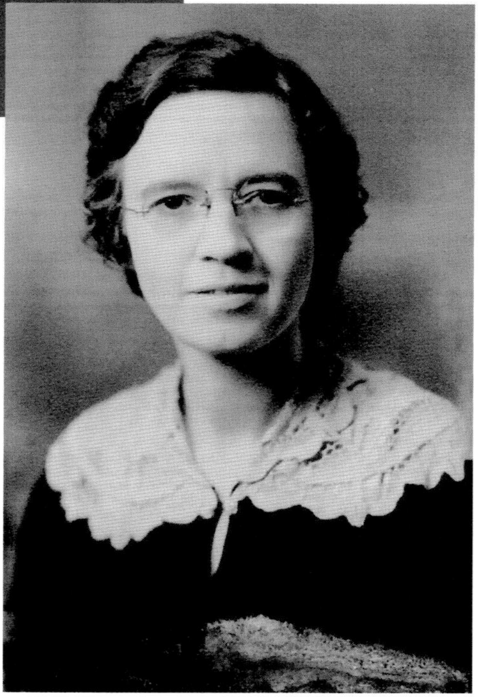

Ruth Huston Whipple.
Ruth Huston Whipple was the first woman on Plymouth's city commission, in 1932. She later served as Plymouth's first woman mayor, from 1940 to 1942. In addition to being the first woman board member on the Michigan Municipal League and the city planning commission, she served on the Wayne County Emergency Relief Commission and the board of supervisors for Wayne County. Whipple, a successful author, teacher, and state debate champion, worked with young students in the district, teaching them the skill of a good debater. In December 1941, she was honored to appear and tell her story in *Woman's Day* magazine. Born in 1894, Whipple died at the age of 59 in January 1953. She is buried at Riverside Cemetery in Plymouth. (Photographs courtesy of Plymouth Historical Museum.)

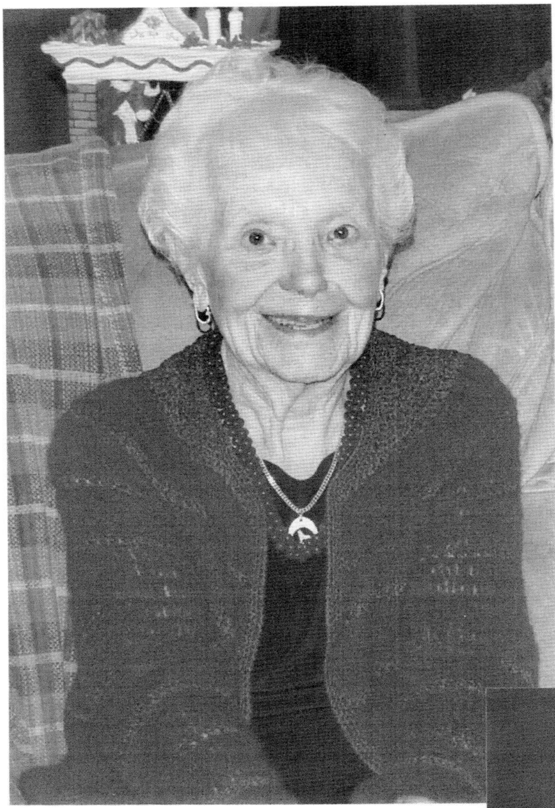

Margaret Dunning.
Margaret, the daughter of Charles and Bessie (Rattenbury) Dunning, was born in June 1910. Raised on a farm, she quickly learned about hard work and responsibility. Her father died in 1923, and Margaret moved with her mother to Plymouth in 1925. She attended a private school in Massachusetts, but then came home and graduated from Plymouth High School in 1929. She attended the University of Michigan and a business school in Ypsilanti, Michigan. Upon graduation, she worked briefly for Henry Ford at the Phoenix Mill Plant in Plymouth, which employed only women. After her time there, she worked locally as a bank teller. In 1947, Dunning decided to go into business for herself and purchased Goldstein's, a popular clothing store in downtown Plymouth. (Photographs courtesy of Plymouth Historical Museum.)

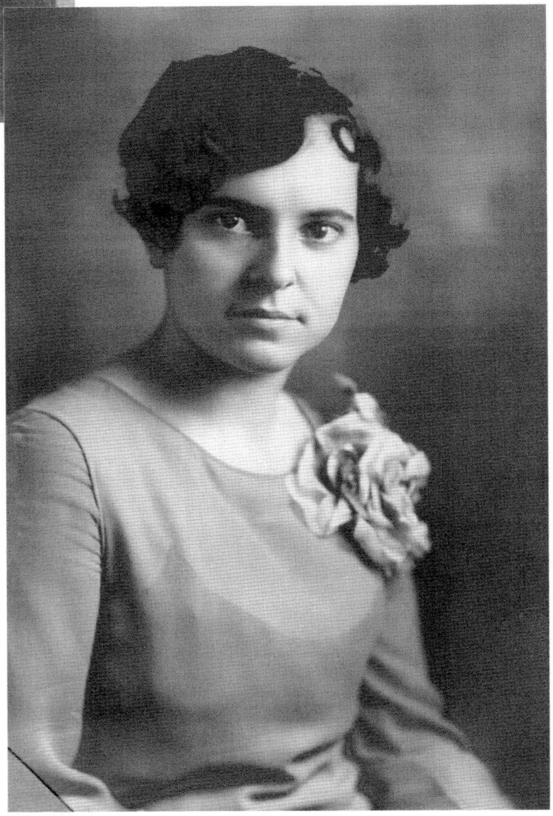

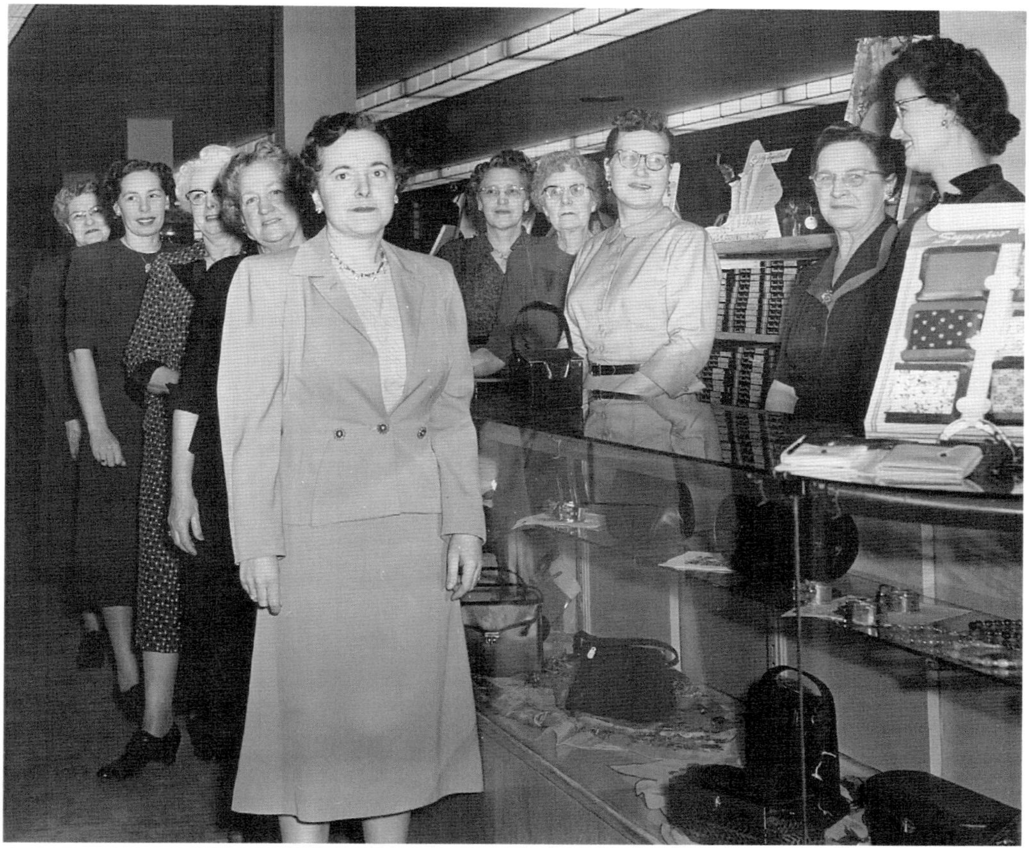

Dunning's.
Margaret (forefront) changed the name of Goldstein's clothing store to Dunning's, and it became the place to purchase quality apparel in Plymouth. In 1950, she moved the store to Forest Street in Plymouth. In 1968, Minerva Chaiken made an offer to purchase the business, and it became known as Minerva Dunning's. The store closed its doors in 1999.

Most known for her philanthropic endeavors, Margaret Dunning, along with her mother, Bessie, presented the City of Plymouth with land and a building for a local library in 1947. In the 1970s, she built the Plymouth Historical Museum and dedicated it in memory of her parents. In 1998, Margaret donated money once again so the museum could expand its space.

At 102, Margaret stays very active in the Historical Society. A very gracious and giving lady, she is a wonderful role model for young and old. She is pictured here in Dunning's store in 1953. (Photograph courtesy of Plymouth Historical Museum.)

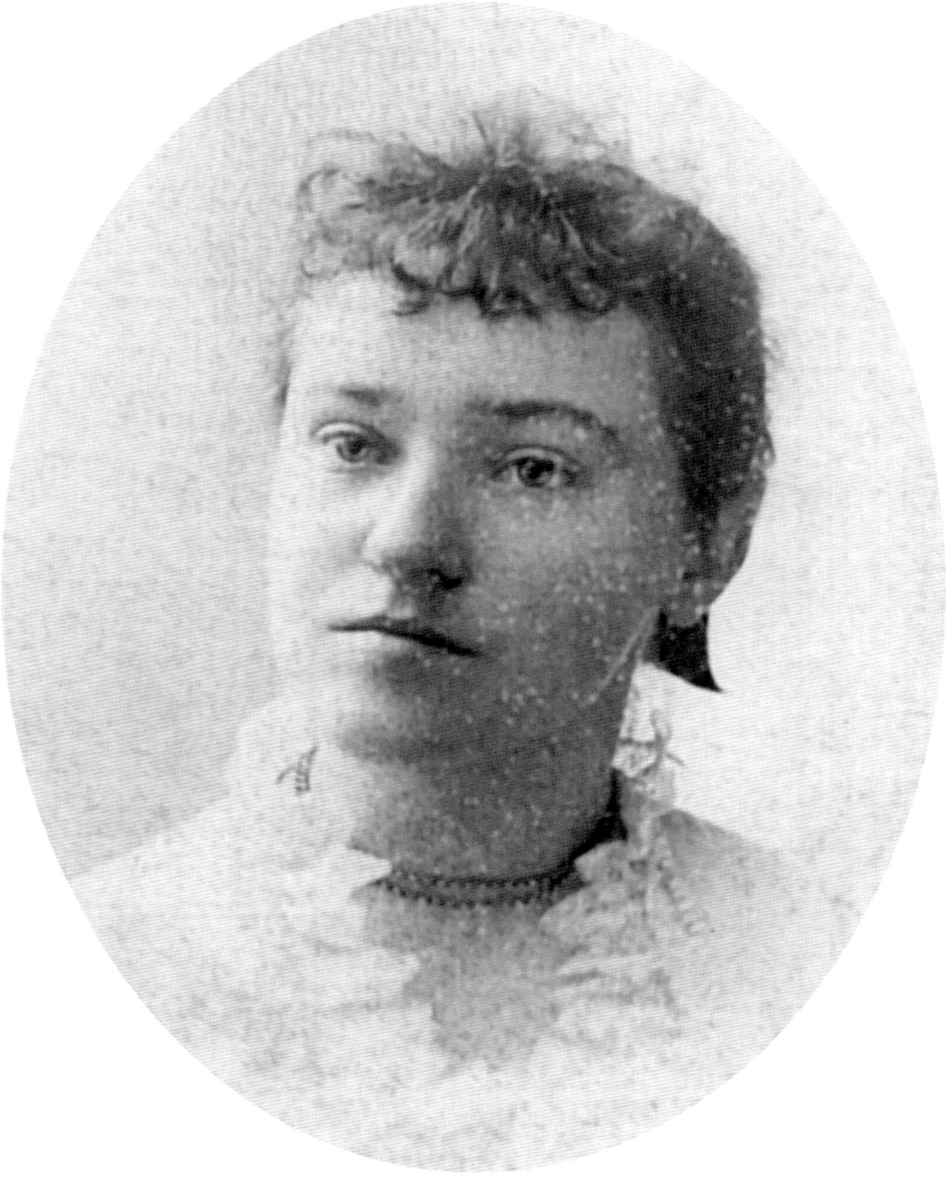

Bessie Dunning.
Elizabeth "Bessie" Rattenbury was the daughter of William and Belle Ewing Rattenbury. Born in July 1871, she married Charles Dunning in March 1898. Charles and Bessie Dunning had one daughter, Margaret C. Dunning, born in June 1910. The Dunnings were primarily dairy farmers, but they also grew potatoes in Redford, Michigan. The farm stood on the corner of Plymouth and Telegraph Roads. The Rattenburys owned farmland in Livonia, Michigan, where the beautiful and charming neighborhood of Rosedale Gardens now stands. Before marrying Charles, Bessie was a schoolteacher and walked approximately five miles from her home to go to work. Often, she went home only on the weekends, which was not uncommon in her day, because only women without family responsibilities would have been hired for a job. (Photograph courtesy of Plymouth Historical Museum.)

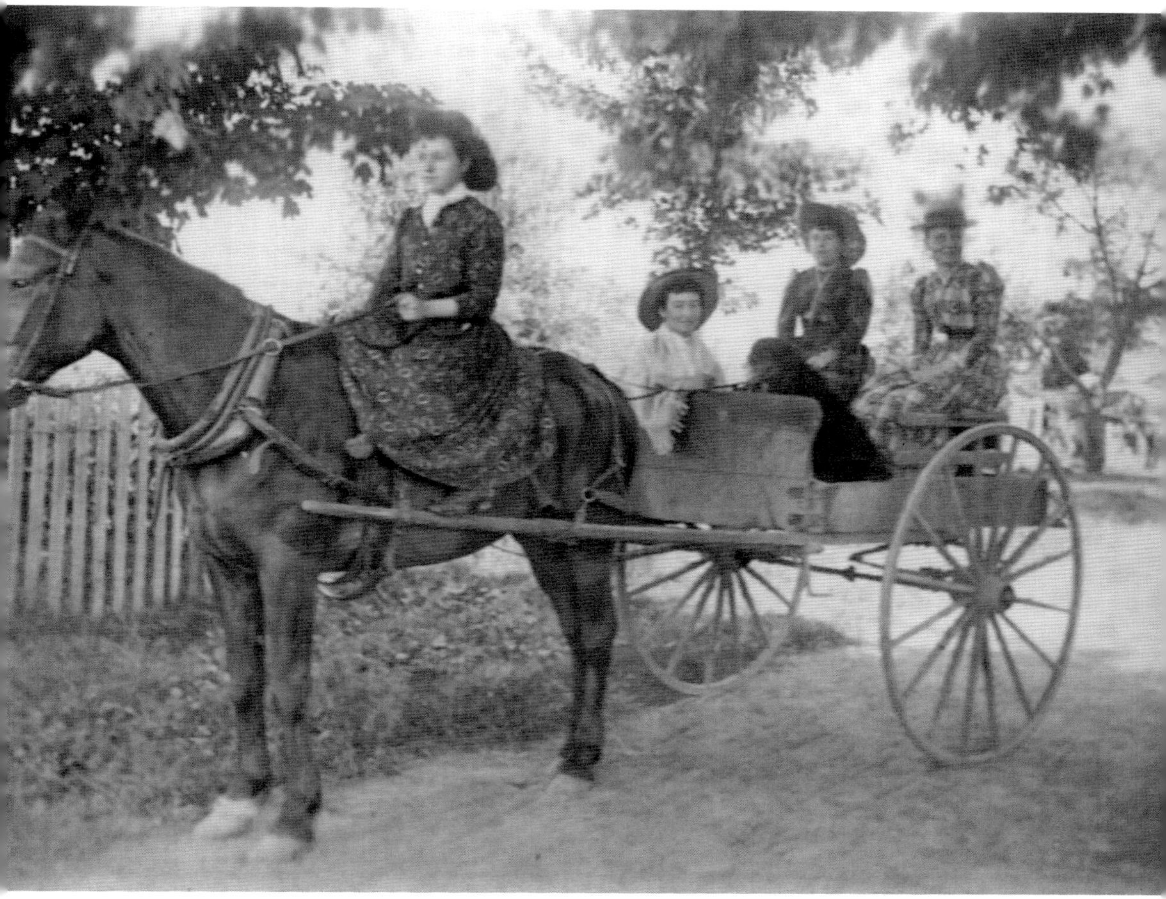

Bessie Dunning, c. 1900.
In 1923, Bessie's beloved husband, Charles, died. In 1925, Bessie and her daughter, Margaret, moved to Plymouth and built a house. Margaret lives in that same house today. In 1947, Bessie and Margaret presented the City of Plymouth with a gift of property for the library. The library, aptly named the Plymouth Dunning-Hough Library, has continued to grow and expand over the years and provides countless activities and resources for its citizens. Bessie Rattenbury, a former teacher and avid reader, saw the importance of having such a building, and Plymouth is grateful to have it and is thankful for her vision. Bessie is pictured here driving a horse and wagon. Her sister Margaret "Maggie" Rattenbury Smith is seated behind her, while two cousins are in the rear of the carriage. (Photograph courtesy of Plymouth Historical Museum.)

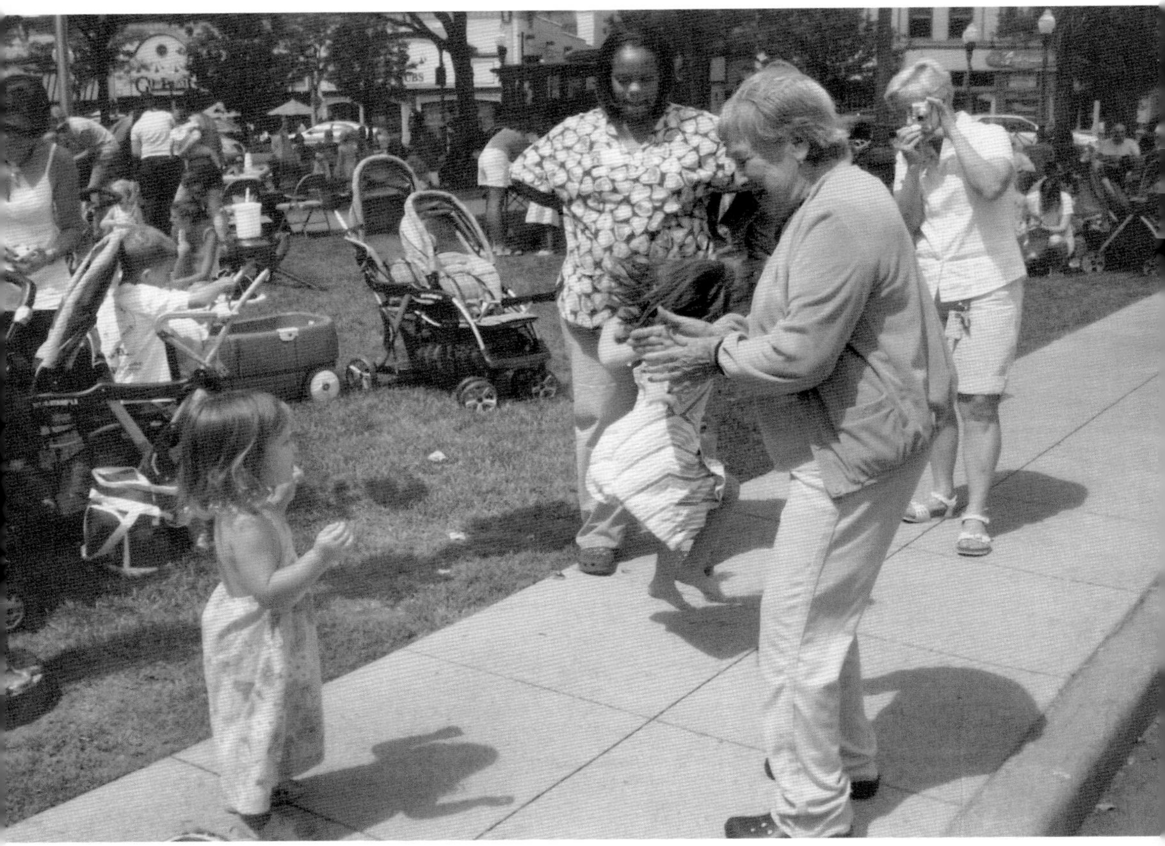

Debra Madonna.
One just might bump into Debra Madonna running around town. An occupational therapist, Debra runs a therapeutic massage business on Main Street in downtown Plymouth and works tirelessly promoting the arts and education in Plymouth. During the summer months, she runs a series called Music in the Park. The lovely event is held on Wednesdays at noon in Kellogg Park and is put on by the Plymouth Community Arts Council and several local sponsors. Debra secures the music and attends every concert to make sure things run smoothly. The concerts, geared toward children, are a fun event where families can lay out a blanket, listen to some music, dance, and eat some lunch, all while sitting under the trees. It's a full summer's day. Debra has been with the Plymouth Community Arts Council for over 20 years and is currently the group's president. (Photograph courtesy of Plymouth Community Arts Council and D. Madonna.)

Sagear Wall of Courage.
In promoting education and understanding, Debra Madonna is responsible for the Sagear Wall, which greets visitors at the front entrance of Plymouth High School. While attending the old Plymouth High School, her friend and fellow student, Sandra Sagear, suffered from the crippling effects of polio. Struck by Sagear's courage, tenacity, and strength, Debra remembered her young friend's struggle but also remembered her smile and resilience and her need to belong and be accepted. Debra never heard Sagear complain about having to climb stairs or try to get to class on time, she just did.

Sagear died at the young age of 42 from her illness. In honor of her memory, and for those current and future students who have their own struggles but overcome and attain their education with dignity and fortitude, the Sagear Wall of Courage was created. A beautiful piece of art, the sculpture is really something to behold. Debra credits her cochair and friend, Jerry Trumpka, with getting the project done. Trumpka, also stricken with polio, has since passed away, but the wall is a reminder of his spirit as well. The artist and architect of the wall is Dennis Jones. (Photograph courtesy of author.)

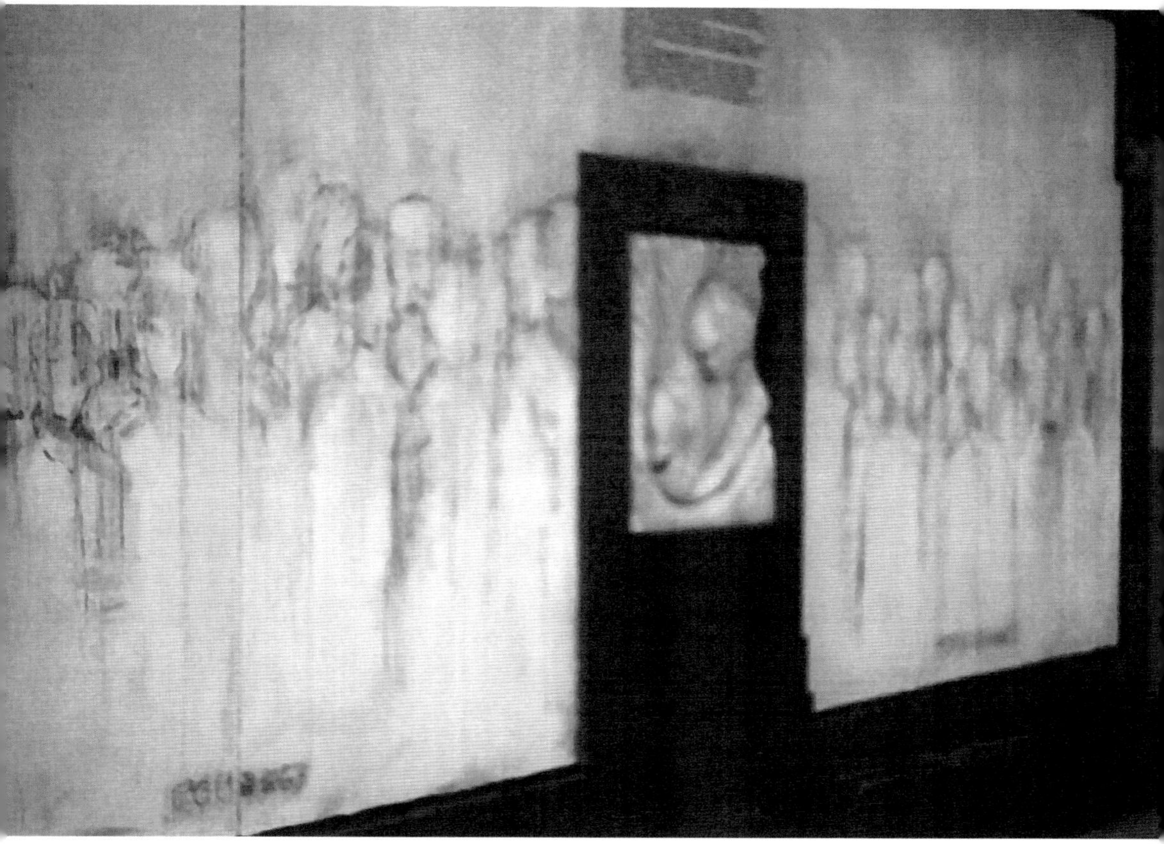

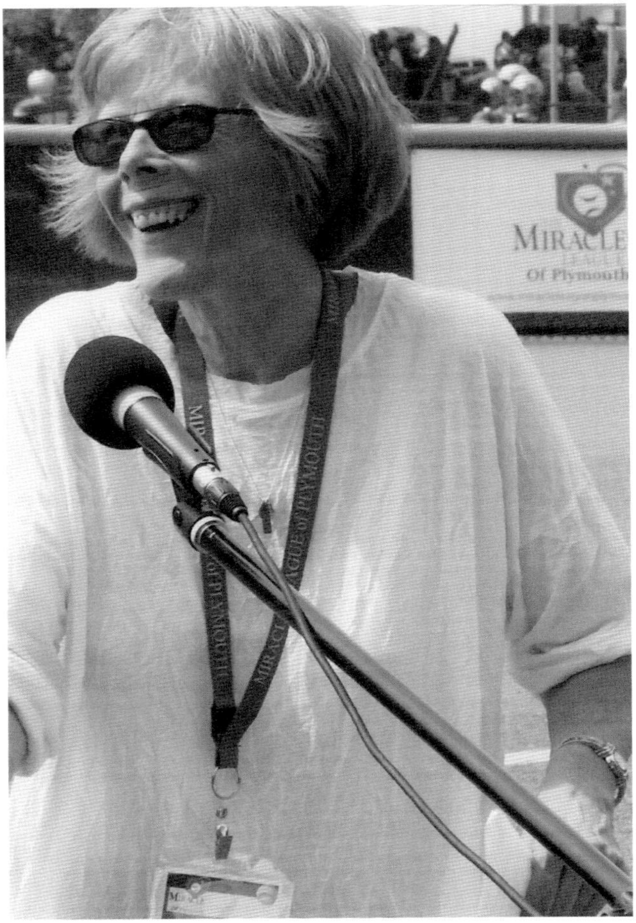

Debra Madonna at Miracle League Ballpark.
Bringing attention to need and understanding is Debra's forte. Most recently, she has been credited with helping put together the Miracle League of Plymouth. This marvelous organization gives children with special needs an opportunity to play baseball. Debra, quoted as saying "It's amazing how much you can get done when no one takes credit," and "Do something bigger than you," credits many people who helped make this project so successful. Ted Barker, a local businessman and resident, was the construction manager. He and his team of workers built a beautiful, quality ballpark, with donations and the support of many in Plymouth and surrounding communities. Barker provided his services at no cost to the organization. Robert Bilkie, the cochair on this project, checked in and, along with Debra, made sure everything ran smoothly. The Plymouth-Canton Schools offered the location, and it has been ideal. The Miracle League of Plymouth is located just behind Central Middle School. Since its dedication on April 29, 2011, it has provided hours of fun and reward for all involved. Debra, shown here in the spring of 2012, currently is president and commissioner for the Miracle League of Plymouth. Readers who are traveling through on a weekend can stop in, say "hi," and watch a game. They will have fun and witness pure joy in motion!

Debra Madonna, a woman who has made an impact and given back to the community she calls home, also served as president of the Rotary Club of Plymouth AM, stepping down in June 2012. To date, under Sandra Sagear's name, the Rotary Club of Plymouth AM has given out 63 scholarships to deserving students. (Photograph courtesy of Miracle League of Plymouth.)

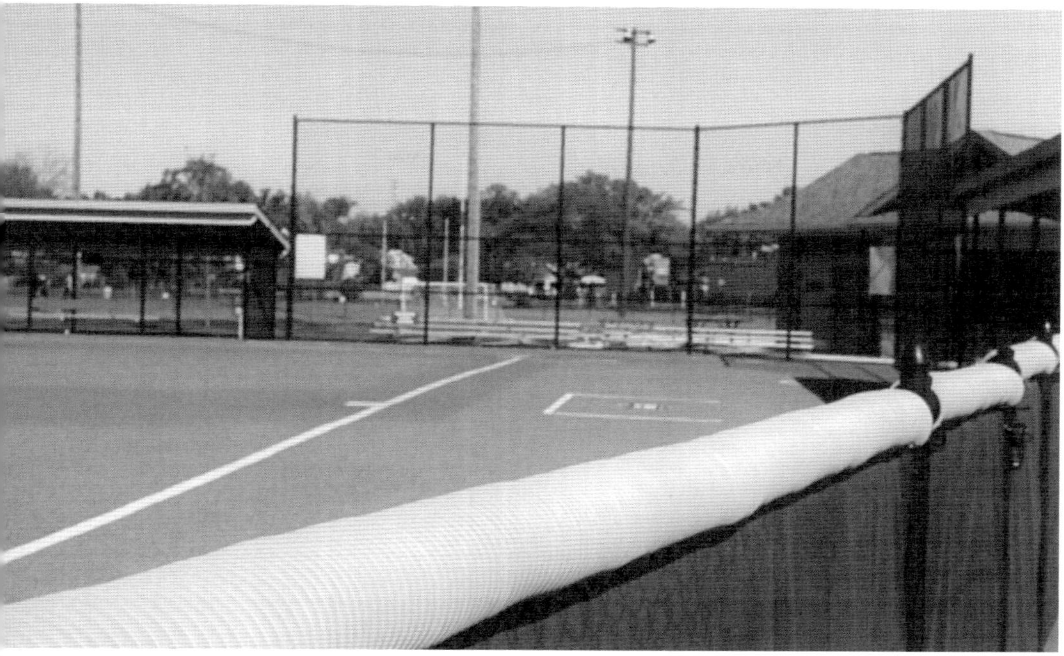

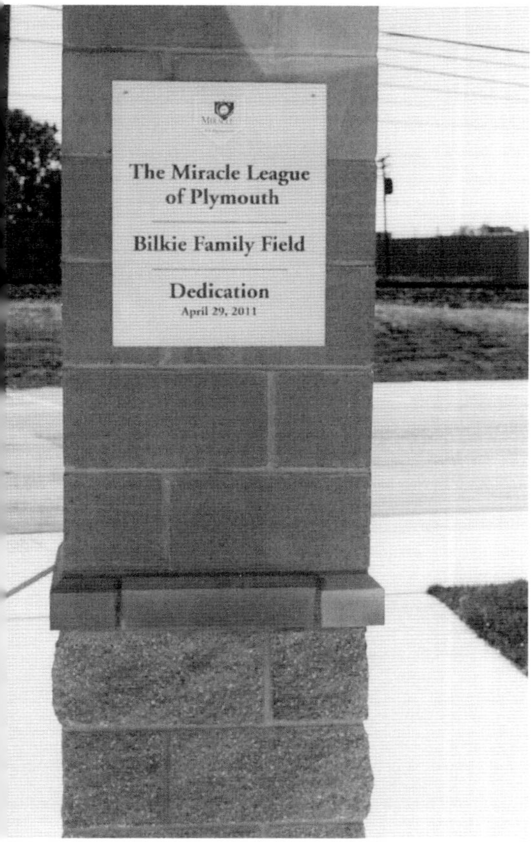

Miracle League of Plymouth Ballpark. Debra Madonna also regularly hosts a local radio program on WSDP 88.1, which airs from the park. The program, called *Community*, is successful for the station, and Debra enjoys talking about local events and newsworthy happenings around town and in the schools. She has been married for 30 years to Marcel Madonna, and they have three sons—Andrew (married to Justine), John, and Mark. Debra—a mom, wife, educator, appreciator of the arts, and an occupational therapist—is a remarkable woman and one to emulate. (Photograph courtesy of author.)

Miracle League Dedication. Pictured is the Miracle League of Plymouth dedication plaque. The field was dedicated on April 29, 2011. The following quote is on a plaque near the front entrance of the field: "If I were to tell you about an organized youth baseball league, you might call it ordinary. If I were to tell you the athletes are physically and mentally challenged, you might call it touching. If you were to see them play, you would call it a Miracle." (Photograph courtesy of author.)

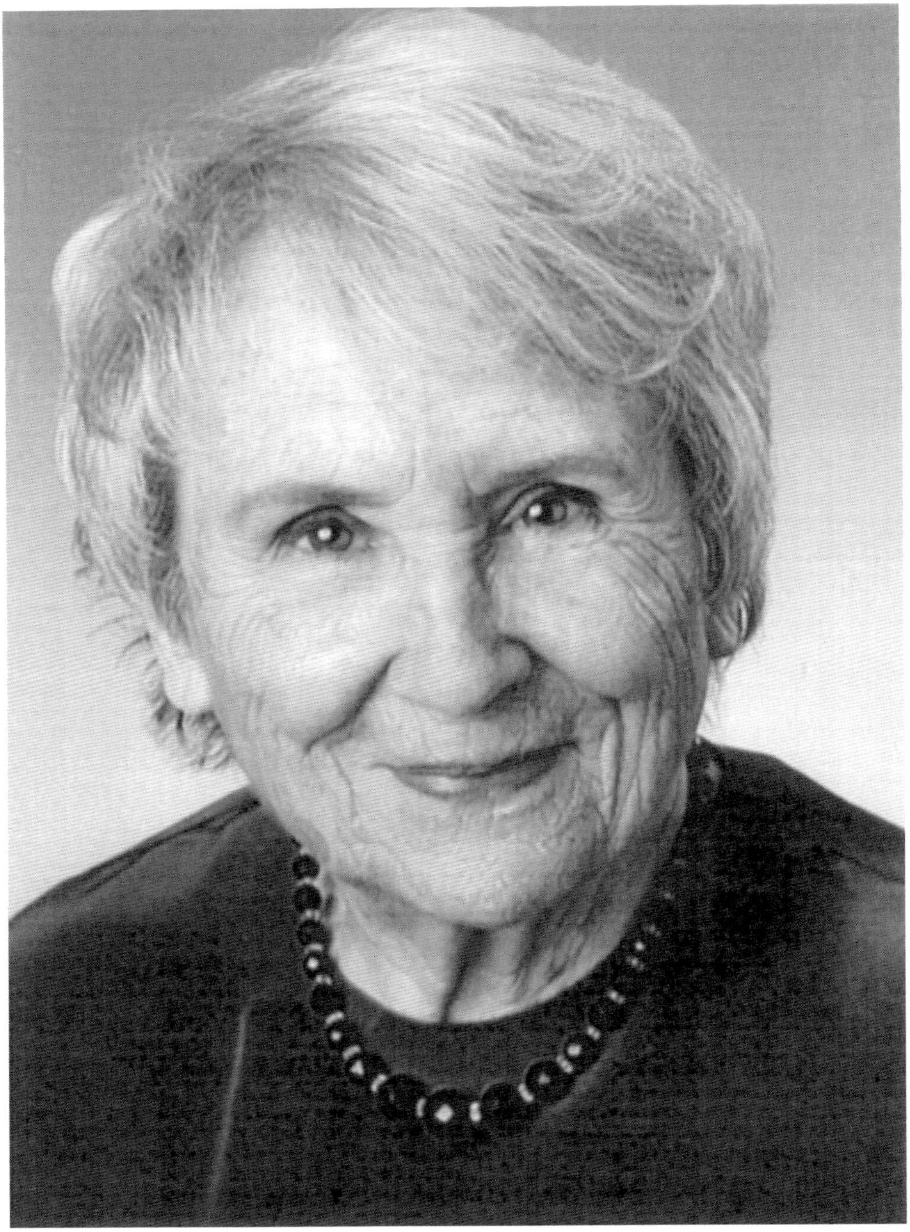

Joanne Winkleman Hulce.
Another very gracious and humble lady of Plymouth is Joanne Winkleman Hulce, known as Jo Hulce. A native of Whitewater, Wisconsin, Joanne attended the Music School of DePaul University in Chicago, where she sang in Grant Park and at Orchestra Hall. In her twenties, she became the featured soloist, "The Golden Voice of Joanne," on the nationally popular radio show *The Hour of Charm*. The show was broadcast from New York every Sunday and toured the United States. Jo moved to Plymouth in 1953 with her husband, Ray. While raising her four children, she sang as a soloist with the Presbyterian Church Choir and the Plymouth Symphony, and joined the League Board. (Photograph courtesy of Joanne Winkleman Hulce's Collection.)

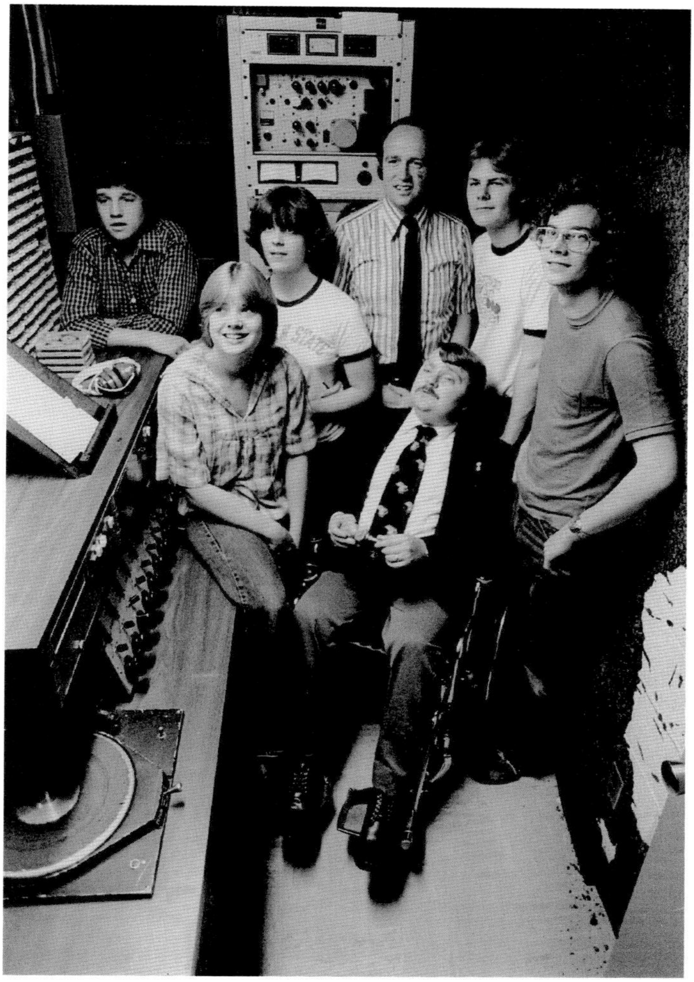

WSDP Radio, 88.1, The Escape, 1970s.
As a board member of the Plymouth Symphony, Jo helped raise awareness for the organization by developing fundraising events such as the popular yearly Symphony Ball. She states, "How fortunate we are to be able to enjoy and claim the Plymouth Symphony, now called the Michigan Philharmonic, as a vision of our community. Their excellence and fine performances are continuing to gain notoriety throughout the state and beyond."

In January 1967, Hulce was appointed to the Plymouth-Canton School Board, serving for six years. While attending a conference in Washington, she saw a school exhibit displaying different artists' work. This "sparked an idea" and was used as a catalyst to develop a program for Plymouth. Jo gathered together her creative friends, made a plan, and presented her vision to the school board. The board honored the request, and this marked the beginning of her leadership of the Plymouth Community Arts Council in 1969.

While on the Plymouth-Canton School Board, she was a big supporter and helped institute the WSDP radio station at the park. Her belief was that hands-on opportunities for students to experience how things work or get done helps to foster responsible individuals and provides a better understanding for business, marketing, and operations. The radio station is currently celebrating 40 years of service to the community. (Photograph courtesy of Plymouth Historical Museum.)

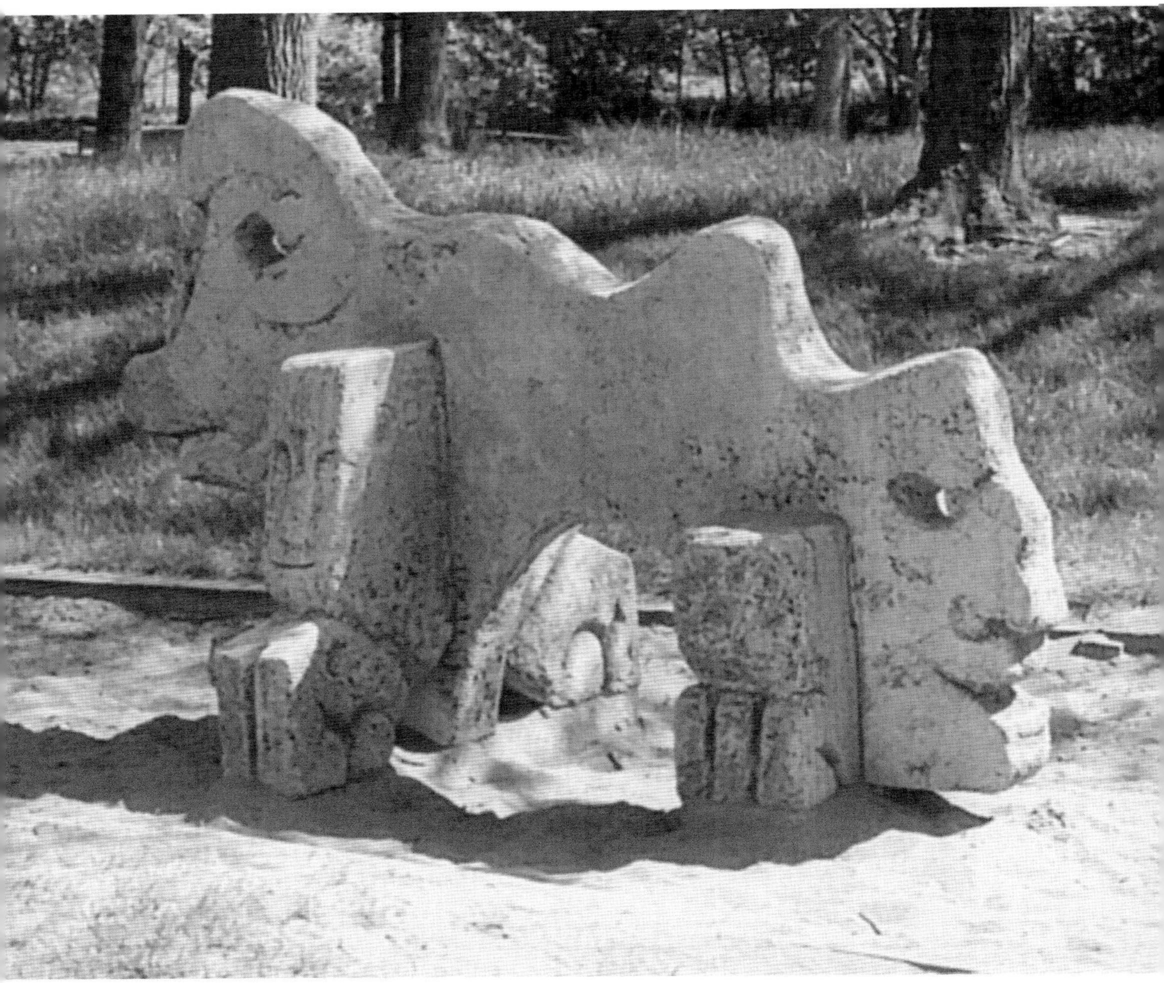

Sculptures at McClumpha Park.
In 1969, the Plymouth Community Arts Council secured the building it still resides in today. The programming offered includes theater, dance, music, and visual arts. Joanne Hulce served as president of the council for five years and has since stayed on as a member of the board. The arts council, committed to working with the community, still works closely with the schools and offers opportunities for students to experience the arts. The arts council also houses the Michigan Philharmonic Orchestra's offices. In 1979, the arts council honored Hulce by naming the building the Joanne Winkleman Hulce Center for the Arts, for her dedication, love, and support of the arts, as well as her goal to make art in Plymouth more present and available for all. (Photograph courtesy of author.)

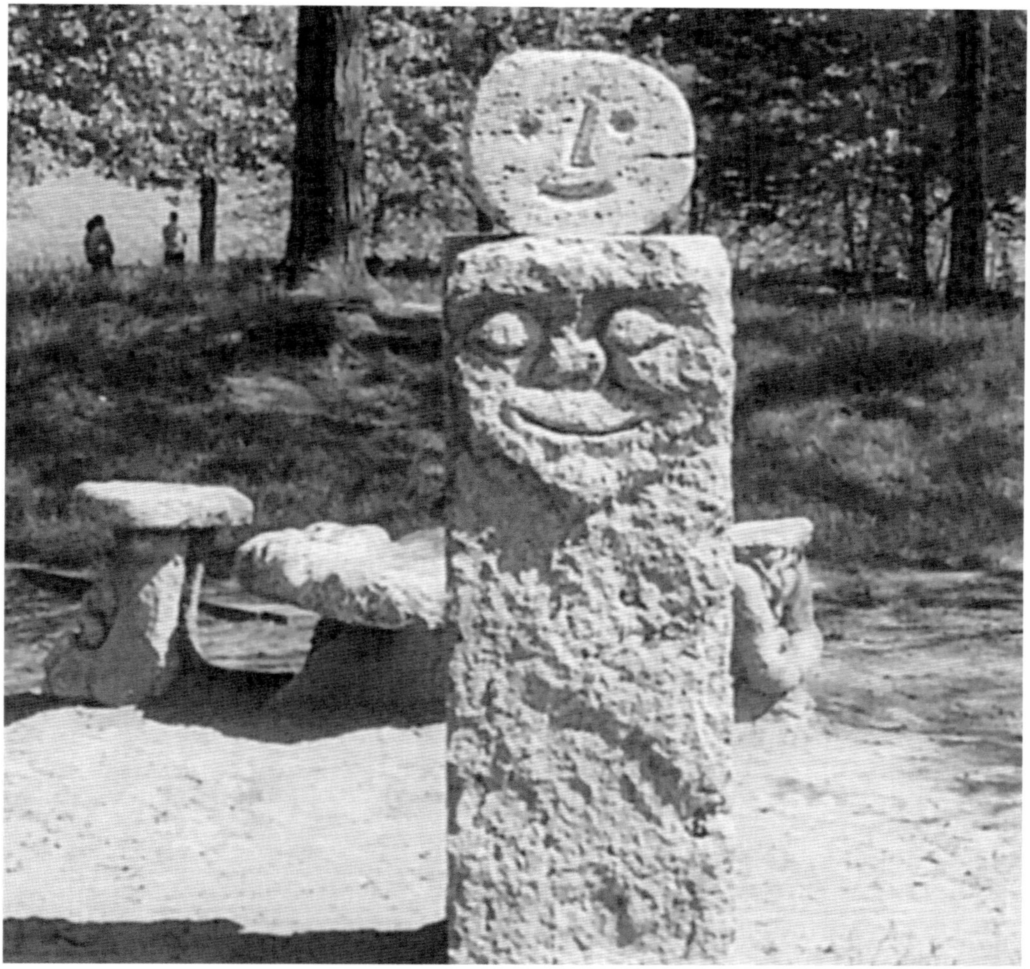

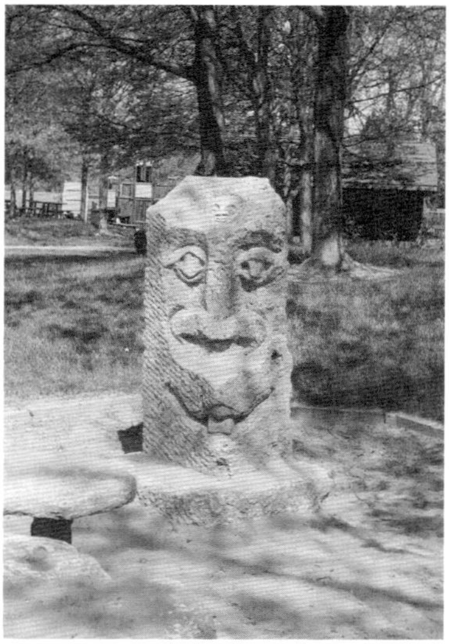

Peter Rockwell's Sculptures.
In 1972, while on the Michigan Council for the Arts Education Committee, Hulce brought the Art Train to Plymouth for two weeks. With total community involvement, it was a memorable experience that provided continued and new support for the Plymouth Community Arts Council. In 1985, at Township Park, she once again brought art to children through play. Sculpted by the famous artist Peter Rockwell (son of Norman Rockwell), several fun "climb-on" sculptures add a magical touch to the playscape. All were made possible by government and citizens of both the city and township of Plymouth. Rockwell spent seven weeks sculpting in the park, inviting many to help. His afternoons were often spent in the schools with projects for the students. For those who recall the event, it is a special memory to have and hold. (Photographs courtesy of author.)

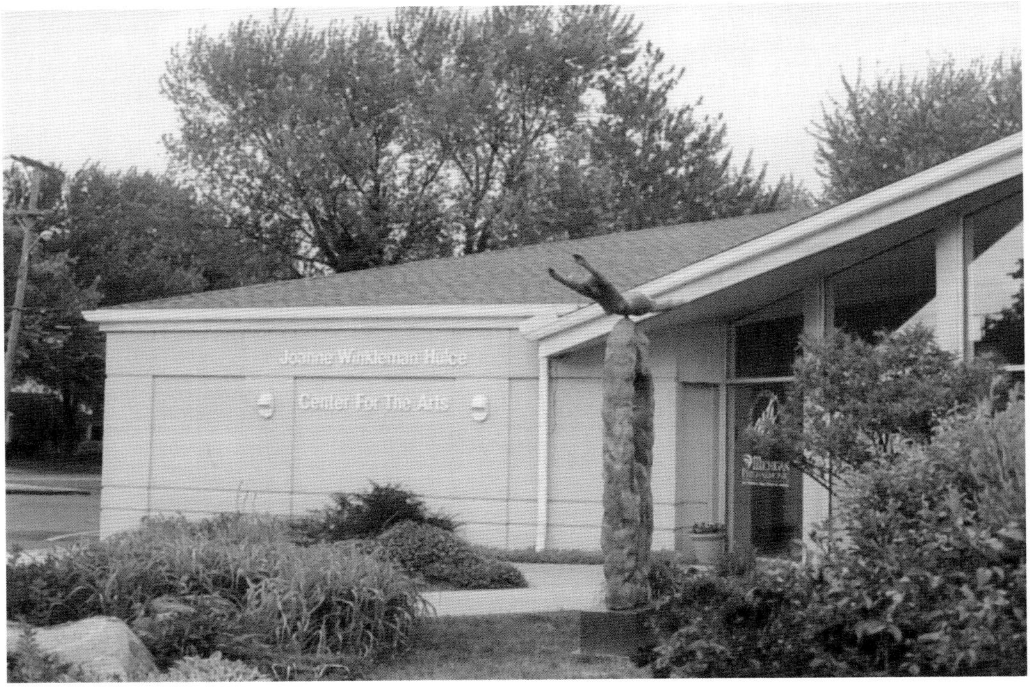

Plymouth Community Arts Council Building.
Joanne Winkleman Hulce, a wife, mother, singer, and lover of art in all its forms, simply saw a need, a void that needed to be filled, and she filled it. Hulce states, "We are so fortunate to live in a community with so many opportunities for a rich life. Much has been provided by the many volunteers giving of their time and talents with so many wonderful friendships being made in the process. There are many needs—a place for everyone to feel the *joy* of giving back. I am grateful." Hulce, still active in Plymouth, enjoys friends and all that life has to offer, and is a proud mother of four and grandmother of seven. (Photograph courtesy of author.)

Nan Washburn. (OPPOSITE PAGE)
The Plymouth Symphony, now the Michigan Philharmonic Orchestra, started in 1945. Now in its 66th season, the orchestra continues to offer beautiful music and entertainment, holding concerts from October through May. Nan Washburn, entering her 14th season with the Michigan Philharmonic, is its director and is one of a few women conducting music in the world today. Born in Denver, Colorado, and raised in Ventura, California, she came to Plymouth in 1999. She is a winner of 17 ASCAP (American Society of Composers, Authors and Publishers) awards and has been featured in several magazines and on National Public Radio. Her fun and innovative programming is pure inspiration and has brought much attention and growth to the orchestra. More recently, the organization has been able to add a youth orchestra. The Michigan Philharmonic Youth Orchestra offers three orchestras and a flute choir, workshops, and an opportunity for students in the orchestras to work with and perform with professional musicians from the Michigan Philharmonic. (Photograph courtesy of Michigan Philharmonic Orchestra.)

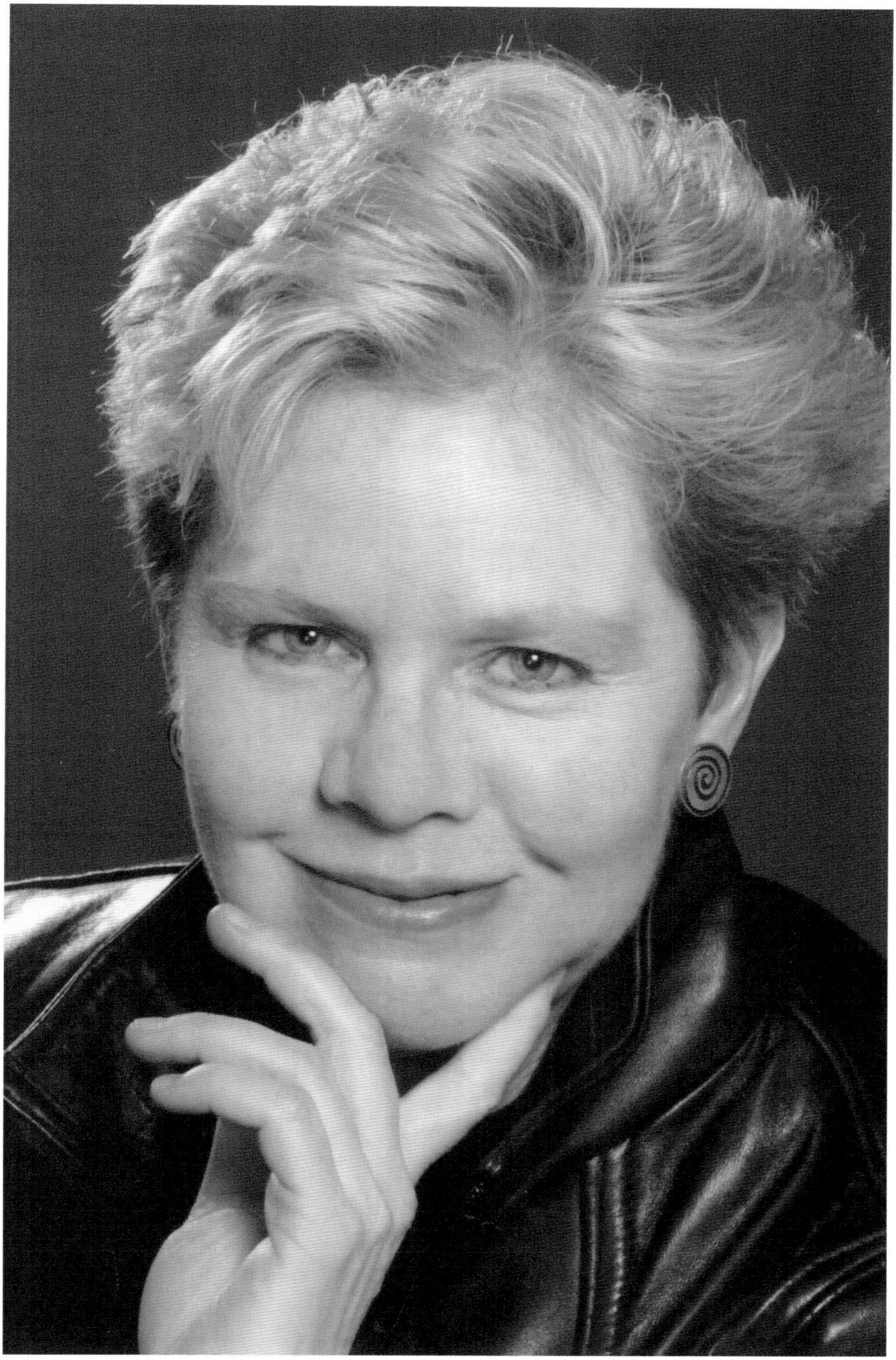

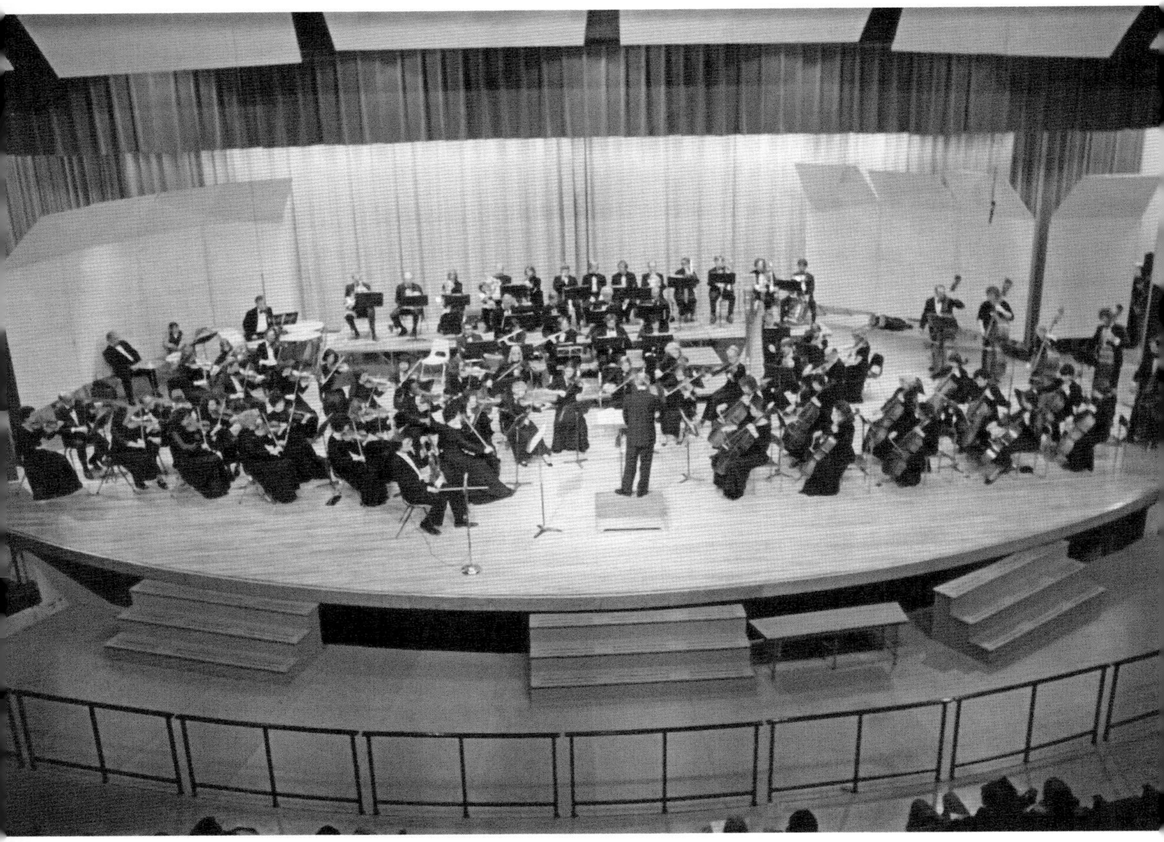

Plymouth Symphony, 1940s.
The programming for the orchestra has included themes such as the Beatles, Hollywood, Made In America, and Beethoven and Friends. Nan Washburn works with young musicians and visits schools, educating students and letting them conduct. This, for her, is the key to opening up minds and hearts to music. Watching Washburn conduct, one can see her passion for the music and her skill in leading the large group of musicians. Plymouth is fortunate to have such a talent. Washburn earned her bachelor of music with highest honors from the University of California, Santa Barbara, receiving the Chancellor's Scholar Award. She earned her master's degree in performance from the New England Conservatory of Music, and received the Alan Memorial Woodwind Award while attending the Music Academy of the West. A trained flutist, Washburn started her studies in conducting in 1984. She has worked and trained with famous conductors and teachers all over the country.

The Michigan Philharmonic started with an idea by local residents Evelyn and Carl Groschke while entertaining a few friends in their home in 1945. The idea was picked up by then music director of the high school, Paul Wagner, and expanded little by little. The first official performance was on April 20, 1947. (Photograph courtesy of Plymouth Historical Museum.)

CHAPTER FOUR

Schools and How They Got Their Names

What is in a name? The answer: many things. Names define, shape, and mold. They give identity and purpose and help develop character. Naming a business or a building is no exception. This chapter will look at how all of the public schools in Plymouth came to receive their names. The Plymouth-Canton Community Schools district is the third-largest school district in the state of Michigan, with sixteen elementary schools, an adult education center, an early intervention program for children with special needs, five middle schools, three high schools, preschool programs, a talented and gifted program, and an extended day program. The district is very busy and strives hard to put forth great programming that is innovative, fun, challenging for students, meets different needs, and gives students opportunities that will assist in the direction of their lives. This is a very big responsibility and one that is taken seriously. The staff, from administration to maintenance, is filled with hard workers dedicated to children and the quality of their school experience. The public schools, while not without challenges, strive to do their very best and continue to create and implement good programming despite tightening budgets. Again, throughout this book, the running theme has been humility and what can be done when people work together and share in the same dream, goal, and purpose. Mountains can be moved when everyone chips in and contributes a little something of themselves. That includes parents as well. Fabulous families dwell in the communities of Plymouth/Canton—parents who know and understand the value and importance of a good education, and parents who are involved and know what it takes to get things done and support the different schools and events through fundraising and the giving of their time and ideas.

What is in a name? Again, many things. The naming of the schools for the Plymouth-Canton district is part of the by-law and policy number No. 7250, and is always marked with a dedication ceremony. The naming of schools and how to go about it was first recorded at a board meeting in 1949. The elementary schools in this chapter will be listed alphabetically. The middle and high schools will be listed by the years they opened.

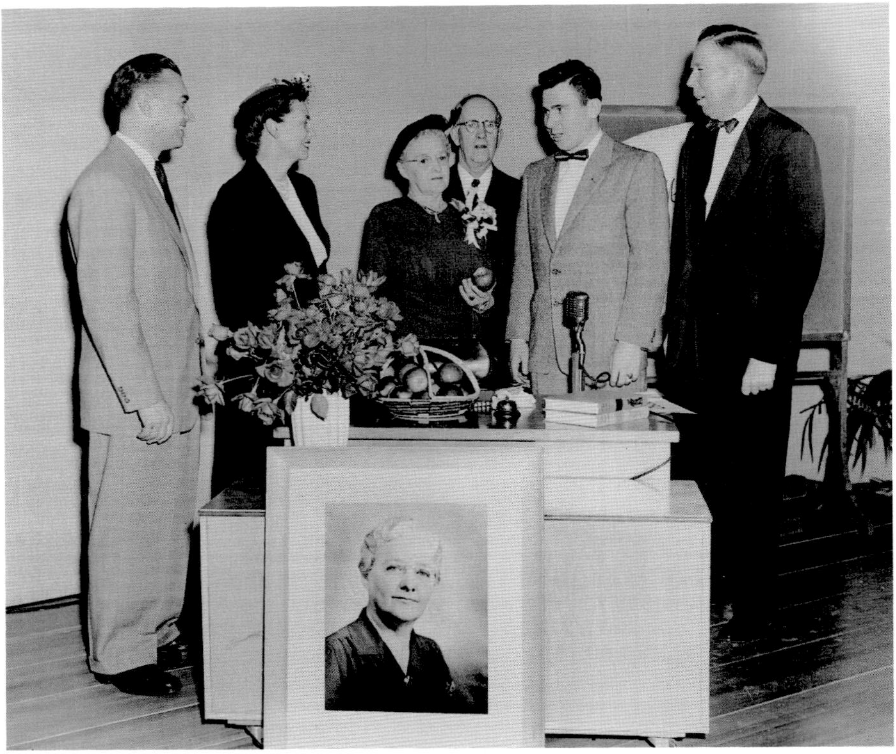

Edna M. Allen (Allen Elementary).
Edna M. Allen came to Plymouth from Bad Axe, Michigan, in the fall of 1913. She first served the district as principal at the high school. She was described as charming, witty, and intelligent. Her favorite subjects were English, philosophy, and reading. She worked in the schools for a total of 38 years, retiring in 1950. She was the eldest of eight children and received her bachelor's and master's degrees from the University of Michigan. Allen never married, devoting herself to her career. She lived her remaining years in Plymouth on Arthur Street. Above, Allen is pictured at the dedication ceremony for Allen Elementary, named in her honor, in 1954. School superintendent Russell Isbister is at the far right. Below is an image of an invitation to the ceremony. (Images courtesy of Allen School Staff.)

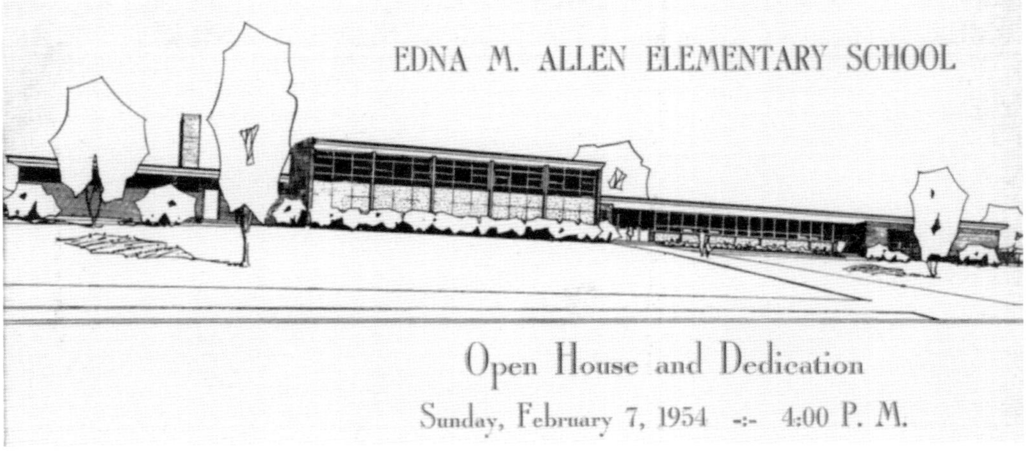

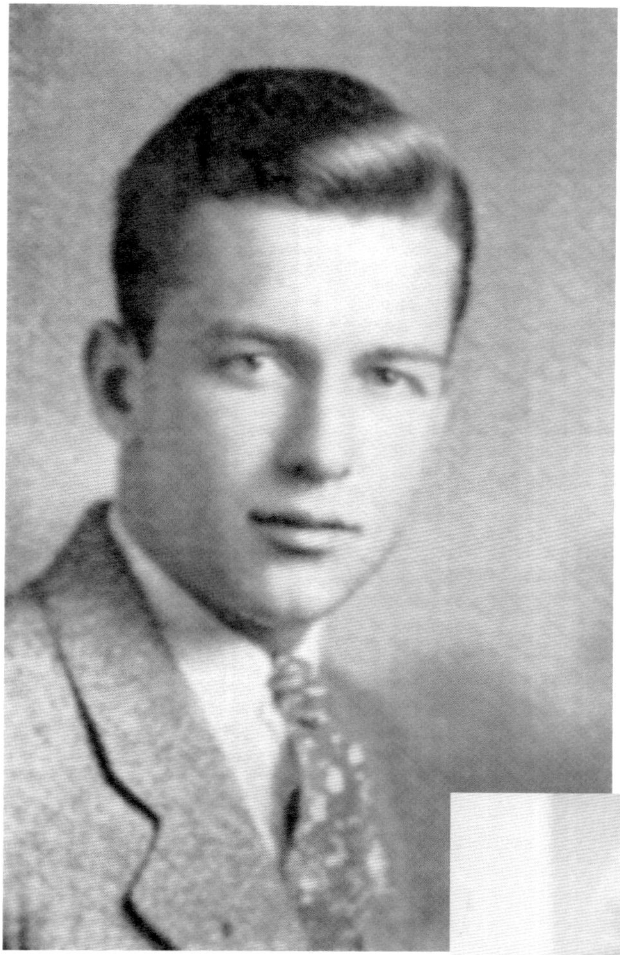

Carvel M. Bentley (Bentley Elementary). Carvel Bentley retired from the Plymouth-Canton Community School District in 1972 after 43 years of service. Many of those years were spent as a principal at the high school. Bentley started working for the Plymouth-Canton Community Schools (PCCS) right out of college, in the fall of 1929. He was known to be a very nice and kind gentleman. Bentley helped to organize a group called the Teacher's Club, which later grew into the Plymouth Educational Association. He served as the group's first president in 1946. At left, Bentley is pictured early in his career with PCCS. Below is a photograph of Bentley in the 1960s. Bentley Elementary opened in Canton in the fall of 1994. (Photographs courtesy of Plymouth Historical Museum.)

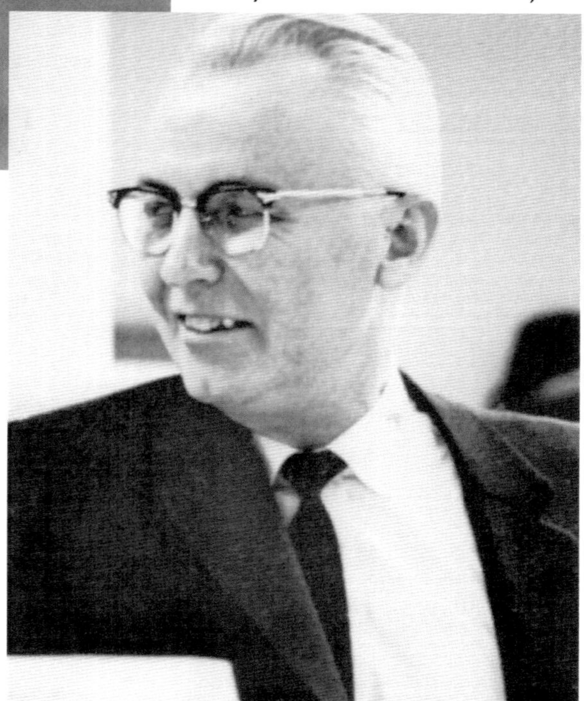

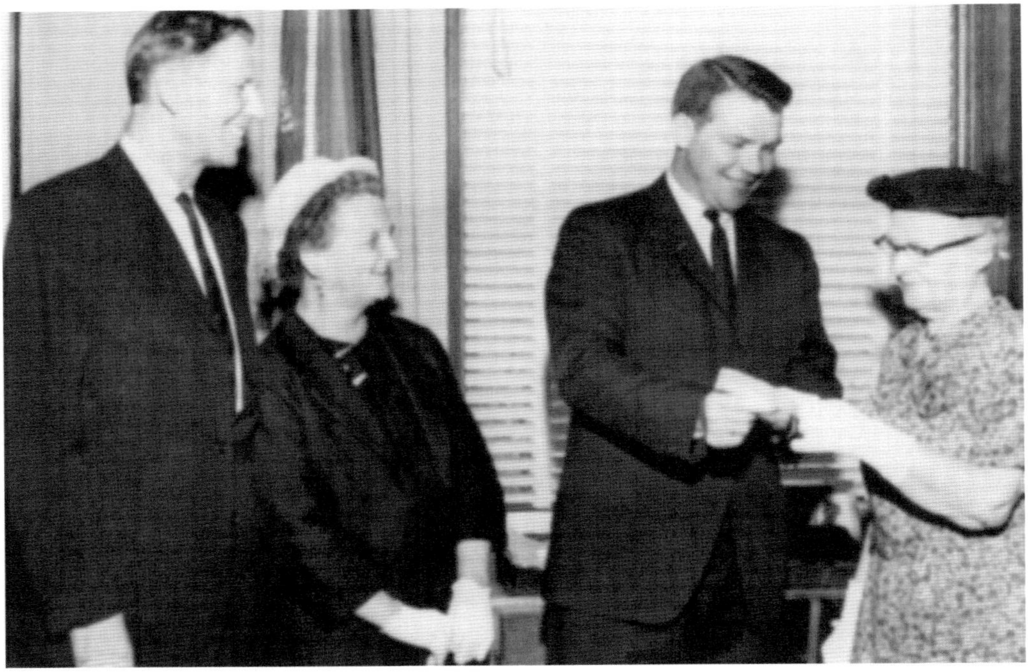

Nellie Bird (Bird Elementary).
Nellie Bird came to Plymouth because her husband had been hired to do construction work at the high school. The year was 1917, World War I was coming to an end, and the superintendent at the time, a Mr. Reebes, was having a hard time filling positions. Hearing about a teacher from the construction crew, he requested a meeting and asked for some help from Nellie Bird. She gladly obliged, and ended up staying for 25 years. Bird loved learning about teaching and enjoyed hearing children's stories and philosophies. It is known she had a warm and gentle nature. Above, she is presented an award by then Michigan governor John Sainson in the early 1960s. Below, Bird is shown with Kenneth Hulsing (right) and an unidentified man at the 1951 dedication of Bird Elementary. (Photographs courtesy of Plymouth Historical Museum.)

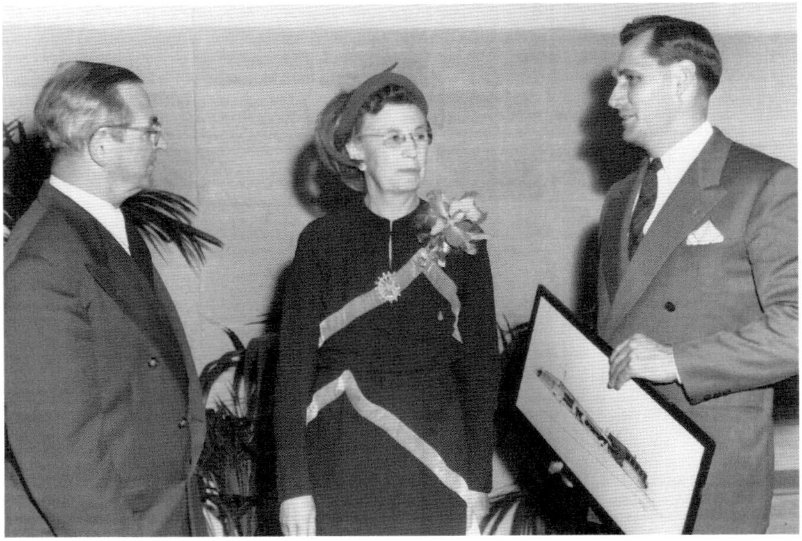

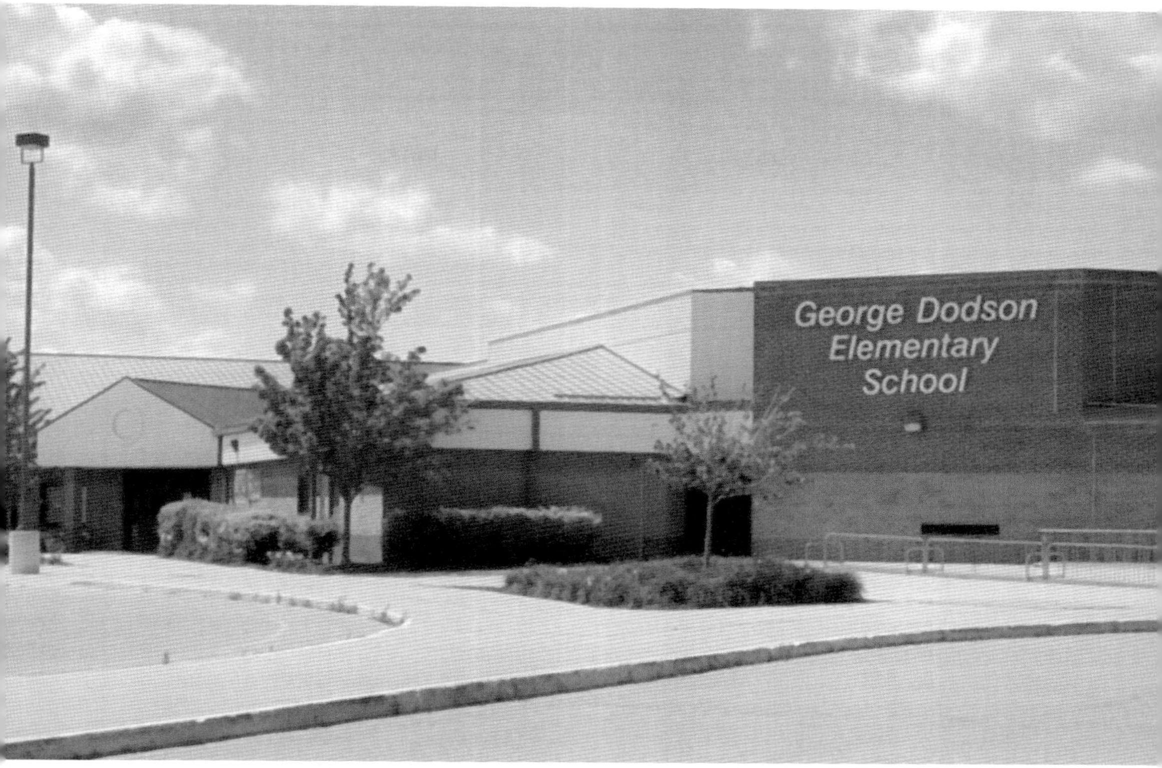

George Dodson (Dodson Elementary).
In 1972, George Dodson was named principal of Gallimore Elementary. Dodson, a lifelong educator, was noted for the respect he had for children. He loved the job of teaching and was a well-respected man. George Dodson Elementary opened its doors and had a dedication ceremony on Tuesday, October 23, 2001. On the dedication plaque hanging in the front lobby are the words "Dedicated for children, our hope, our joy." Home of the Dolphins, Dodson Elementary, like several of the schools in Canton, was built to accommodate a growing population. The school is located in the southern part of Canton. (Photograph courtesy of author.)

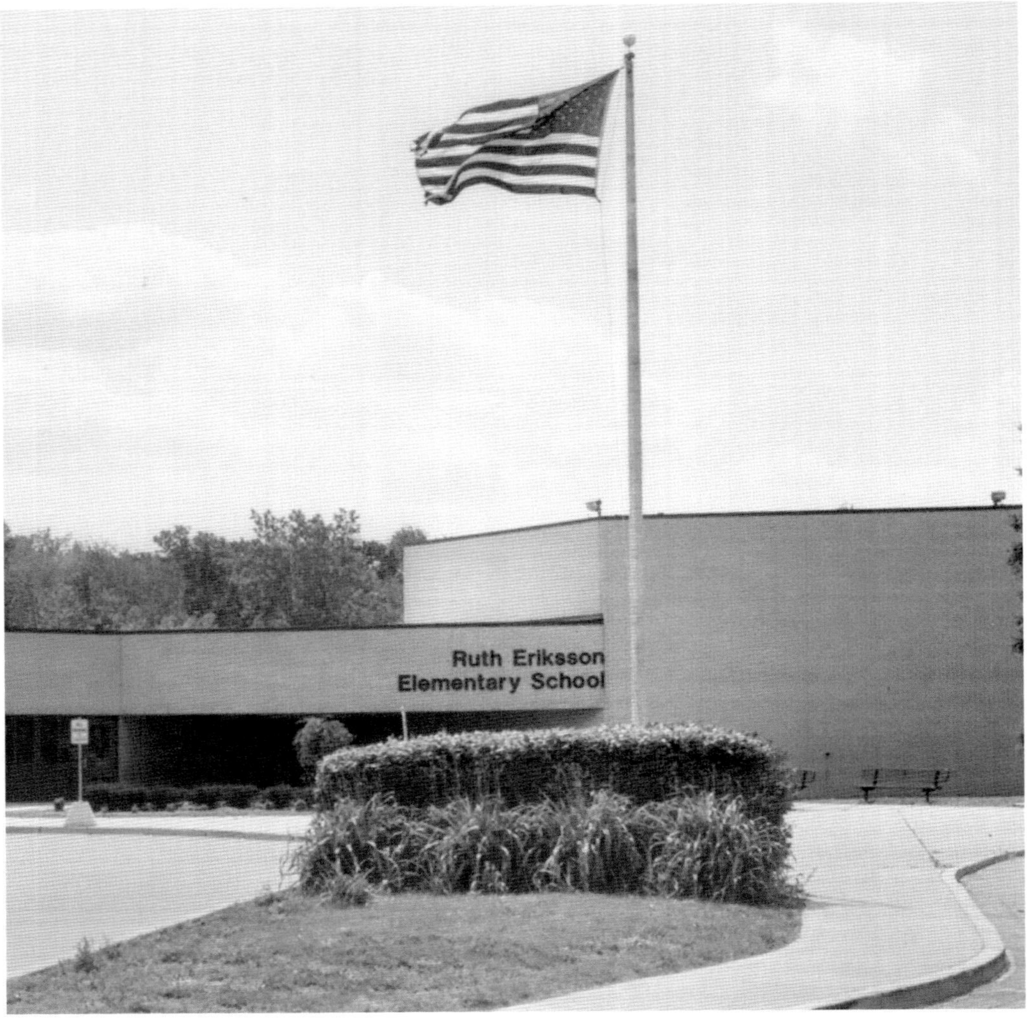

Ruth Eriksson (Ruth Eriksson Elementary).
Ruth Eriksson retired in 1971 as principal of Smith Elementary. She had come to the district in 1939 and spent most of her career in the Plymouth Schools, for a total of 32 years of service. Interestingly, in 1928, the school board elected to not hire married women, and, if married during the term of the contract, the employee's contract would then be void. Two years later, that ruling was changed. Only if recommended by the superintendent could a woman stay employed as a teacher, and she had to have additional help at home so that the domestic sphere would not interfere with her duties as a teacher. Ruth, just out of school and not married, started her career in Plymouth as a sixth-grade teacher. How the times changed during her career in the schools! Named in her honor in 1976, Ruth Eriksson Elementary School and Field and Hulsing Schools were coined "Bicentennial Schools." Eriksson, too sick to attend the dedication, was represented by her brother. She died in 1979. (Photograph courtesy of author.)

Helen Farrand (Farrand Elementary). Farrand Elementary was dedicated in 1958, the same year Helen Farrand retired after 31 years of service to the Plymouth-Canton School District. Raised on a farm off of Ann Arbor Road, Farrand graduated from Plymouth High School in 1911. Taking a six-week course in teaching at Ypsilanti Normal (now Eastern Michigan University), she often joked that it took her 37 years and many summers to get her teaching degree. Farrand lived quietly the rest of her years and died in 1977. Tucked inside Lakepointe subdivision, Farrand Elementary School is a charming little structure. Its design and construction followed plans similar to that of Gallimore Elementary, with a couple of changes. When built, the school had 12 classrooms, large kindergarten spaces, and a couple of multipurpose rooms. The cost to build the school in 1957–1958 was about $500,000. (Photographs courtesy of Plymouth Historical Museum.)

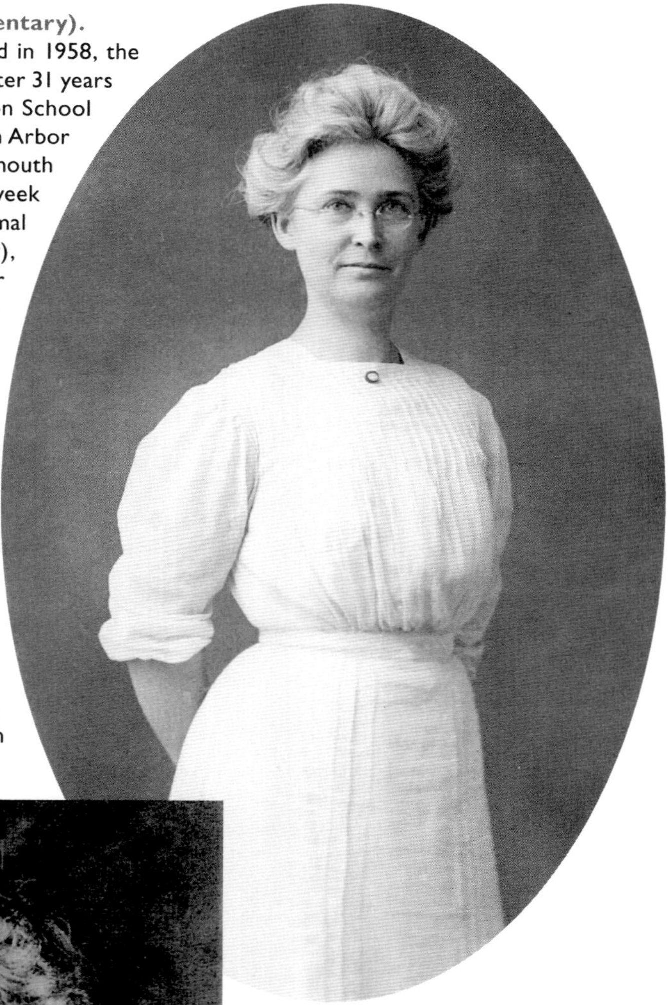

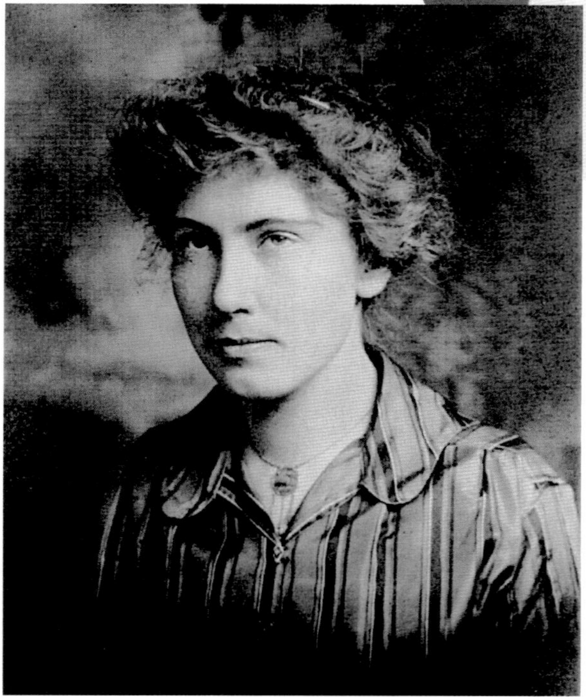

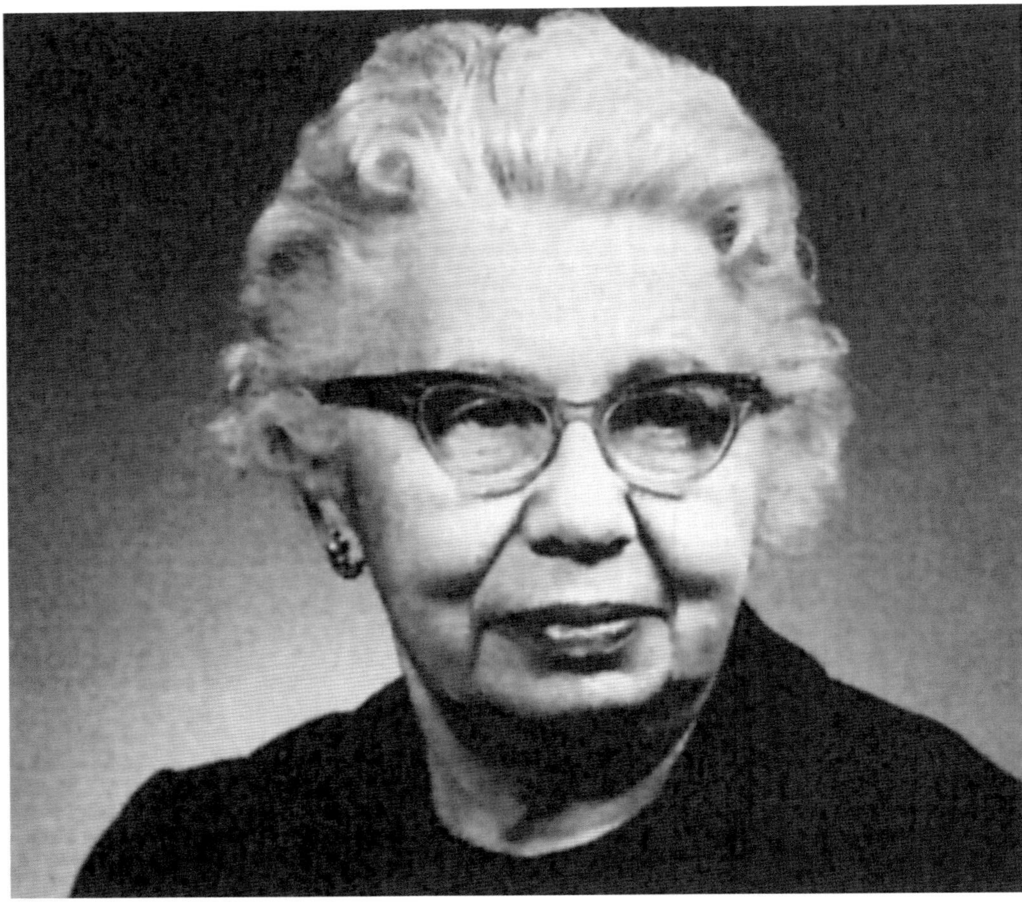

Gertrude Fiegel (Fiegel School).
Fiegel School opened its doors in 1968 and was named after Gertrude Fiegel for her 36 years of service to the district. She was born in Ann Arbor, Michigan, and earned her bachelor's and master's degrees from the University of Michigan. She came to teach in Plymouth in 1929, and her favorite subjects were government and history. It is recorded that many of her students could not wait to get to her classes, because she made them fun and interesting. In the 1950s, studying international relations and government, Gertrude and another teacher by the name of Jerry Fisher decided to take a field trip to New York and see the United Nations in action. The money was raised, parents gave their support, and the trip was undertaken. More such trips took place over the next 14 years. (Photograph courtesy of Plymouth Historical Museum.)

Mildred Field (Mildred Field Elementary).
In May 1967, Mildred Field was honored during a board meeting, when her 19 years of service as a principal for Starkweather School were recognized. Almost 10 years later, Mildred Field Elementary was dedicated in honor of her 24 years of service and dedication to the Plymouth-Canton Community School District. In all, Field dedicated 40 years of service to education. She had served other school districts before coming to Plymouth, and was also a social worker. She retired to South Haven, Michigan, in 1972. (Photograph courtesy of Plymouth Historical Museum.)

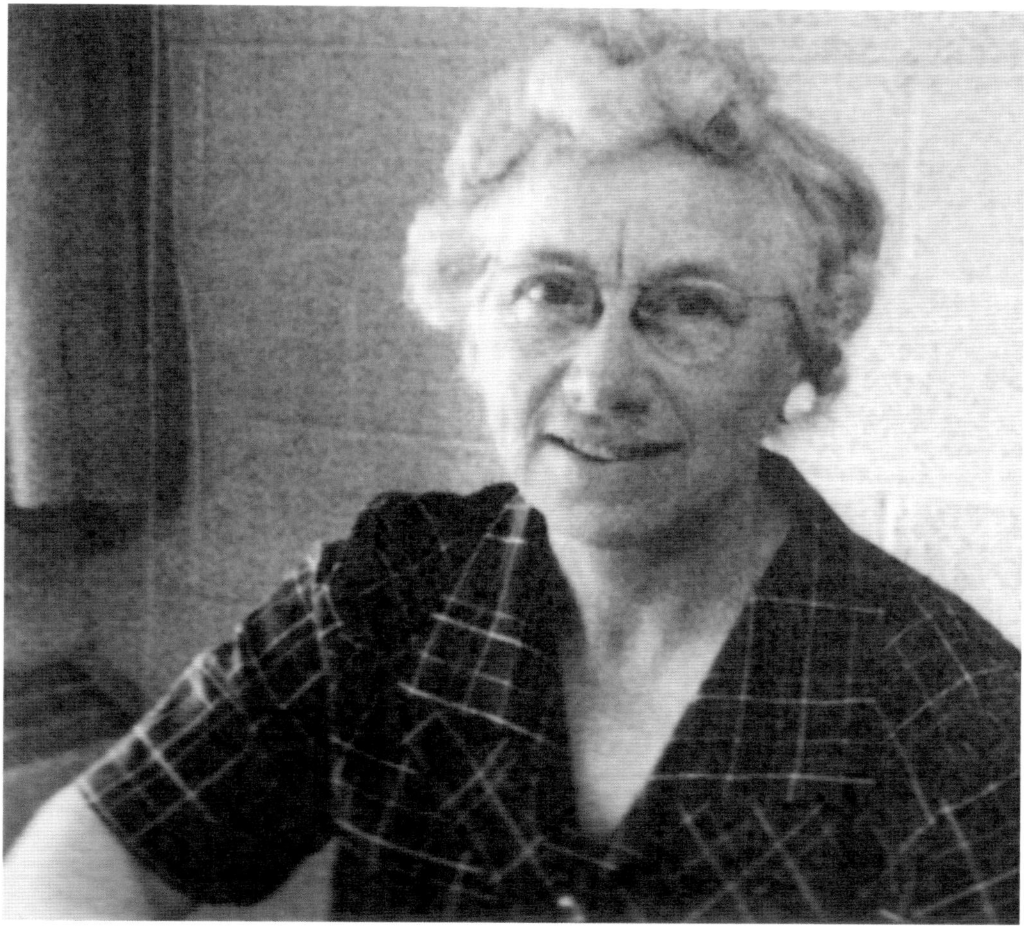

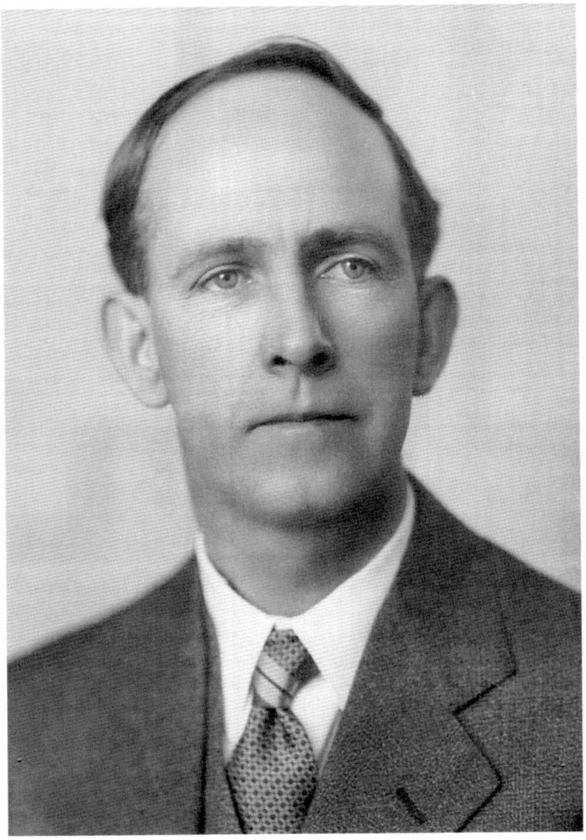

James Gallimore (James Gallimore School). Gallimore Elementary opened in 1956, and its dedication ceremonies were held in March 1957. James Gallimore served on the school board for 12 years and was president of the board for several of them. Trained and educated in toolmaking, Gallimore also worked for Burroughs Inc. and Ford Motor Company. In the mid-1940s, he took a position teaching a shop class at Wayne High School in Wayne, Michigan. In 1967, the school board voted to preserve 10 acres of woods around Gallimore Elementary to serve as an outdoor nature center and learning laboratory for current and future students. (Right, photograph courtesy of Plymouth Historical Museum; below, photograph courtesy of author.)

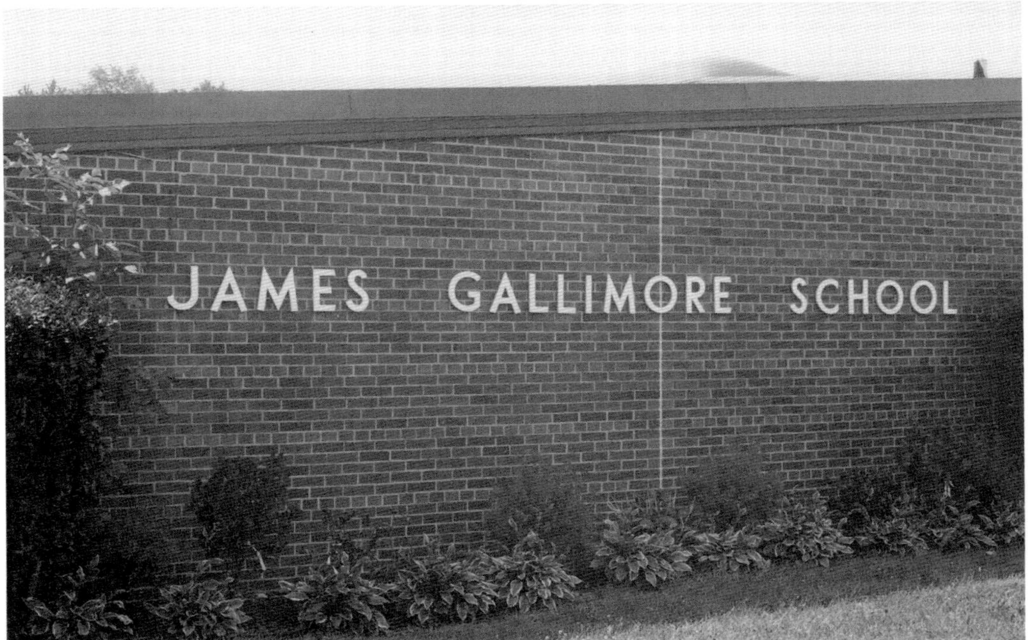

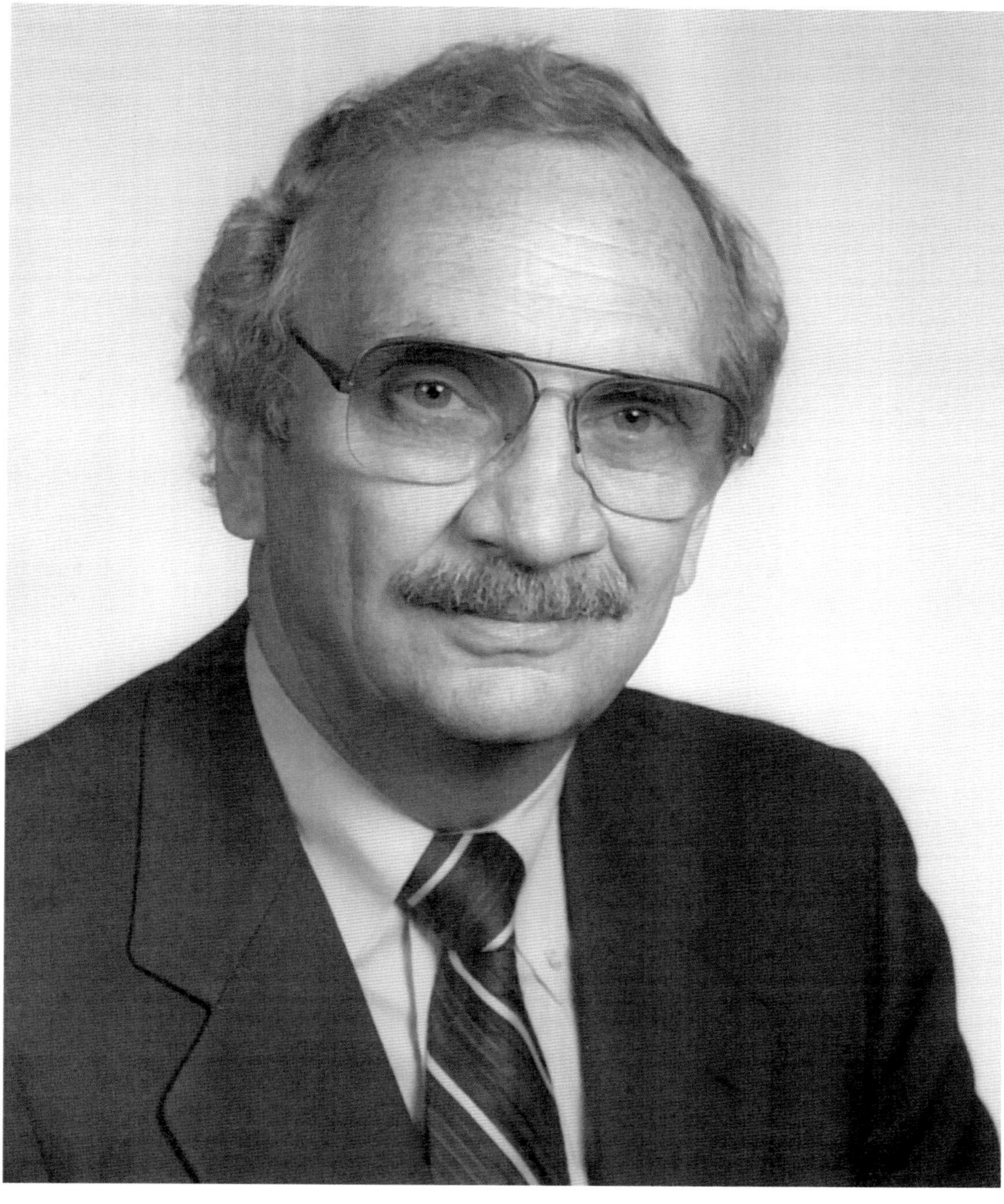

Dr. John Hoben (Hoben Elementary).
John Hoben came to the Plymouth schools in 1955 and worked as a math teacher. He had served in the Marines for six years before attending Adrian College, where he earned a bachelor's degree in education. While working to attain his degree, he served in the Korean War. A sports star at Adrian College, he was inducted into its hall of fame. Shortly after college, he was drafted by the Boston Celtics and had a two-year career as a professional basketball player with the Toledo Jeeps. He earned both a master's and, in 1979, a doctorate from Wayne State University. Hoben served Plymouth-Canton Schools as a counselor, an assistant principal, and a coordinator of secondary education. Hoben Elementary, home of the Hoben Hornets, opened in 1988. (Photograph courtesy of Plymouth Historical Museum.)

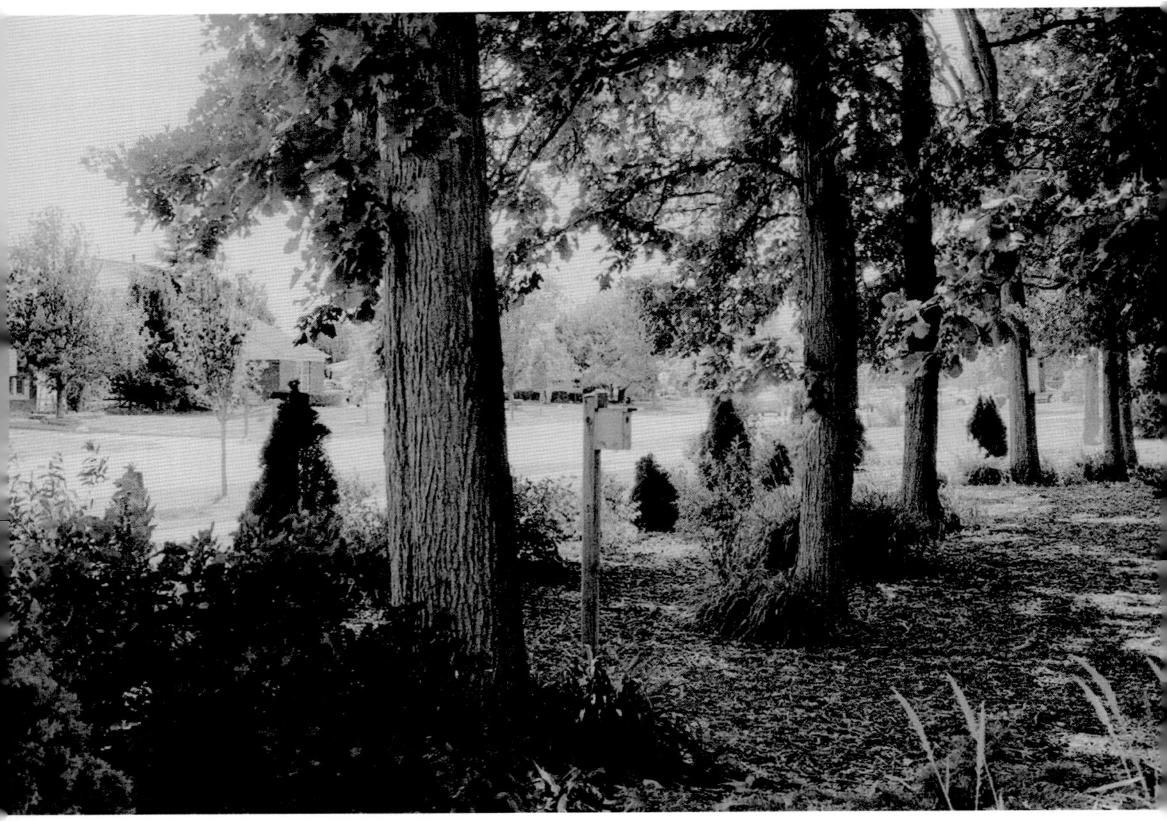

Hoben Elementary Nature Area.
Dr. John Hoben served Plymouth-Canton Schools as a counselor, an assistant principal, and a coordinator of secondary education. In 1971, he was appointed assistant superintendent, and in 1972, superintendent. Hoben was a well-liked, civic-minded individual and is credited with innovation and forward thinking in taking the district into the future. He participated in many different community groups and organizations. This 2012 photograph shows Hoben Elementary's beautiful nature area, complete with birdhouses, feeders, and paths on which to walk. This area is located near the front of the building, and is a lovely greeting to students and guests. (Photograph courtesy of author.)

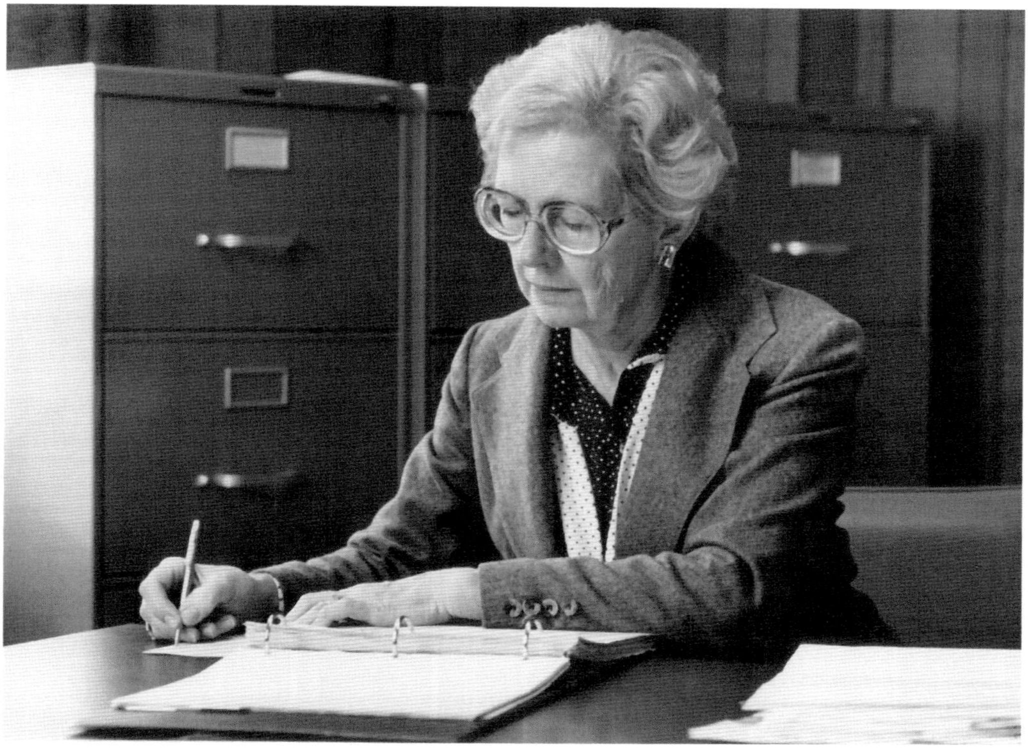

Esther and Kenneth Hulsing (Esther and Kenneth Hulsing Elementary). Hulsing Elementary is the only school in the district named after a husband-and-wife team. The Hulsings served many years as trustees on the school board, and received this honor in 1976. Esther served for eighteen years, some as president, and Kenneth served for six years, also serving some as president. Esther worked as the Plymouth township clerk for many years, and Kenneth worked for General Motors. The Hulsings had three daughters who attended school in the district, and Mr. and Mrs. Hulsing were always active within their schools and with the community. Above, Esther Hulsing is pictured at work in the 1960s. Hulsing Elementary is shown in the below photograph. (Above, photograph courtesy of Plymouth Historical Museum; below, photograph courtesy of author.)

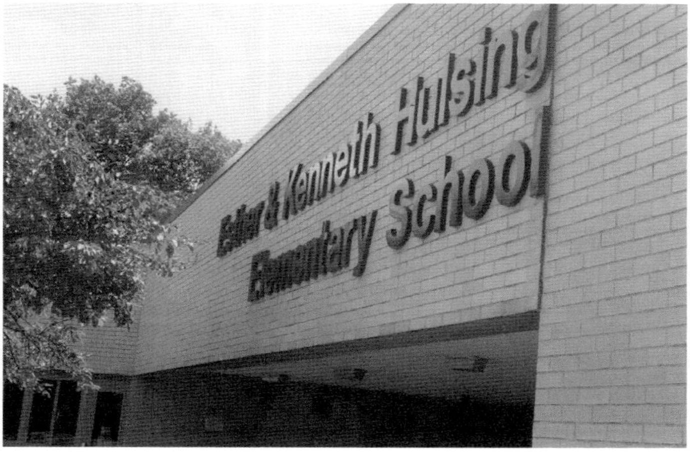

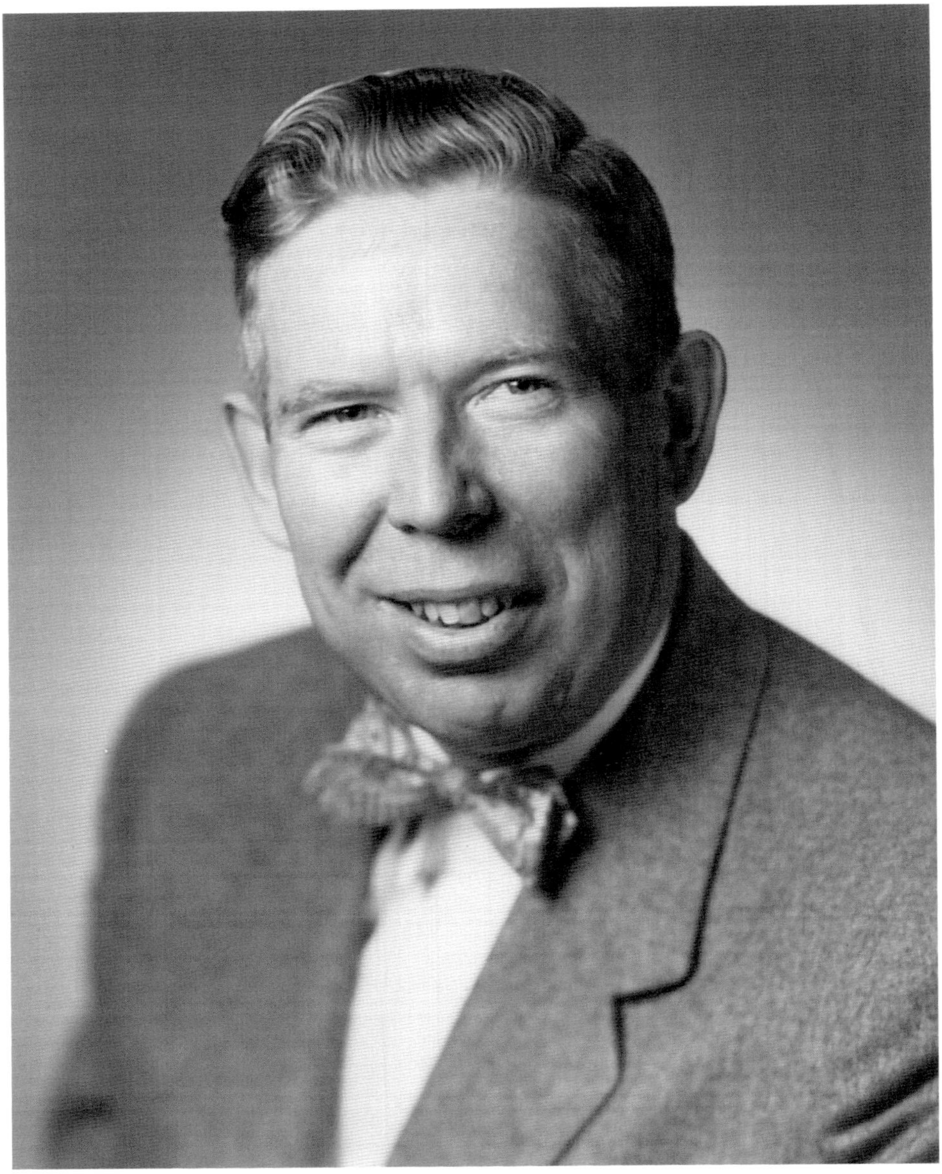

Russell Isbister (Isbister Elementary).
Russell Isbister was superintendent for 16 years. Well-liked and always sporting a bow tie, he was instrumental in the development of Schoolcraft College, located in nearby Livonia, in 1961. Schoolcraft was built to address the overcrowding at universities and has been very successful, recently celebrating its 50th birthday. Isbister was also very civic-minded and did not limit his abilities to only school matters. He was a member of the Plymouth Community Fund Drive and of the chamber of commerce. Isbister was also instrumental in the purchase of the land where the high schools now stand. After retirement in 1967, he went on to teach at Eastern Michigan University. He was described as kind, professional, and truly devoted to the education of children. Sadly, Isbister died of a heart attack in 1968, one year after his retirement as superintendent. Isbister Elementary opened in 1968 and was dedicated in his memory. (Photograph courtesy of Plymouth Historical Museum.)

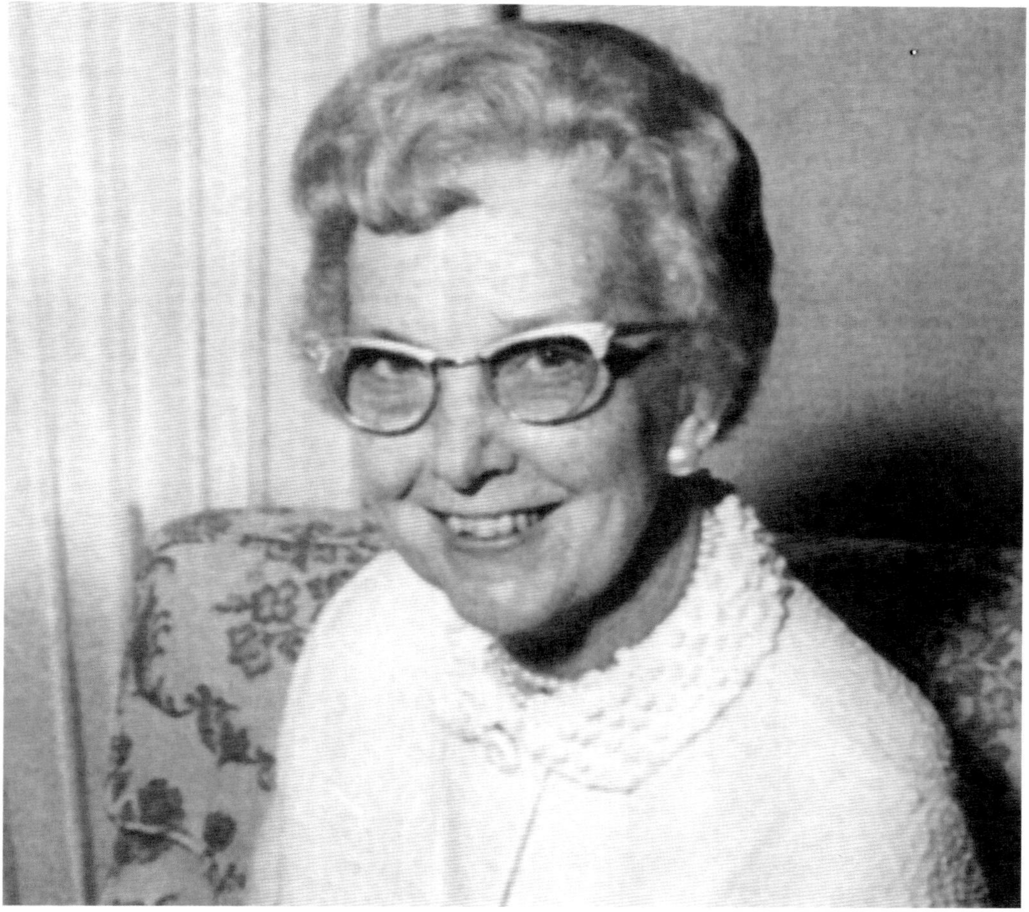

Dorothy T. Miller (Miller Elementary).
Miller Elementary opened its doors in 1973 and was named after Dorothy Miller for her 24 years of service. Miller attended Eastern Michigan University. Coming to the district in 1944, she worked as a kindergarten and first-grade teacher. Her time spent in the district was at Starkweather and Bird Schools. She retired in 1968 from the district and stayed very active in community affairs. A member of the Plymouth's Women's Club, the Arts Council, and the Symphony Society, she was known for her kindness and dedication to children. She died in 1984. (Photograph courtesy of Plymouth Historical Museum.)

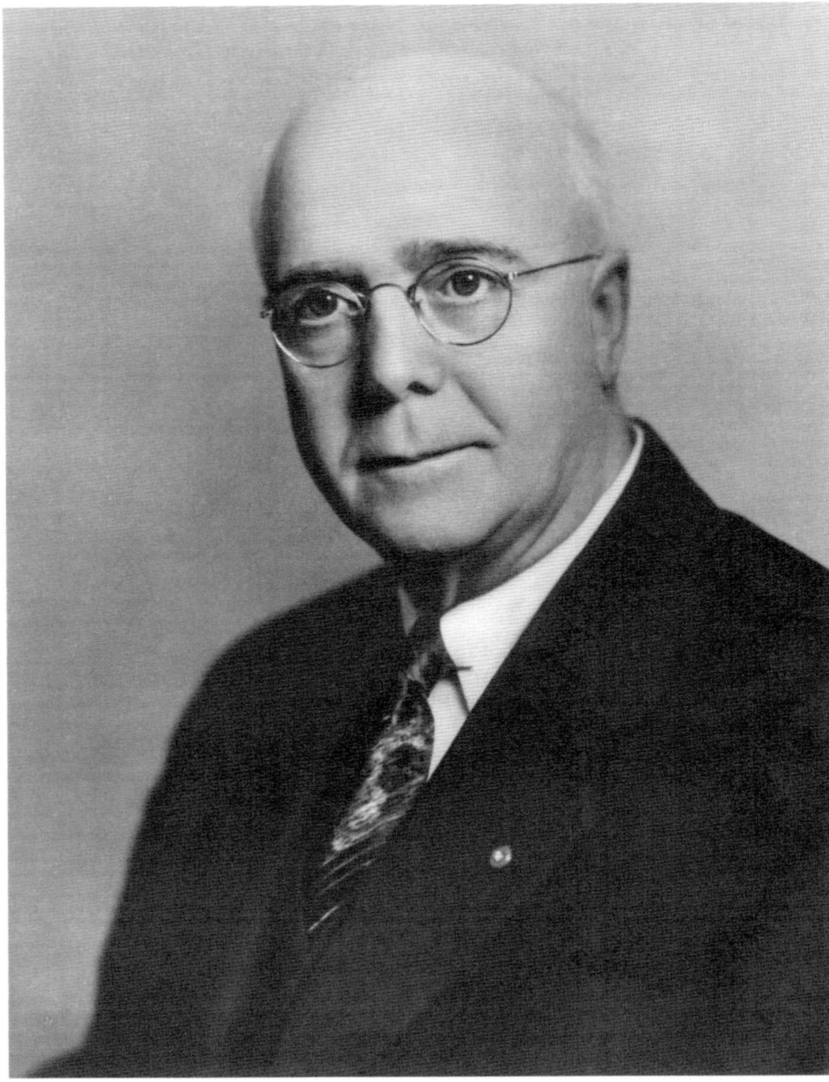

George Smith (Smith School).
George Smith came to the school district in the fall of 1913. At the time, Superintendent Reebes was asked to take a position with Bowling Green University. Smith, a superintendent for Manchester School District, applied for the job in Plymouth. He was a very driven young man. Self-taught in many areas, he experienced great success in the field of education. He was orphaned at the age of six, and in his adolescent years, a lovely couple took him into their home and loved and cherished him. George went back to school and earned his degree shortly after arriving in Plymouth. He was very well liked, and it was reported that he possessed a positive, can-do attitude, a trait that served him well in his position. He worked in the district for 27 years, and in that time experienced many challenges and innovations, including World War I, women's rights, sicknesses, and vaccinations, to name a few. Smith School, named in his honor, was built in 1950 and dedicated in 1951. Until 1950, there were only three schools in Plymouth: the high school, Central Grade School, and Starkweather. Between 1950 and 1976, another 15 schools were built to accommodate the growing population in the Plymouth and Canton areas. (Photograph courtesy of Plymouth Historical Museum.)

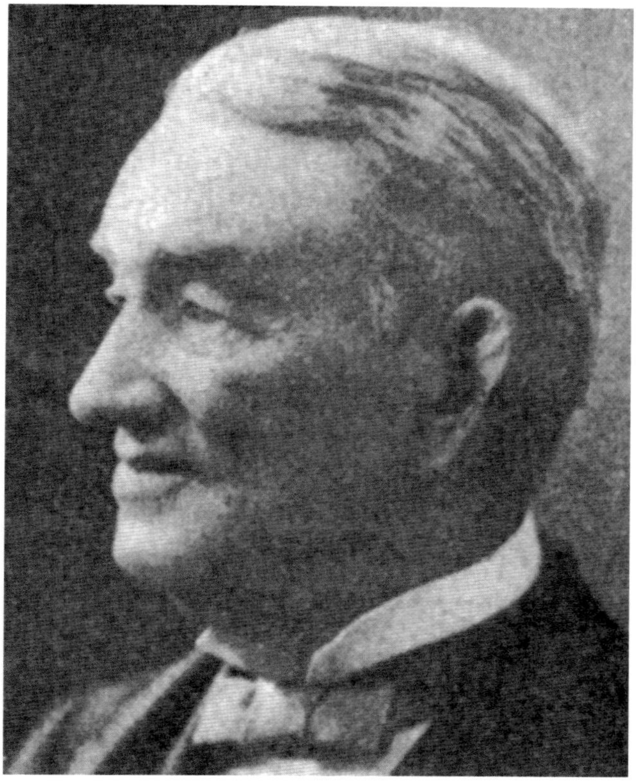

George Starkweather (Starkweather Building). Named after founding settlers to the area, Starkweather is one of the oldest buildings in Plymouth. Nellie Bird was the school's first principal when it was built in 1927. The school taught many local children whose names readers may be familiar with: the Houghs, Bennetts, McClumpha, and Kellogg, to name just a few. George Starkweather (left) taught in one of the earlier schoolhouses in Plymouth and was said to have very good, serious study habits. The photograph below shows the laying of the first cornerstone of the Starkweather Building on May 2, 1927. Today, the building holds adult education classes and is located in what is known as Old Village. (Photographs courtesy of Plymouth Historical Museum.)

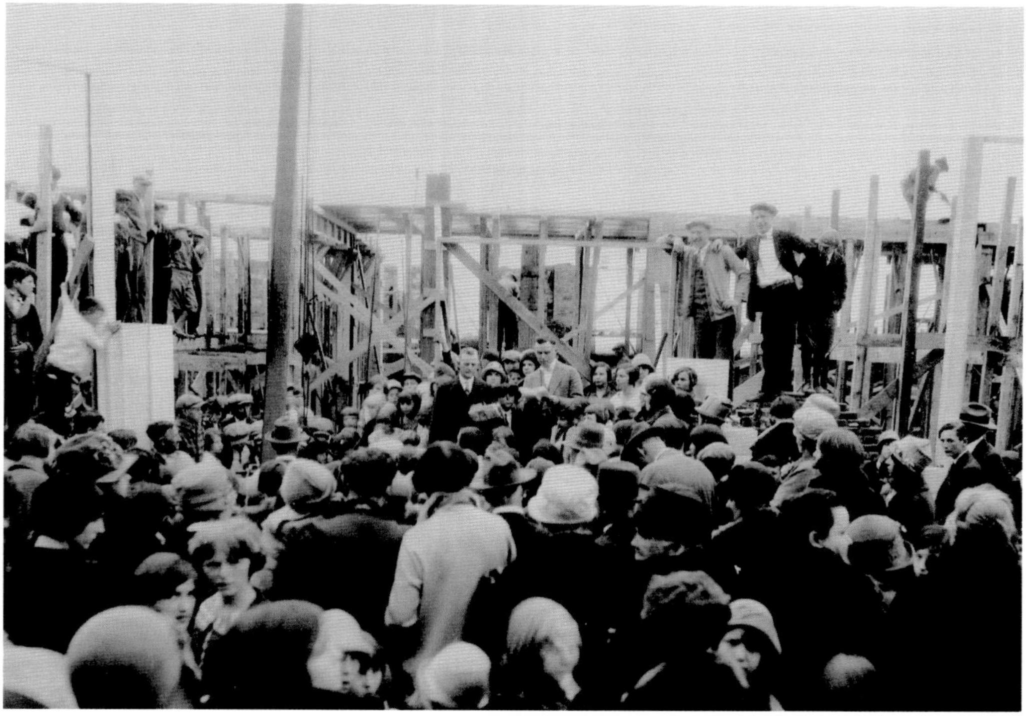

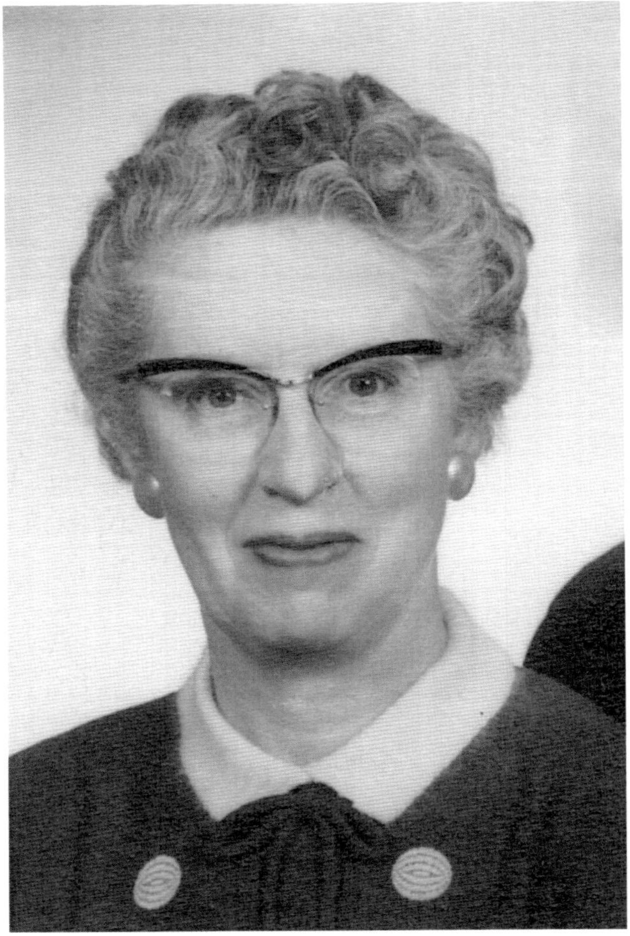

Nancy Tanger (Tanger Elementary). Nancy Tanger served the school district for 34 years. She taught fourth and fifth grades and also served as principal at Starkweather and Central Schools. Tanger was Bird Elementary's first principal when it opened. She had taught with Nellie Bird and was very flattered and honored to work in the school named after her fellow teacher. At Madonna College in nearby Livonia, Nancy worked for five years as a consultant for their teaching program. Today, Madonna University is widely recognized for its teaching program and, as at Schoolcraft College, its program offerings and attendance have soared. Tanger Elementary opened its doors and was dedicated on June 4, 1967. Today, the building is used for the Infant Preschool Special Education Program, which helps identify and work with students who have special needs. Early intervention is critically important in a student's success in school and in life. It is a wonderful program and has assisted many families over the years. Tanger retired in 1961. (Photograph courtesy of Plymouth Historical Museum.)

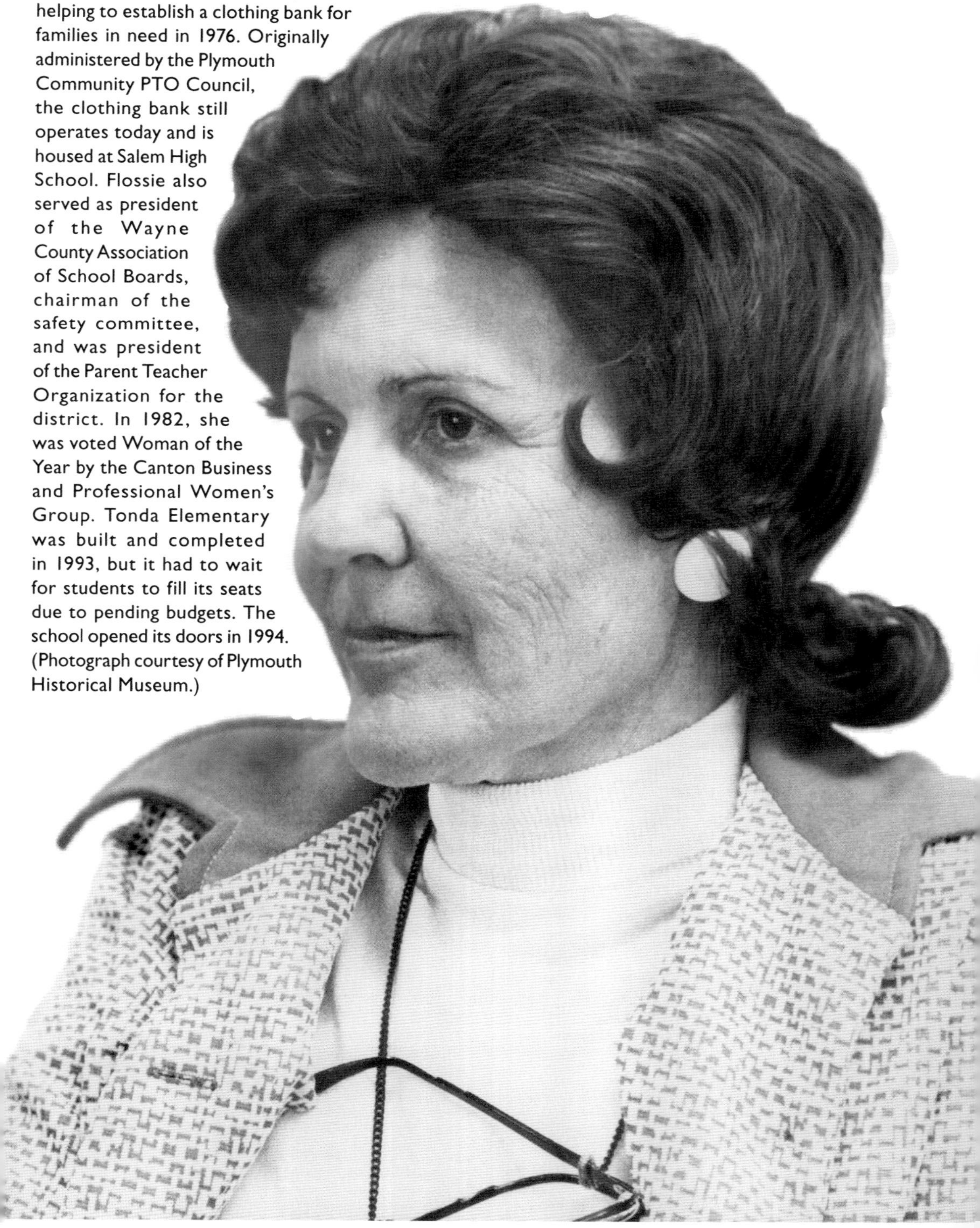

Flossie B. Tonda (Tonda Elementary). Flossie Tonda served on the Plymouth-Canton School Board from 1975 to 1984. In that time, her devotion and dedication to serving Plymouth and Canton students were inspirational. A hard worker, Flossie was responsible for helping to establish a clothing bank for families in need in 1976. Originally administered by the Plymouth Community PTO Council, the clothing bank still operates today and is housed at Salem High School. Flossie also served as president of the Wayne County Association of School Boards, chairman of the safety committee, and was president of the Parent Teacher Organization for the district. In 1982, she was voted Woman of the Year by the Canton Business and Professional Women's Group. Tonda Elementary was built and completed in 1993, but it had to wait for students to fill its seats due to pending budgets. The school opened its doors in 1994. (Photograph courtesy of Plymouth Historical Museum.)

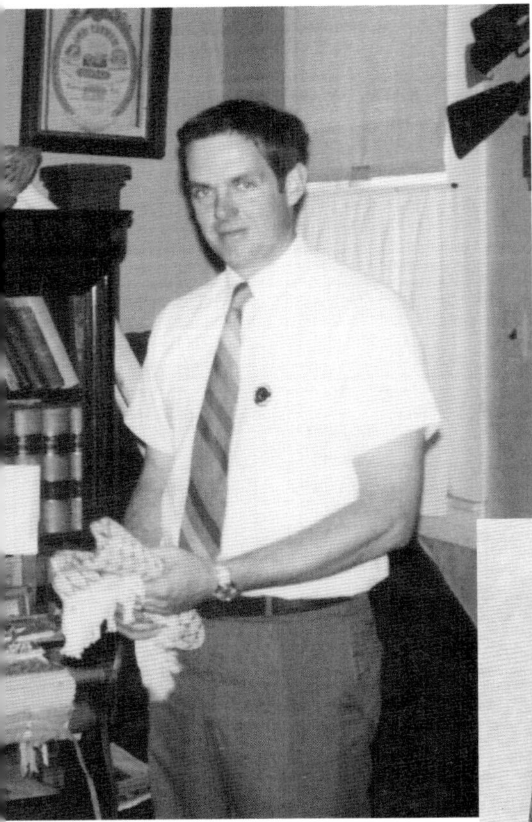

Thomas Workman (Workman Elementary). It was in 1967, just prior to his retirement, that Russell Isbister recommended Thomas Workman as principal for Allen Elementary. His career with the district had begun in 1960, when he worked as an elementary schoolteacher and a coach in several of the schools. Workman served as Allen's principal for 20 years. In 1985, he took a principal position at East Middle, and decided to retire in 1995. In the fall of 2006, Workman Elementary opened, and the building was dedicated in Workman's name. He is still active in the community and drops in on the school regularly to read and work with students, who look forward to his visits. Shown below is the invitation to the Workman Elementary dedication. (Left, photograph courtesy of Plymouth Historical Museum; below, photograph courtesy of Workman Elementary School staff.)

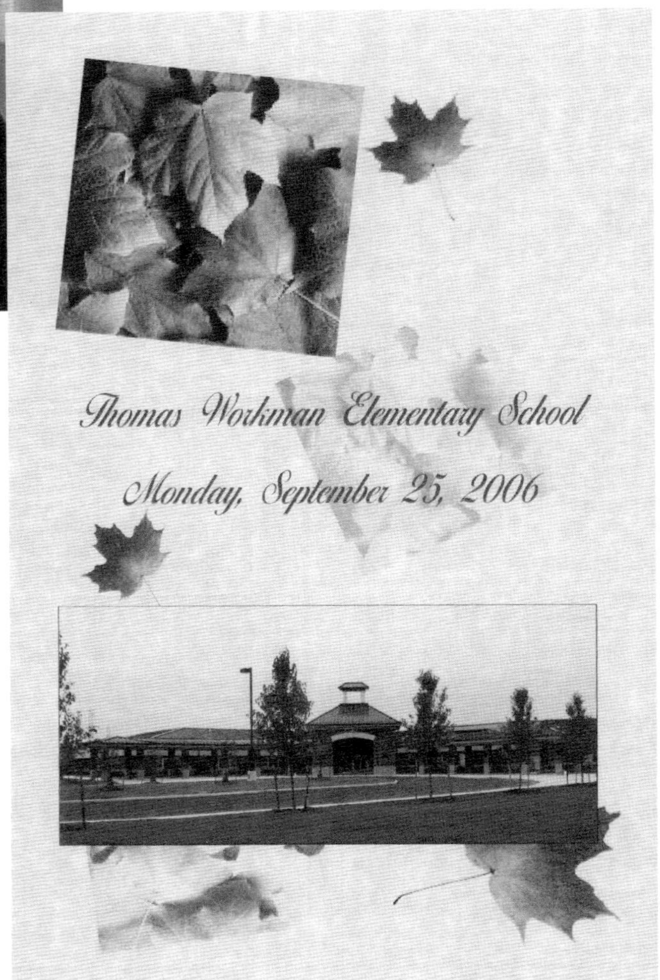

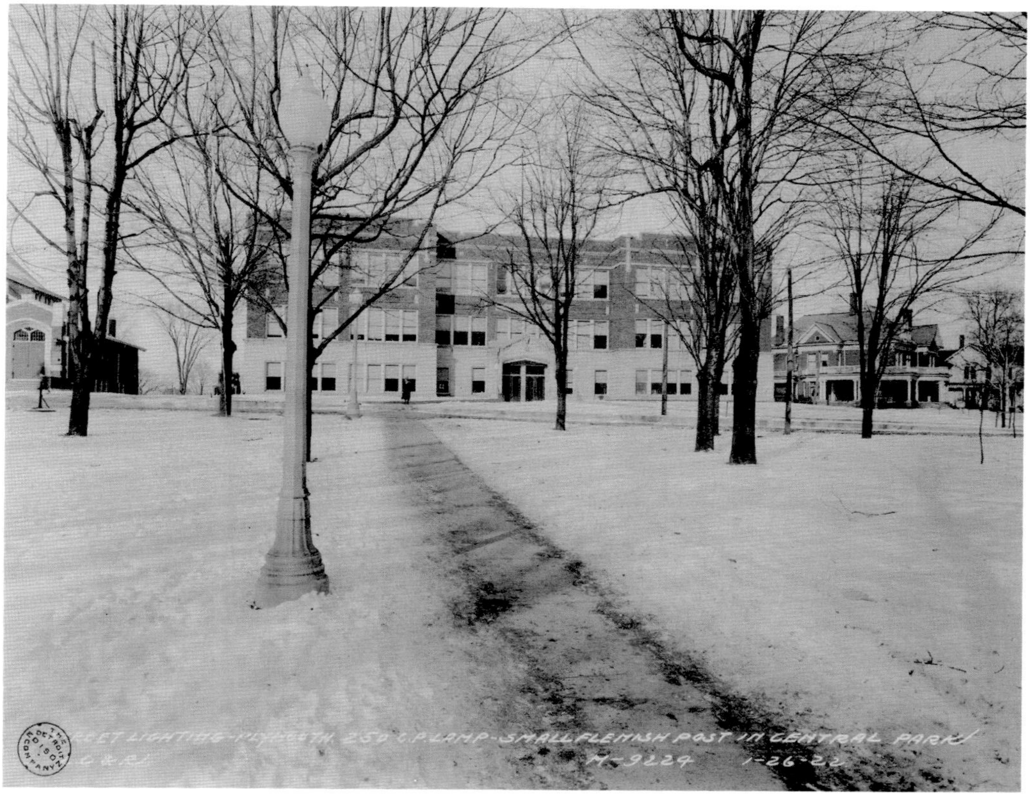

Ebenezer J. Penniman and Central Middle School.
The naming of the middle schools, while not as exciting or imaginative as that of the elementary schools, still serve a purpose. Plymouth-Canton Community School District guidelines state that middle school names must tie in with a geographic location or philosophy. The schools named are Central, East, West, Pioneer, and Discovery. Central Middle School opened in 1924 and has been a very big part of downtown Plymouth.

Many people who grew up in Plymouth and walked the halls of Central have fond memories. Once called Plymouth High School, the building is large and has a wonderful pool and grounds, including tennis courts and baseball fields, on which the Chargers compete. The building's location allows students the opportunity to access the town after school, including visiting the library and local eateries.

In 1858, Ebenezer J. Penniman donated to the school district the property on which Central Middle School now stands. The site originally housed the seminary that Penniman had built to honor the memory of his first wife. Penniman was a very influential man in Plymouth. In 1837, he vetoed the idea of the University of Michigan establishing a branch in town. In 1857, he objected to the idea of *Webster's* dictionary being used in the classroom, but later recanted and changed his vote. The school board at the time allowed $5 in the budget for the purchase of the dictionaries. For more on Ebenezer J. Penniman, see chapter one. (Photograph courtesy of Plymouth Historical Museum.)

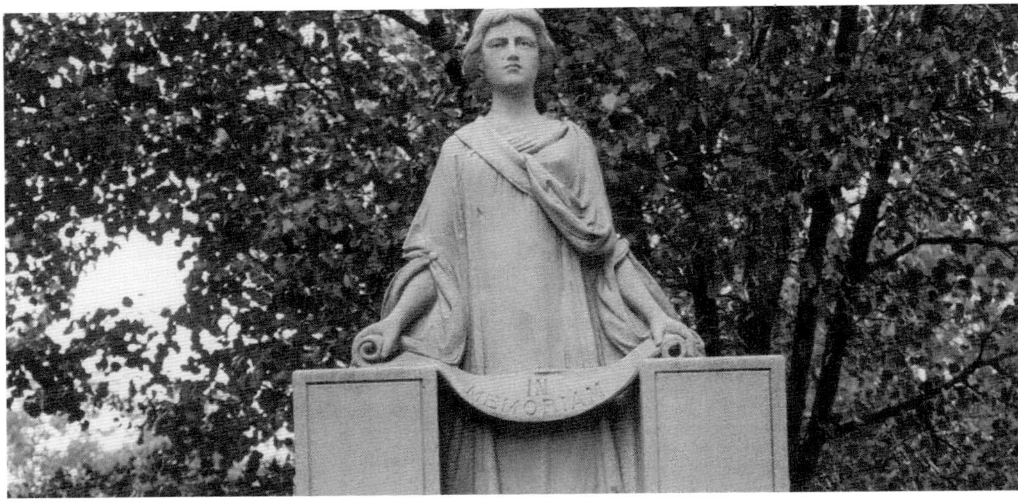

Plymouth Community Veterans' Memorial Park.
In front of Central Middle School stands the beautiful Plymouth Community Veterans Memorial Park. The park, dedicated on July 4, 2006, honors all soldiers from the Civil War and all subsequent conflicts. Pictured above is the Civil War Monument. Meticulously landscaped, and featuring flags raised high, the park is an honorable and beautiful tribute to those who have given their time and service to the country. (Photographs courtesy of author.)

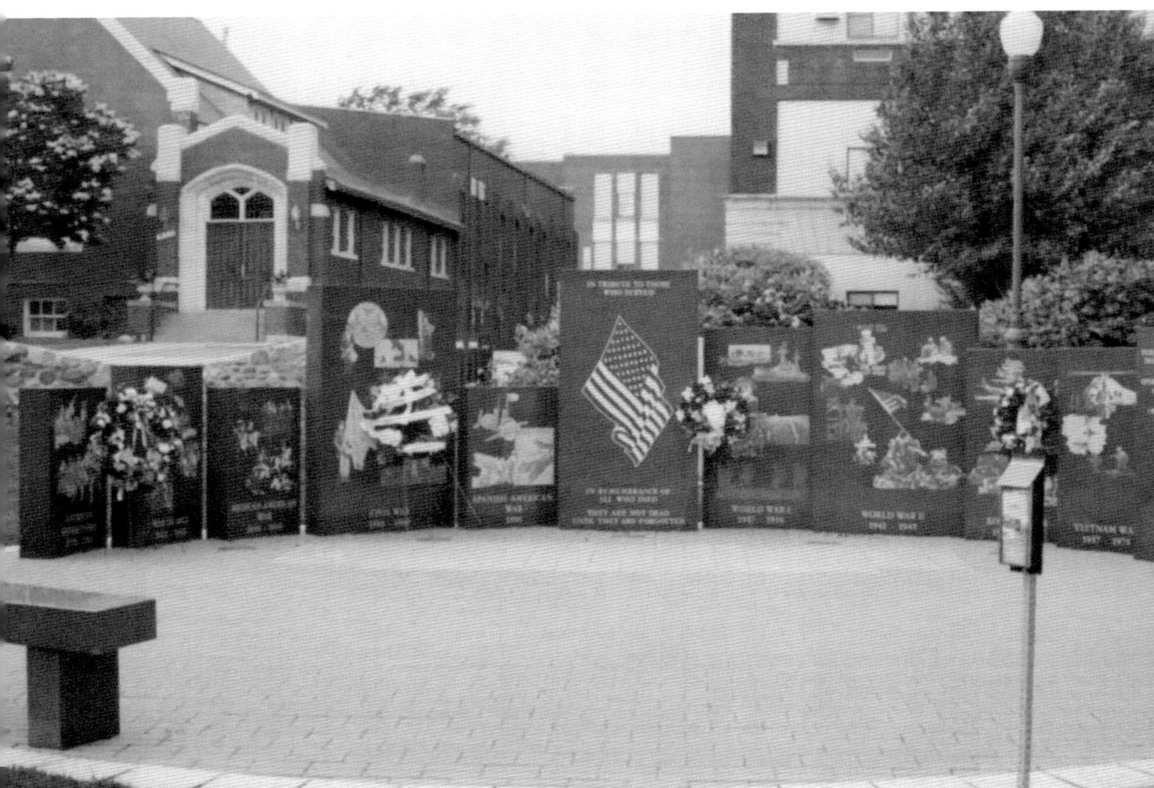

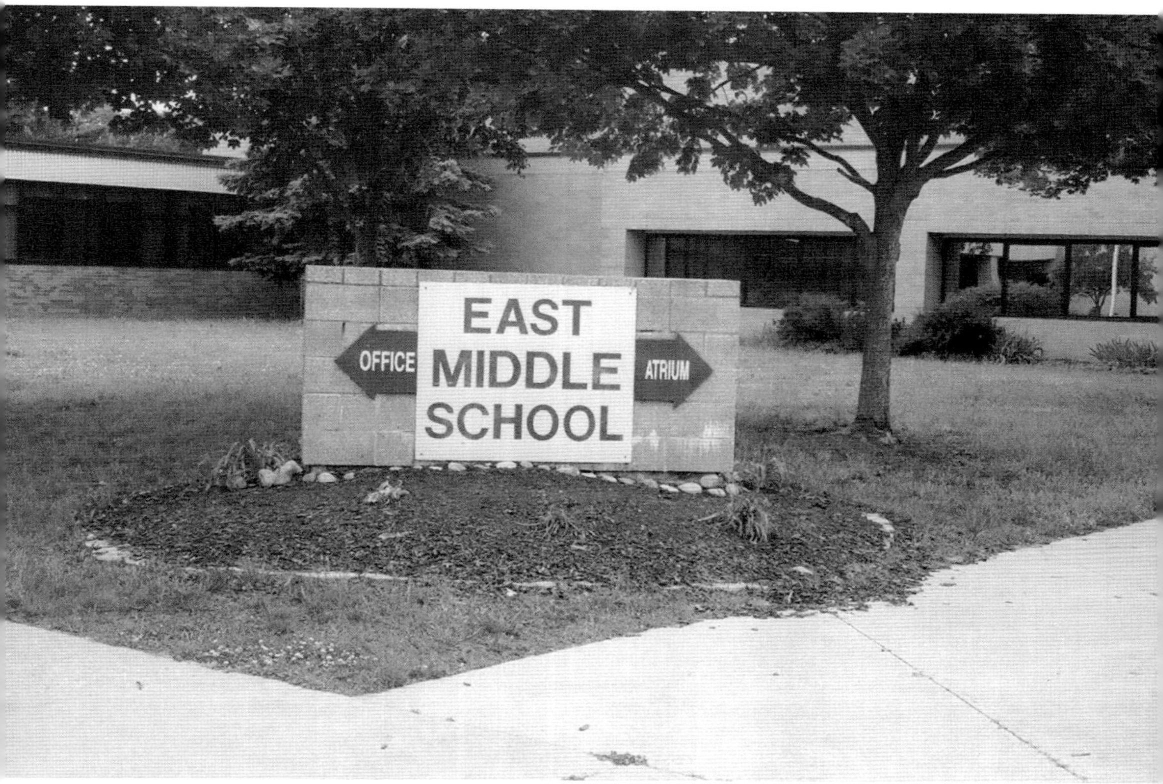

The Plymouth Rotary and East Middle School.
East Middle School, opened in 1957, resides in the eastern part of the city and township. Tucked off of Mill Street, the school was originally called Junior High East, but the name was quickly changed to East Middle. Situated on about 18 acres, the school is home to the East Rockets. Located nearby are the district's transportation department and curriculum center. East Middle School houses the Talented and Gifted Program for middle school students. It is also important to note that, originally, the grounds were used by the Plymouth Rotary for its annual chicken barbeque. That event developed into what is now known as the Fall Festival. The Plymouth Rotary raises money and awareness for many charitable causes in the area. For more information on this group and other wonderful organizations, see chapter seven. (Photograph courtesy of author.)

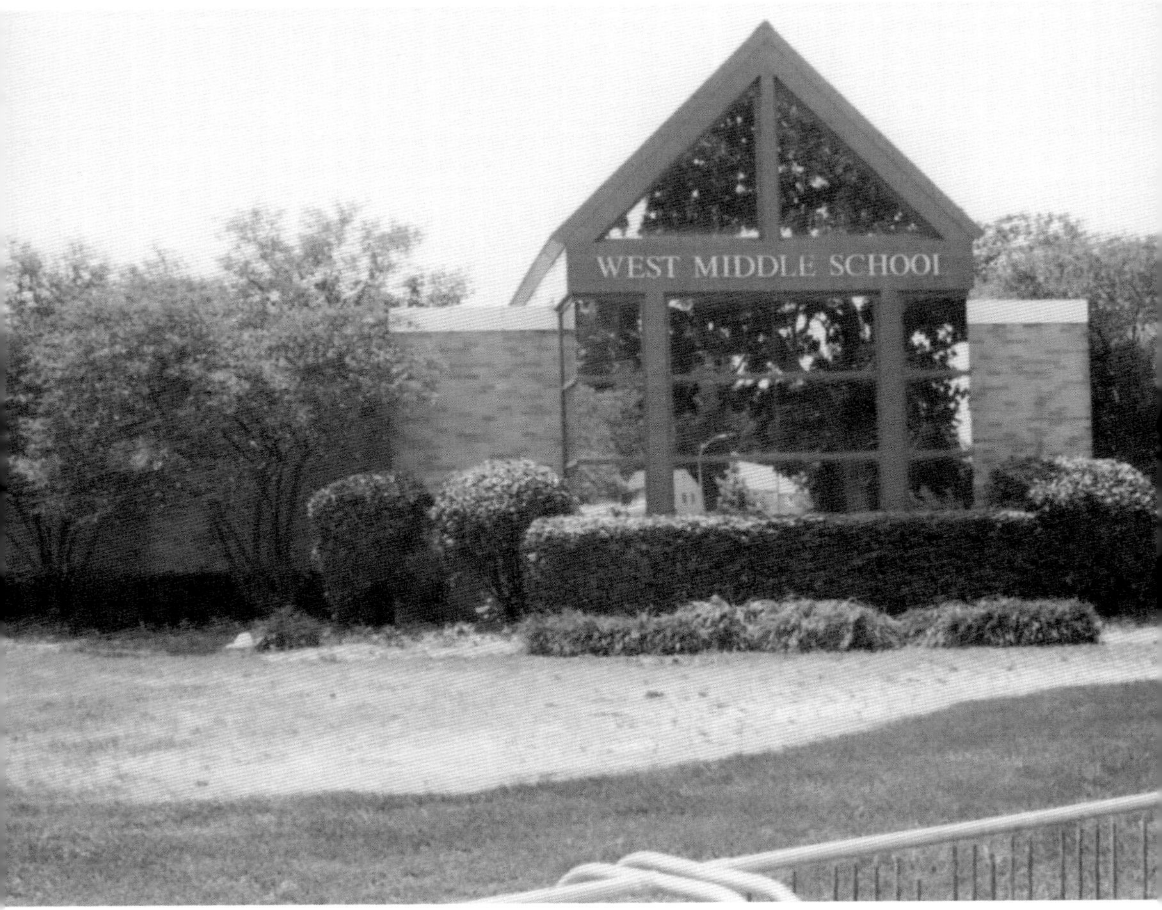

Robert Smith and West Middle School.
West Middle School, situated on the city and township's western end, broke ground in 1961. The first principal for the school was Robert Smith. He served the district for 20 years and retired in 1984. Smith started his career with the district as a chemistry and physics teacher, working his way up and earning his master's degree from Wayne State University. West, home of the Bulldogs, will be celebrating its 50th birthday. All of the schools in the district sit on nice-sized parcels of land. Outdoor spaces are used by students during recess and gym class, and for any number of after-school sports activities. Many of the schools also have nature areas used for science classes. (Photograph courtesy of author.)

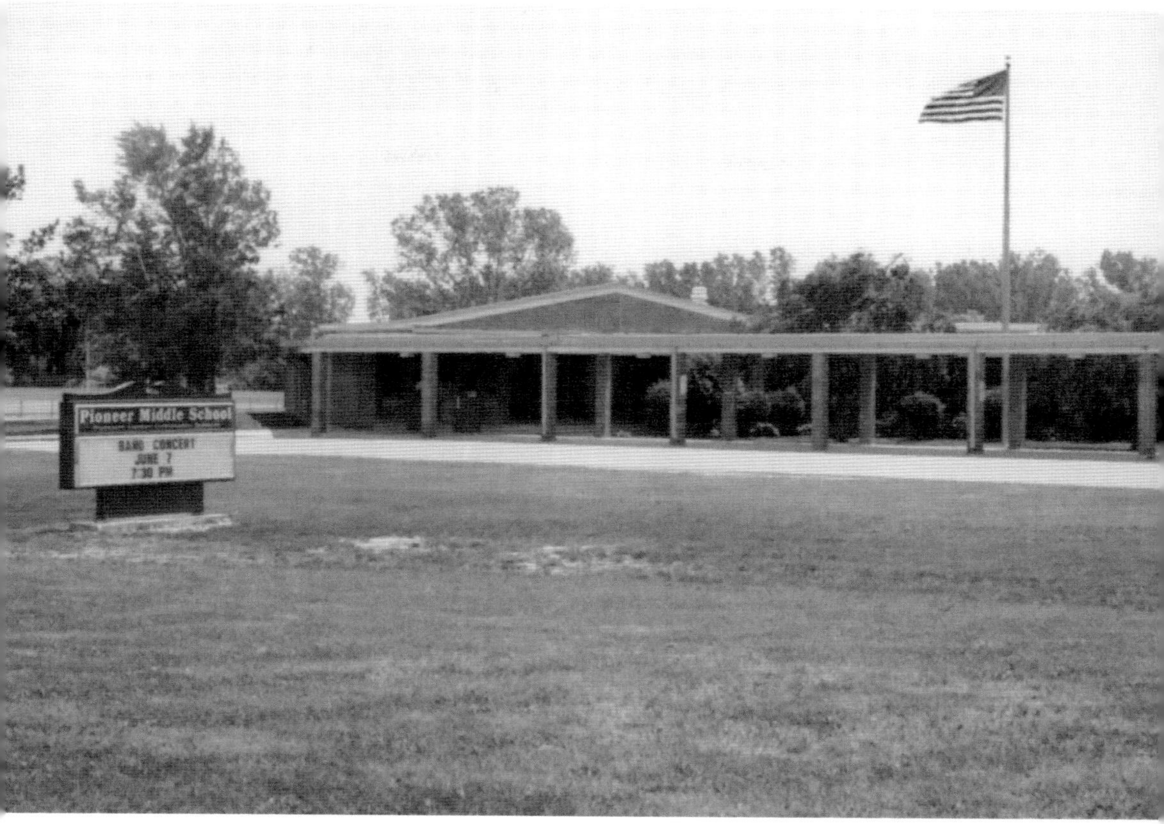

Gerald Elston and Pioneer Middle School.
Pioneer Middle School opened in the fall of 1968. It was named Pioneer because it was the first middle school in the district planned with a philosophy specifically geared toward junior high students. Home of the Panthers, its first principal was Gerald Elston, who had served in that capacity at Farrand Elementary when it opened in 1958. Elston retired from the district in June 1984 after 33 years of service to the schools. (Photograph courtesy of author.)

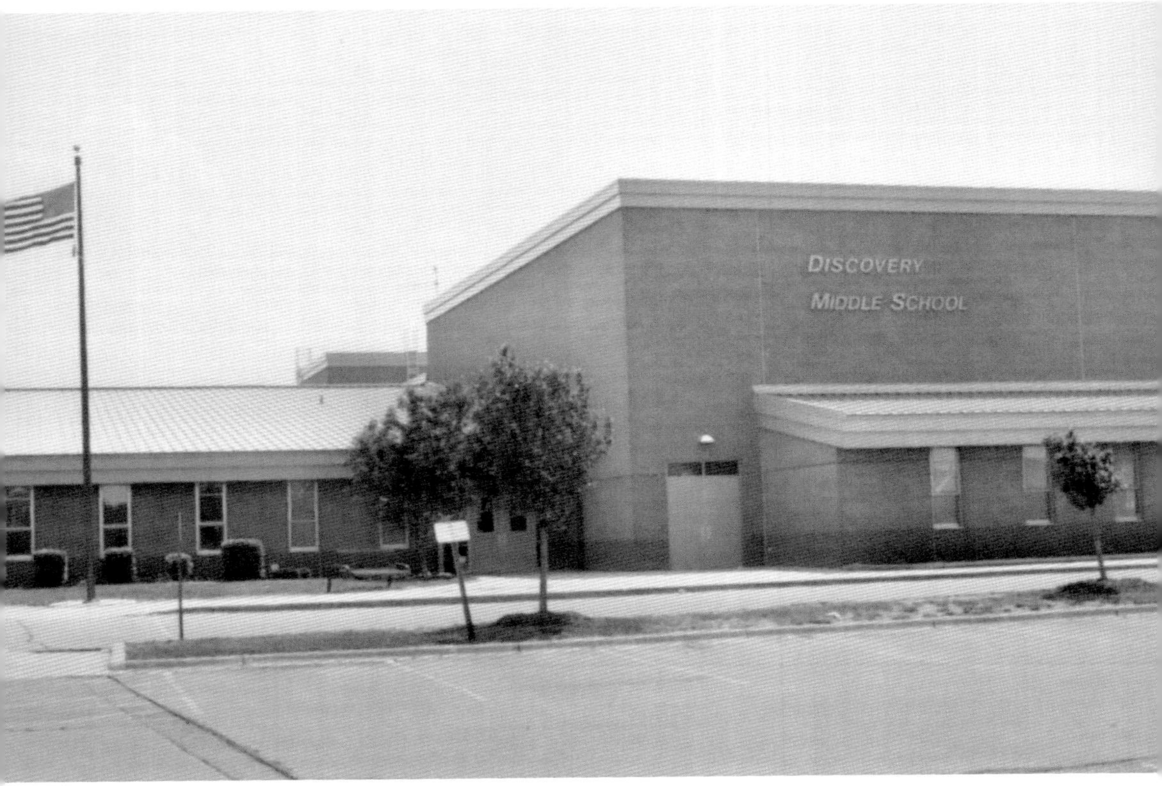

Discovery Middle School.
Discovery Middle School, built in Canton and situated in a neighborhood, is the district's most recent middle school. Opened and dedicated in 2000, the school is the home of the Eagles. The modern building's ample space and up-to-date technology are often used for larger school board meetings and informational gatherings. The school board made the decision to have the school built when, due to an ongoing population boom in Canton, it was evident that the district was in need of more classrooms and facilities space. (Photograph courtesy of author.)

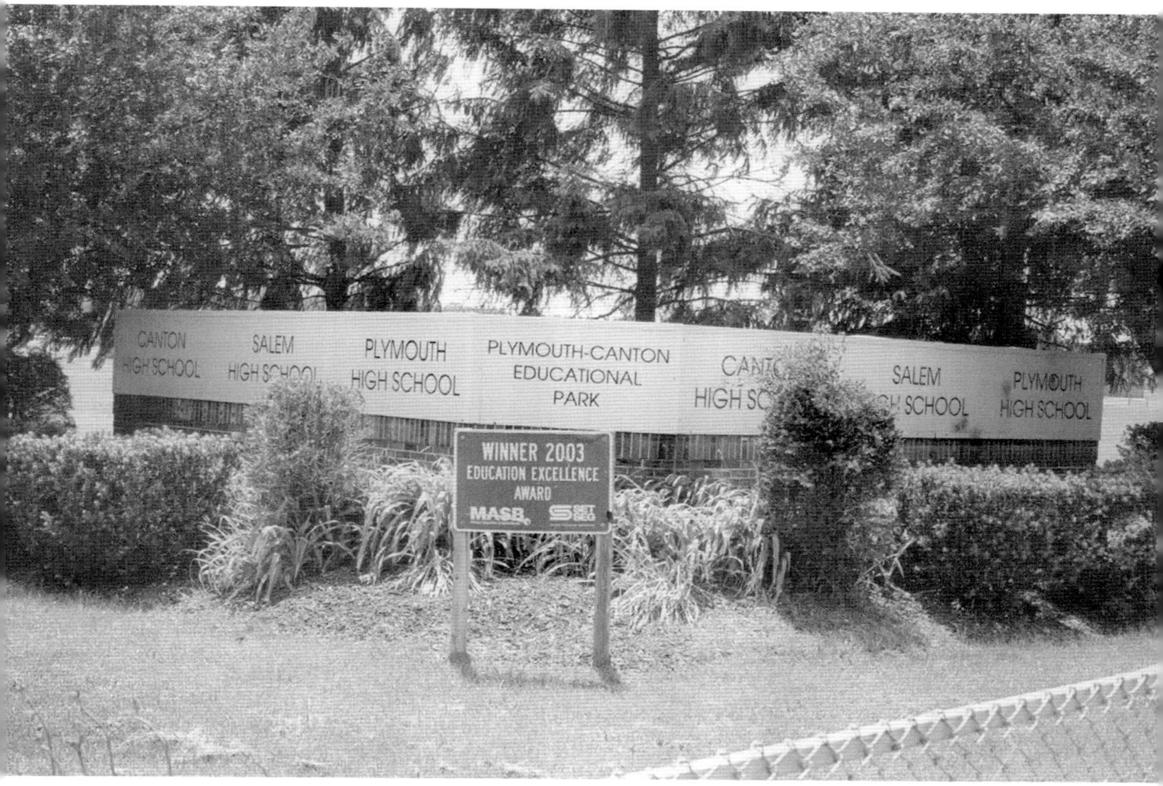

Russell Isbister and the Plymouth-Canton Educational Park.
For many years, the high school had been in the center of downtown Plymouth. The old high school is now used as Central Middle. In the 1950s, the school board recognized and addressed the area's growing population, realizing that it would need to start planning for future schools to accommodate that growth. A committee was assembled, and it recommended that the new high school be on at least 40 acres. Parcels of land that size were hard to find near downtown Plymouth. The board considered expanding the old high school, but found it more prudent to start fresh. In May 1959, the school board sent letters to landowners, asking if they were interested in selling, and 16 responded. Russell Isbister, a proponent of building new, also proposed the purchasing of land big enough to hold four high schools. Having multiple high schools in one location would be more cost effective, as they could share facilities and services. Times were changing, and the need for such a plan seemed to exist.

In 1967, after obtaining voter approval, land became available on the corner of Canton Center and Joy Roads in Canton. The land meeting all the requirements totaled 305 acres. In April 1968, the board voted on a name, and it became known as the Plymouth Community Centennial Educational Park. Today, it is referred to as Plymouth-Canton Educational Park.

In 1976, the school district's name was formally changed to Plymouth-Canton Community School District, due in large part to the increasing population of nearby Canton. It was the League of Women Voters who brought to the attention of the school board that a change needed to be made and that the two areas needed to work together as one.

Russell Isbister was instrumental in much of the progress during his career with the district. For more information on Russell Isbister, please see the text on Isbister Elementary on page 68.

Policy states that the high schools must be named for the township or community encompassed within the district's 54 square miles. Thus, the district has Salem, Canton, and Plymouth High Schools. (Photograph courtesy of author.)

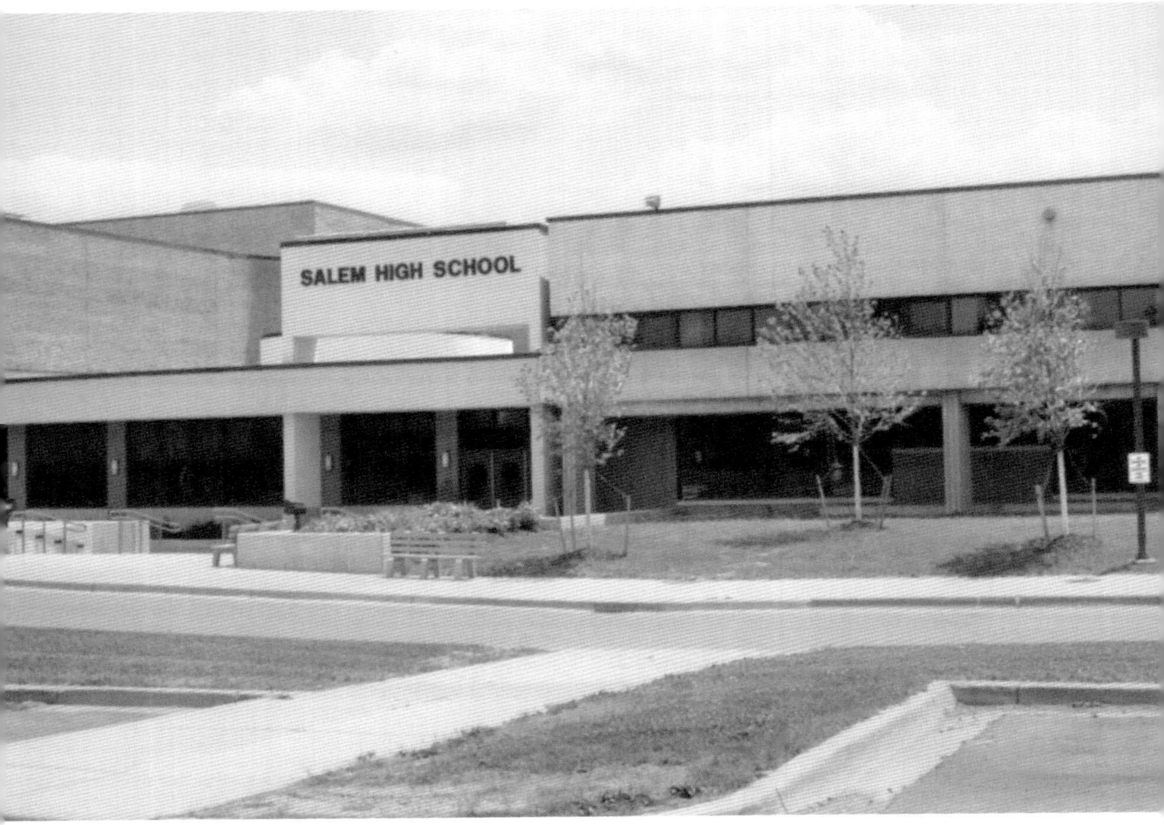

Esther Hulsing and Salem High School.
Opened in 1970, the ground-breaking for Salem High School took place in May 1968, and it was Esther Hulsing (of Hulsing Elementary) who laid her shovel into the earth and turned over the dirt for the new high school. Construction took place from 1968 to 1971. When the building was done, it totaled 313,000 square feet and offered many amenities. It was considered to be state of the art. Its dedication took place on December 5, 1970, followed by an open house. When Salem opened, its enrollment was over 2,000 students. Shortly after it opened, and as the second high school was under construction, the topic of names came up again. Parents and past graduates, upset that the next school would be named Canton, were concerned that Plymouth was nowhere in the school names and that the area of Plymouth would not receive proper recognition. After the board was petitioned, it was decided that the schools would be known formally as Plymouth Salem and Plymouth Canton. (Photograph courtesy of author.)

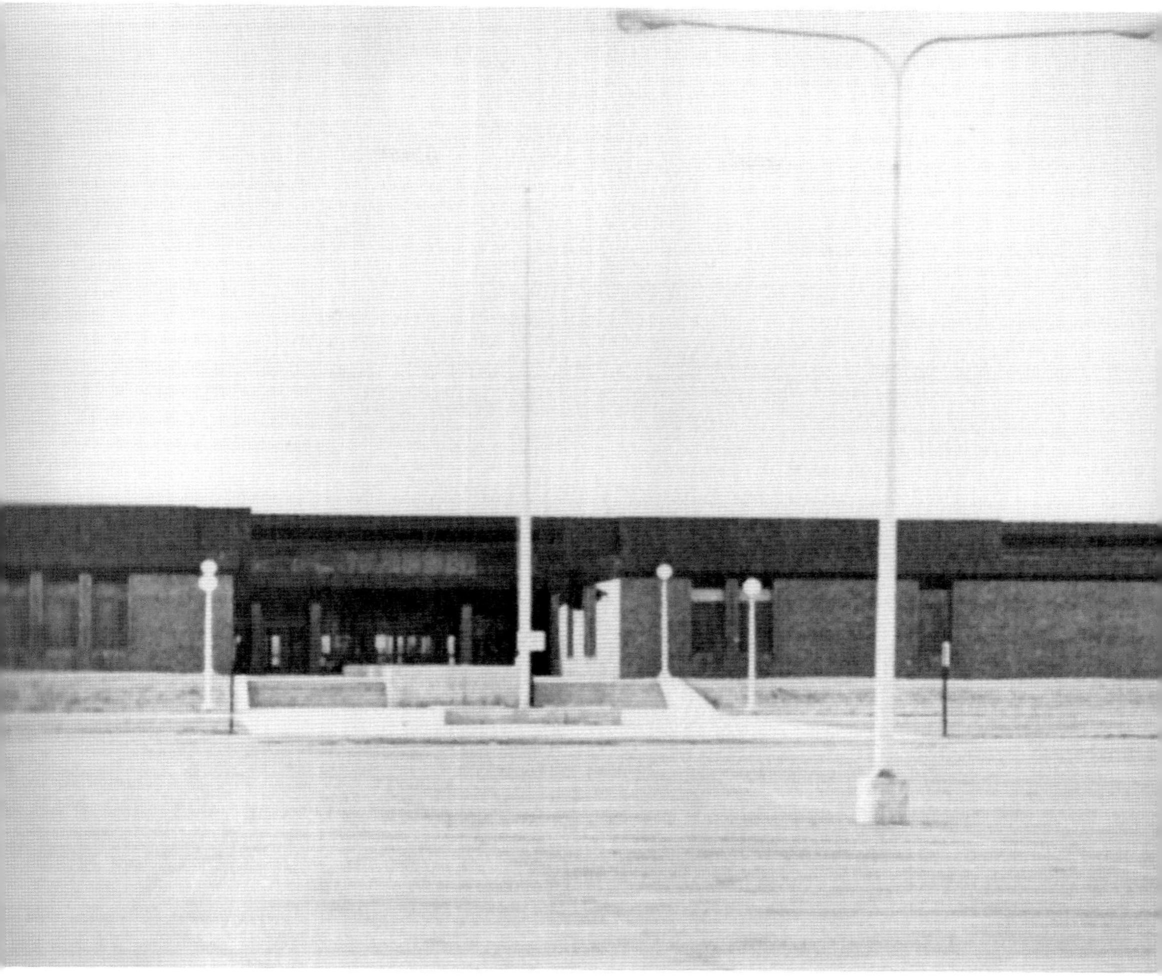

Russell Isbister and Canton High School.
Canton High School opened in 1972. With the opening of two new high schools, the Plymouth Community School Council was formed. Begun in 1968, it is still going strong today and is made up of representatives from each school and from the community interested in the schools. Their job is to assist the district in getting correct information to the public, as well as to help support the district through steering committees, information distribution, and the exchange of ideas. The third phase of Canton High School, called Phase 3, sits between Salem and Canton. It houses a gymnasium and music facilities and was opened during the 1976–1977 school year. With all high school students attending either Canton or Salem, Central, in town, was now free to be used as a middle school. Russell Isbister sadly did not get the opportunity to see his vision of the high schools come to fruition. He died suddenly in November 1968 at the age of 60. Much loved and respected in the community, his legacy continues. (Photograph courtesy of Plymouth Historical Museum.)

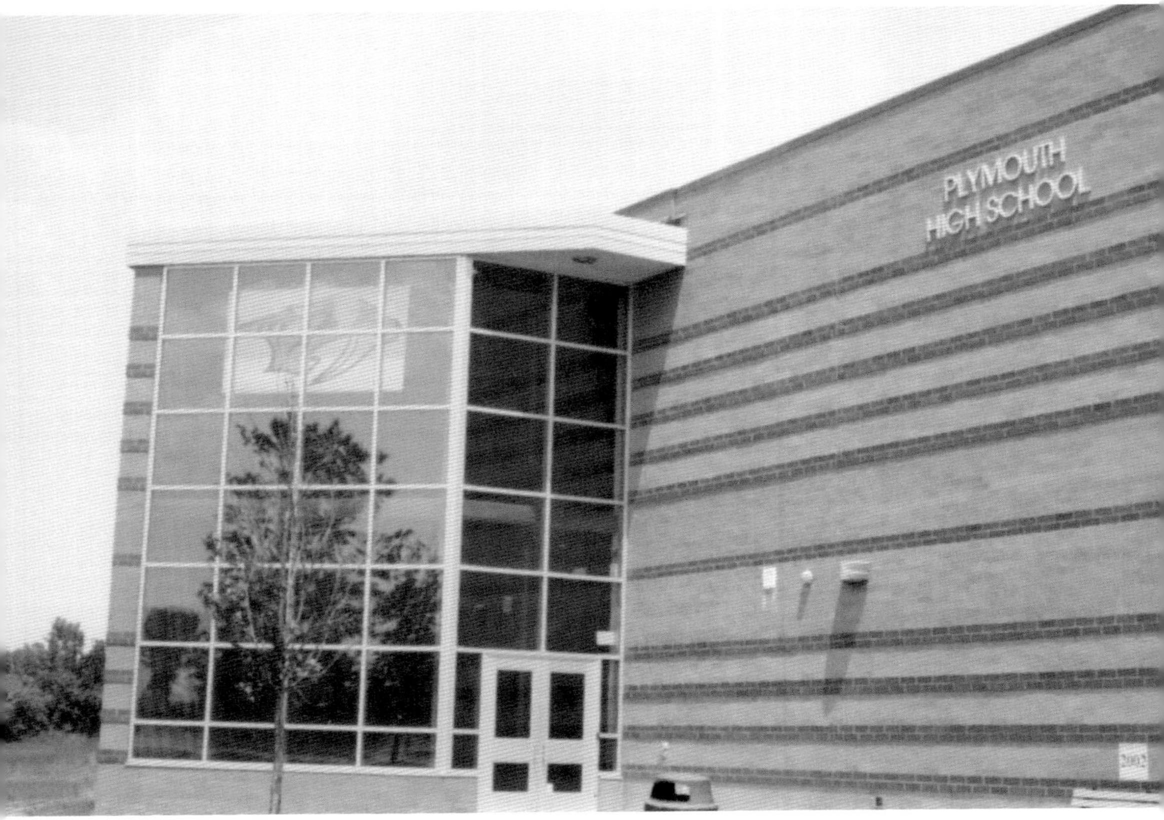

Plymouth High School.
Plymouth High School opened in 2002 and sits southwest of Salem High School. When the school opened, it was the job of the first graduating class (2006) to come up with a school mascot and colors. After much thought and discussion, it was decided that they would be known as the Plymouth Wildcats, and that the school colors would be black and silver. The other two schools' mascots are the Canton Chiefs, with red and white team colors, and, at Salem, the Rocks, in blue and white. The "Park," as the Plymouth-Canton Educational Park is affectionately called, has over 50 clubs and organizations, including the radio station, a debate club, and its first robotics team. There are also clubs dedicated to different languages and cultures. Many parents and staff are very involved in the schools and share a sense of pride and ownership. These factors are what makes the school district distinctive and attractive to families. (Photograph courtesy of author.)

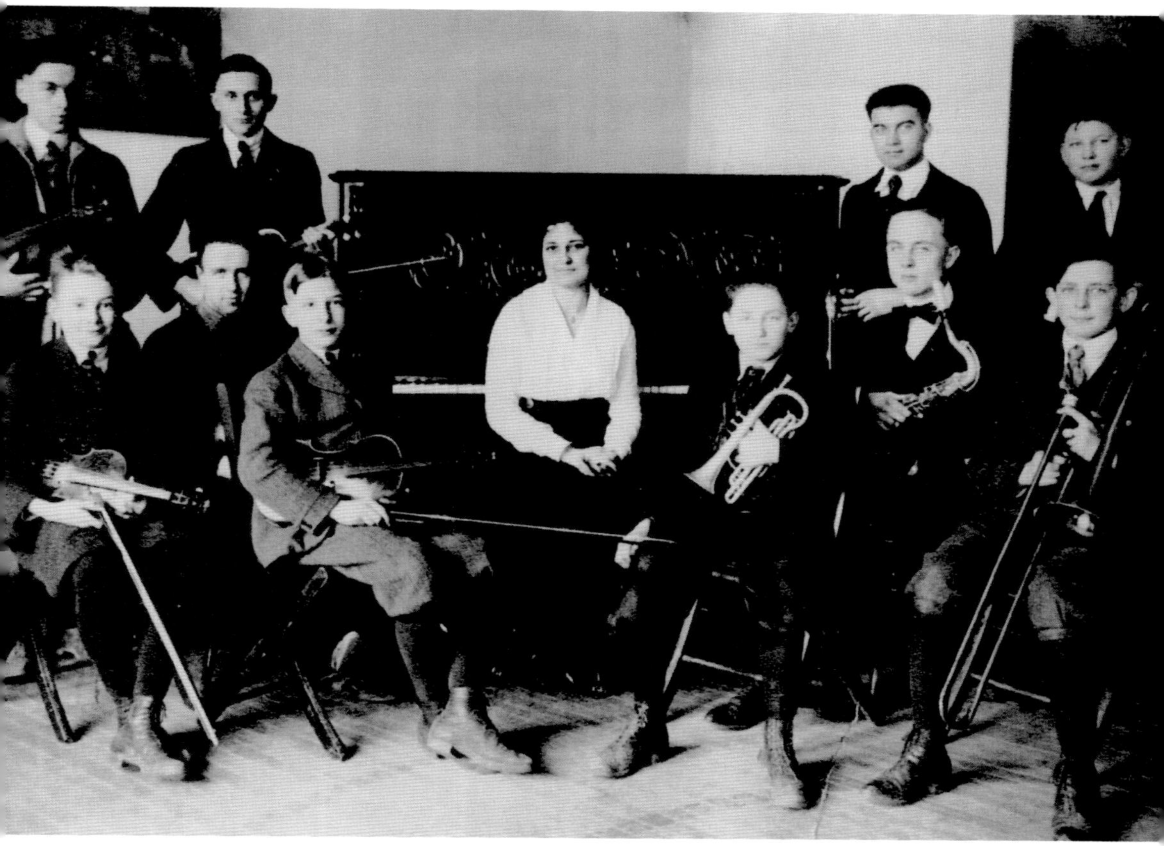

Clubs and Plymouth High School Orchestra.
Clubs are a huge part of the high school experience at the park. Theater at the park has two groups, and there is no shortage of talent. In 1970, the Salem staff started what is now known as the Park Players. At Canton High School, there is a drama group known as the Second Stage Players. Every year, the groups stage at least two shows directed by the faculty, and every semester, they produce one play and a musical. The school bands, orchestra, and choirs grew in popularity with students in the 1980s and have continued to expand as the area has grown. Starting in middle school, students in the district get an opportunity to learn a musical instrument. Dedicated music teachers and band directors work their magic and in a very short time create wonderful musicians. (Photograph courtesy of Plymouth Historical Museum.)

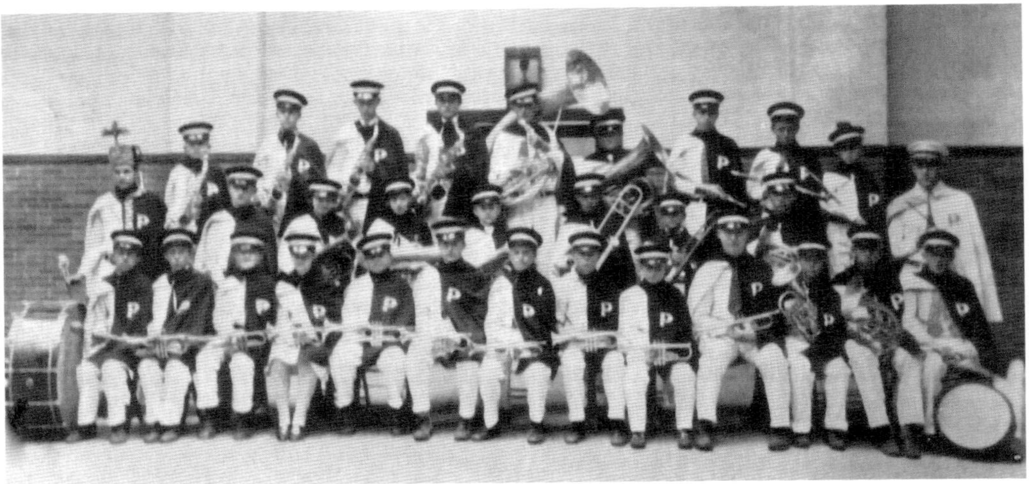

Plymouth High School Band, c. 1928.
The residents of Plymouth love their music, and the Plymouth-Canton Educational Park Marching Band is one they are always proud of. The band has won numerous regional and national awards. It has performed at Ford Field, the Pontiac Silverdome, and, in 2011, marched in the Macy's Thanksgiving Day Parade in New York City. Its performances are packed with spirit and energy. (Photograph courtesy of Plymouth Historical Museum.)

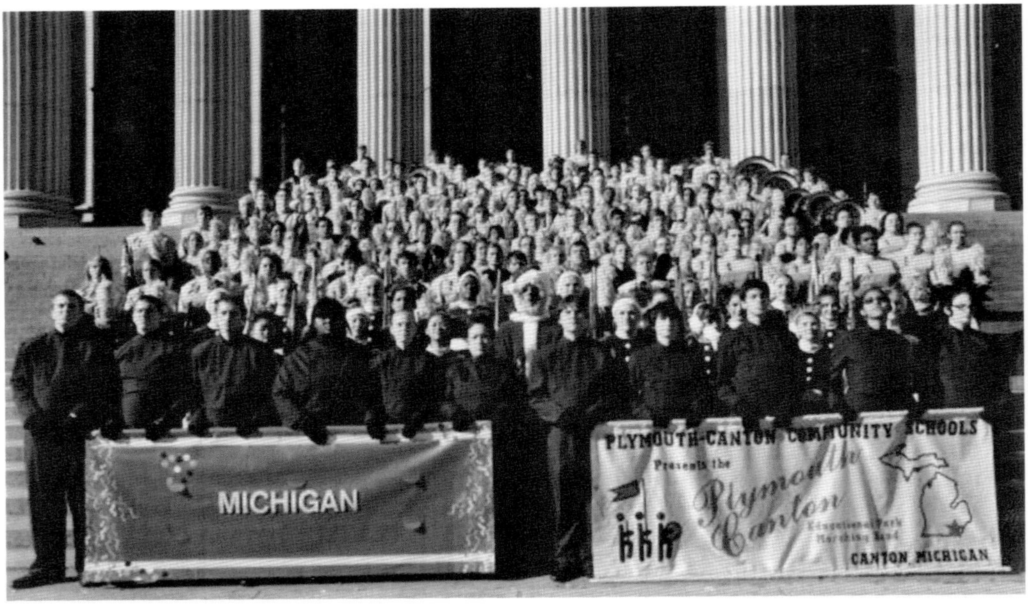

Plymouth Marching Band at the Macy's Thanksgiving Day Parade.
In Dick Well's book *Our Times, Our Stories: Plymouth High School Class of 1960*, it is written that band director Laurence Livingston "did for Plymouth band what John Philip Sousa did for the US Marine Band. He raised the standard in an immediate and dramatic fashion." James Griffith followed, and through the years the program has grown stronger. The band shown here stops for a photo opportunity after performing in the Macy's Thanksgiving Day Parade in New York City in November 2011. (Photograph courtesy of Plymouth Marching Band.)

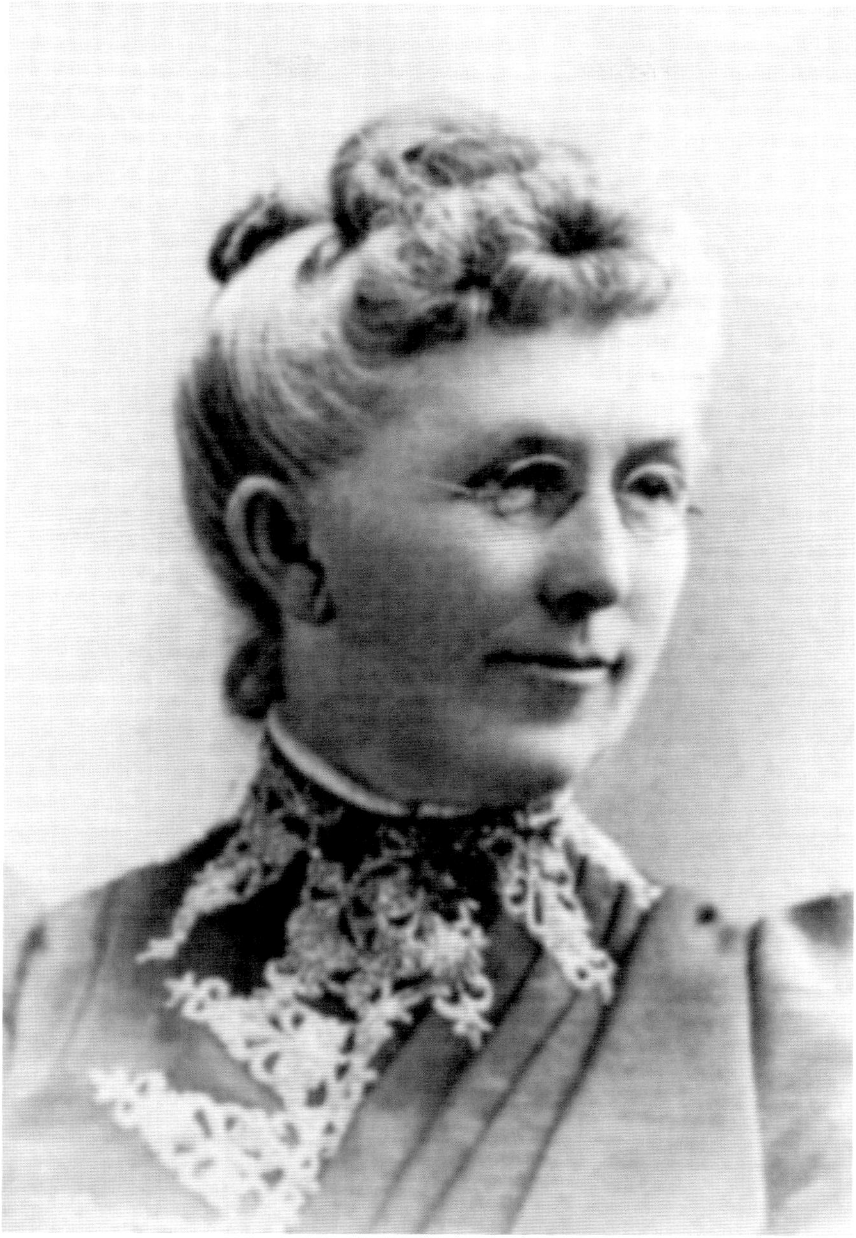

Anna Smith.
There are no buildings named after her, no wings in hallways dedicated to her. But those that do remember, or perhaps have learned about her, help to keep her legacy alive. Anna Smith worked as a teacher and librarian for a record-breaking 62 years. She began her career at the age of 16, working in a one-room schoolhouse. She taught for five years in Northville Schools and then moved to Plymouth, where she taught for 46 years. Her last nine years in Plymouth were spent as a school librarian. It is recorded that her dedication to her job and students was exceptional. Anna died suddenly while getting ready to go to work in 1932 at the age of 84. (Photograph courtesy of Plymouth Historical Museum.)

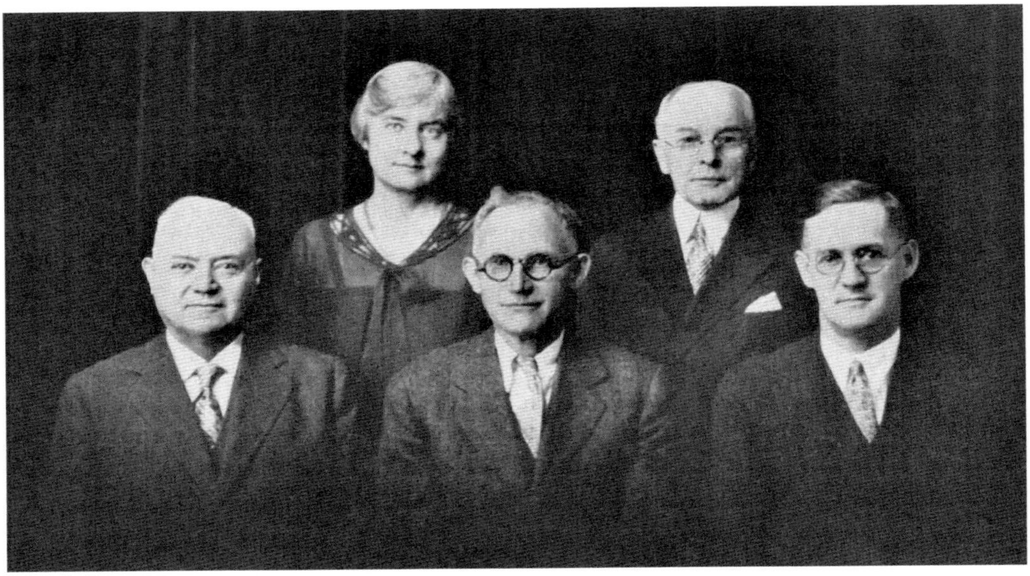

Ada Murray and the Plymouth School Board, 1930s.
School board members elected to their positions carry a lot of responsibility and need to weigh their decisions carefully. Shown above are, from left to right, (back row) Ada Murray and Charles Bennett; (front row), Mr. Pierce, Mr. Sutherland, and Claude Buzzard. Every decade brings about different challenges in terms of curriculum, population growth or decline, budgets, and policies. Sitting on a school board is an enormous job. Ada Murray also held the position of village librarian for 25 years. Initiated by the Woman's Club of Plymouth, Plymouth's first library opened in 1923. (Photograph courtesy of Plymouth Historical Museum.)

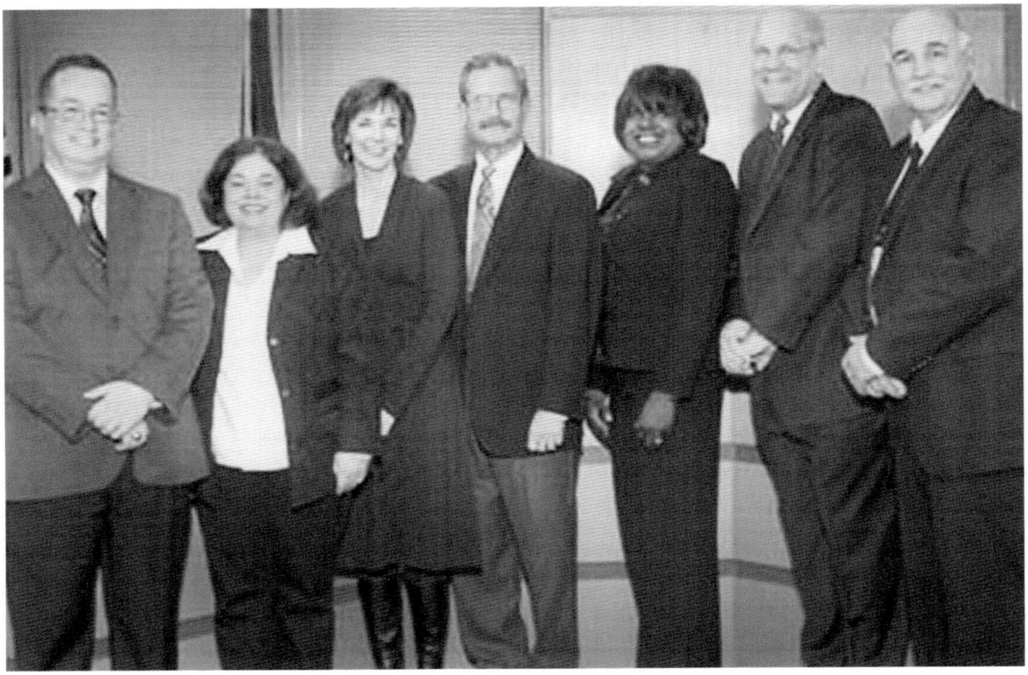

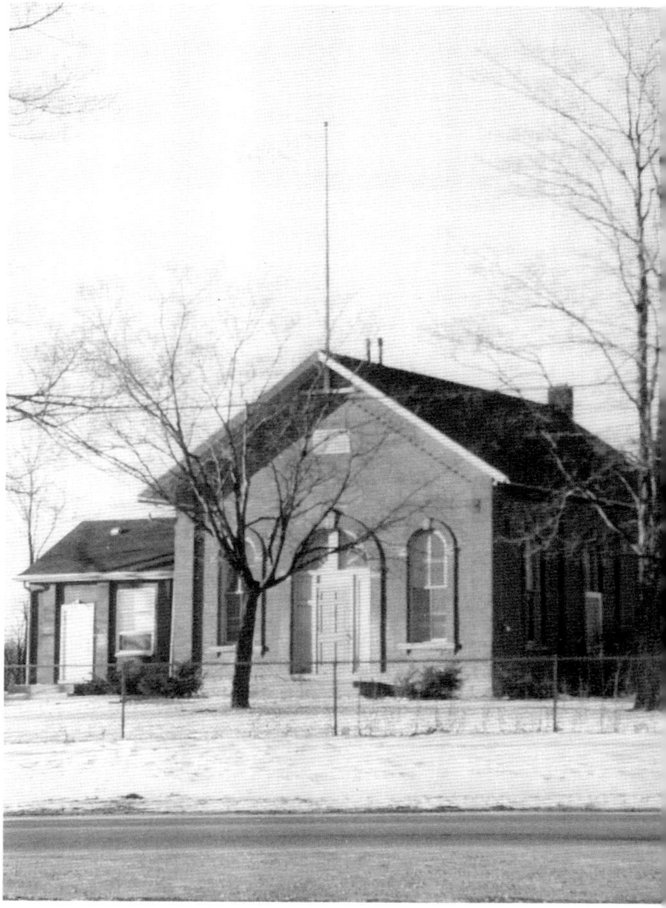

The Geer School.
In 1827, Michigan passed territorial legislation to the effect that each township or area of 50 or more residents needed to employ a schoolmaster. The person hired would need to be of high moral character and be able to teach reading, writing, arithmetic, French, and spelling. The teacher would also have to teach good manners. The teaching of good manners and proper behavior was attributed to the attitudes of the New England Puritans. The notion of a free education was considered by many to be the most significant contribution that New Englanders settling in America had given to the new country, and it was taken very seriously. People did not want the next generation to decline in terms of acceptable and appropriate behavior. A schoolmaster's position carried a lot of responsibility. When the legislative act regarding territory passed, the township of Plymouth was still not divided. The first school built in Plymouth township was in 1827, and it stood on Baseline Road, which later became part of Northville. The next school, built in 1829, was Geer School. (Photograph courtesy of Plymouth Historical Museum.)

Plymouth-Canton School Board, 2012. (OPPOSITE PAGE)
School board members in today's fast-paced world work hard to stay informed and up-to-date with the latest in programming and curriculum. Members give of their time, an important element in any school district. Many of today's board members have given several years of dedicated service to the district. Sheila Paton (pictured here, third from left) was instrumental in starting the Legislative Action Network Committee, which travels to the state capital of Lansing to represent Plymouth-Canton Schools. Representatives stay informed on legislative issues regarding Michigan schools and share the information with local groups. Helping parents stay informed and involved makes for a stronger school district and community. Pictured here are, from left to right, Mark Horvath, Judy Mardigian, Sheila Paton, John Barrett, Adrienne Davis, Mike Maloney, and Barry Simescu. (Photograph courtesy of Plymouth-Canton Schools.)

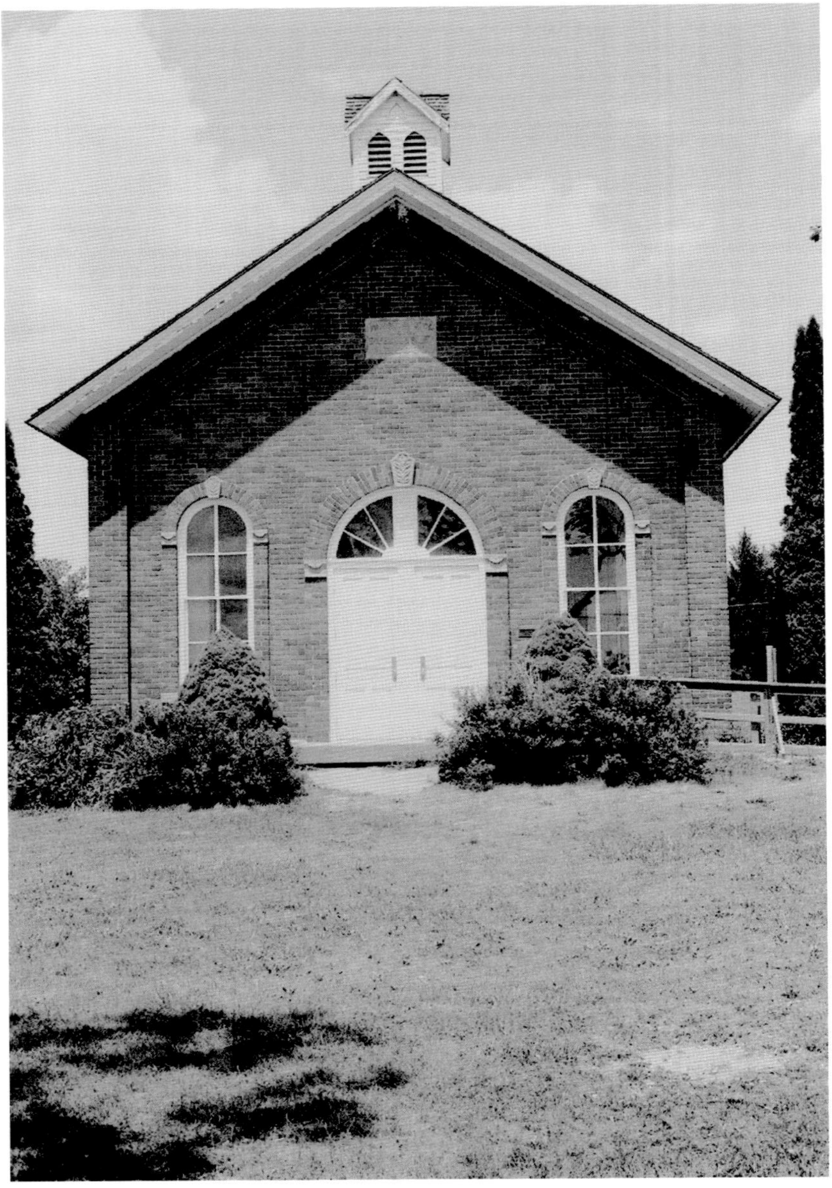

William Geer and the Geer School.
Geer School is in Superior township and stands on the corner of Gotfredson and Ann Arbor Roads. The school was named in honor of William Geer in 1880, when he became the school director. Geer was also responsible for the post office and the general store in the area. Today, Geer School is used as a field trip destination for Plymouth-Canton elementary students. Students dress up and attend class in the old schoolhouse, getting the chance to feel what school might have been like in the early 1900s. (Photograph courtesy of author.)

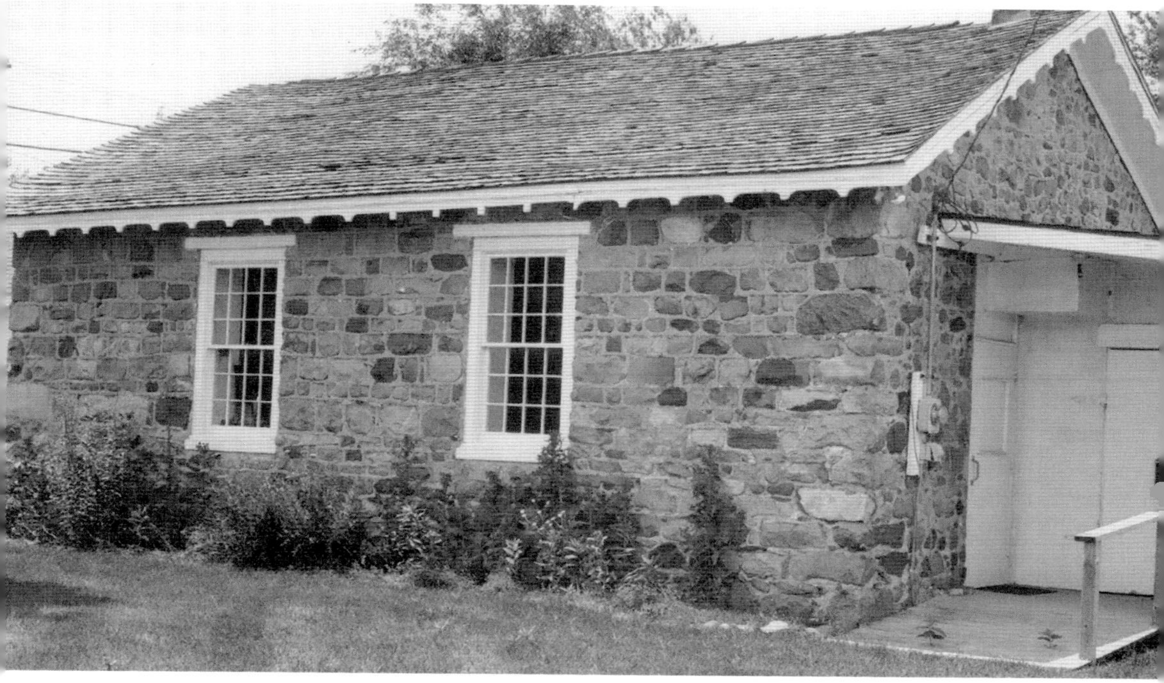

Salem's Stone School.
Stone School, also built in 1829, sits on the corner of North Territorial and Curtis Roads in Salem township. Stone School, annexed, like Geer School, in 1965, sits on a small plot of land and is believed to be one of the oldest existing schools in Washtenaw County. Horace Mann (1796–1859) was an early leader in education. He served in the Massachusetts House of Representatives and Senate, and is responsible for establishing a public school system. Rev. John D. Pierce, in 1837, is on record as Michigan's first superintendent of public schools. Reverend Pierce and a lawyer by the name of Issac Crary are credited with designing a school system in the state of Michigan. Reverend Pierce died in 1882 and is buried in Marshall, Michigan. His monument was purchased by a group of teachers to honor his dedication to the field of education. Today, throughout the great state of Michigan, there are many schools that bear his name. Stone School is owned and maintained by the Salem Historical Society. (Photographs courtesy of author.)

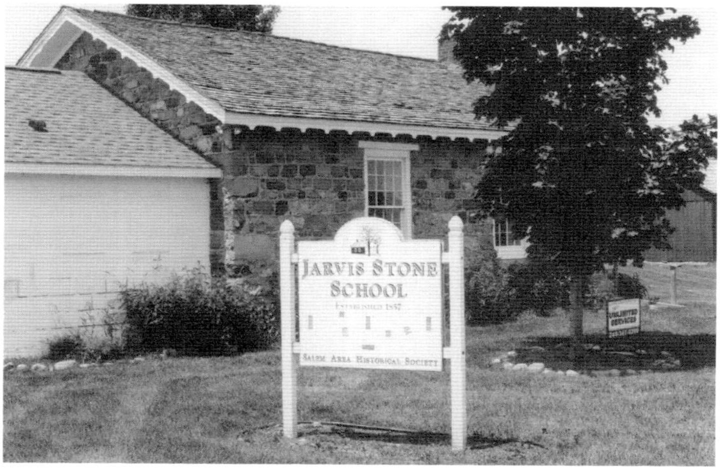

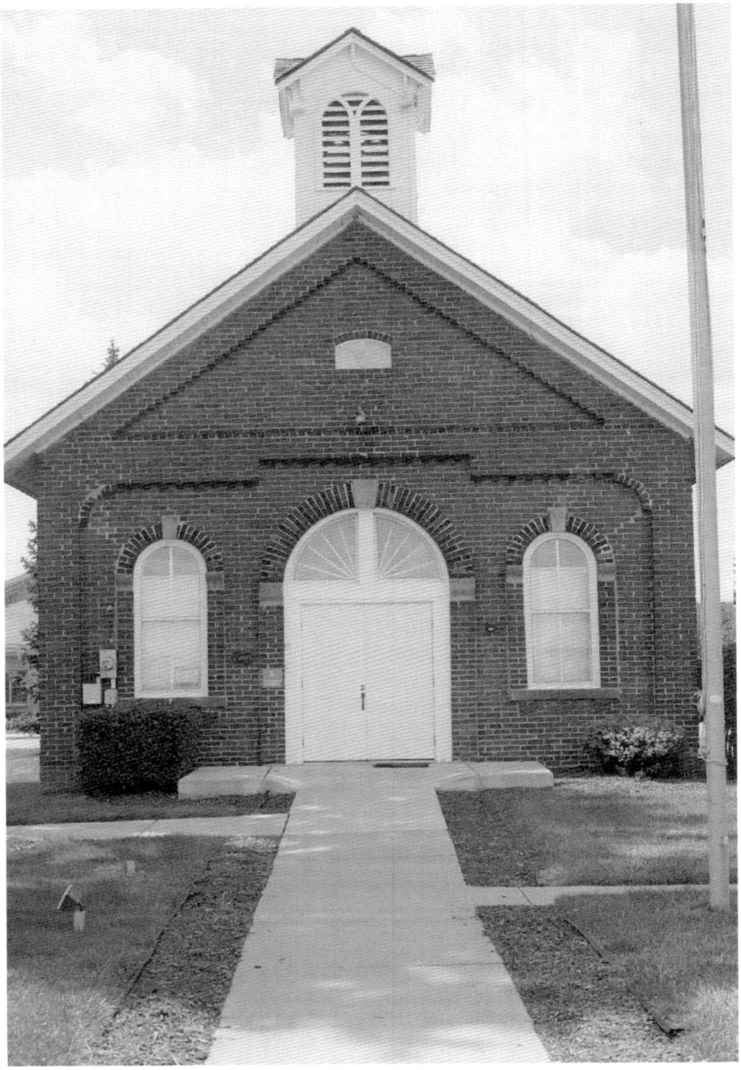

Canton Center School.
Canton Center School stands on Canton Center Road near the township's municipal buildings. The school joined the Plymouth-Canton Schools in 1955. Built in 1884, the building is made of bricks made in a clay pit on a nearby farm. Classes were held in the building for kindergarten through eighth grade until 1954. In 1977, the school board deeded the property and the building to Canton Township. It is now used as the Canton Historical Museum and was dedicated as such on December 5, 1982. All three of the old schoolhouses had uncertain fates during the 1970s for economic reasons, but residents of Plymouth and its surrounding communities felt it important to keep their history alive.

Canton became a township in 1834. Known for corn and dairy farms, Canton took its name from a city in China due to the popular trade business between the United States and China. Early settlers to Canton came from New England and placed importance on a good "moral" education. Nine schoolhouses originally stood in Canton, each built at crossroads so that students could walk to the schoolhouse. Today, four still stand. One is privately owned, and two are used for public facilities. Canton Center School is used as a museum and is cared for by the Canton Historical Society. (Photograph courtesy of author.)

CHAPTER FIVE

The Penn Theatre

For many, the only way to see a movie is on the big screen. The experience of standing in line, getting the tickets in one's hot little hands, with the anticipation bubbling up inside, can be positively exhilarating. Seeing the latest dreamy hunk or beautiful starlet in a screwball comedy, scary movie, or serious drama and escaping the problems of the day is a treat. Popcorn and candy complete the event, and moviegoers sit down in their seats. The lights dim, and the audience members are taken away for 90 minutes.

Along with the arts and music, the residents of Plymouth love movies and, more so, the theater. This chapter will look at the history of the popular Penn Theatre. Located in downtown Plymouth on Penniman Street, across from Kellogg Park, its marquee has become an icon in the small city. Movies, while entertaining, allow viewers to reflect, dream, organize their thoughts, and sometimes see the past, present, and future. Theaters like the Penn are becoming extinct, and that is why this structure is such a treasure. The theater has added so much to the community over the years, and it is the rare person who does not have a special memory tied to it. Going on a first date, meeting up with old friends, or taking one's children to see their first movie at the Penn—each and every memory is special, and the Penn holds a place of honor in many hearts. The Penn Theatre, the future of which was uncertain for a time, has been preserved thanks to a very resourceful and passionate group called Friends of the Penn. The residents of Plymouth are indebted to them and are grateful for their efforts and diligence. In these pages, one will read about Kate Penniman Allen, who owned Plymouth's first theater, and Harry Lush, who came to own the current Penn Theatre. Margaret Wilson also owned and operated the theater for many years, and possessed a beautiful smile few would forget. Readers will also be introduced to the man many called "the voice of the Penn." The following pages will entertain and inform regarding the wonderful and lustrous history of the beautiful, beloved Penn Theatre.

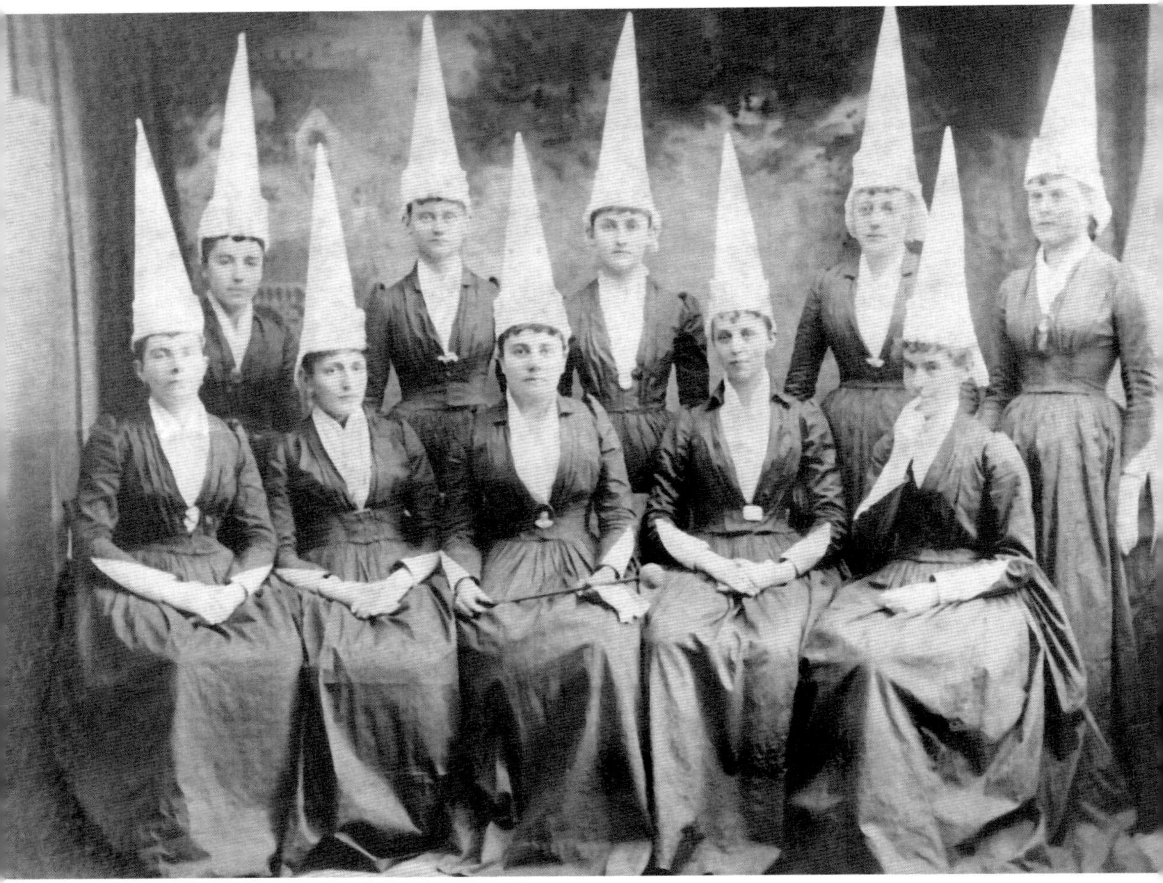

Kate Penniman Allen.
Kate Penniman Allen truly enjoyed entertainment and was responsible for much of what Plymouth did to have fun. Allen opened the Penniman Allen Theatre on Penniman Avenue on Friday, November 22, 1918. She showed motion pictures with titles such as *Hell's Angels* and *Scarface*. She also produced local plays in the theater. The first recorded play was called *Modes and Manners*. The theater also housed concessions and a bowling alley and was always very busy. Allen was also responsible for the construction of the nearby Northville Marquis Theater. The Marquis, still in operation today, specializes in children's theater. Allen changed how people lived in the small community of Plymouth. She is pictured here, seated third from the left in the first row, around 1890 as a Peak Sister. (Photograph courtesy of Plymouth Historical Museum.)

Penniman Allen Theatre, Early 1900s.
In 1922, Kate Penniman Allen began showing movies on Sunday afternoons. This really upset conservative churchgoers in Plymouth, so much so that the issue had to be put to a vote. On March 13, 1922, the controversial question was put to ballot. Allen was victorious when a record number of voters showed up to the polls to vote on the issue, and it was decided that movies could respectfully be viewed on Sundays. Sadly, on January 7, 1968, the Penniman Allen Theatre burned down in a very serious fire. Several buildings were lost, and the theater was never reconstructed in the same location. (Postcard courtesy of Plymouth Historical Museum.)

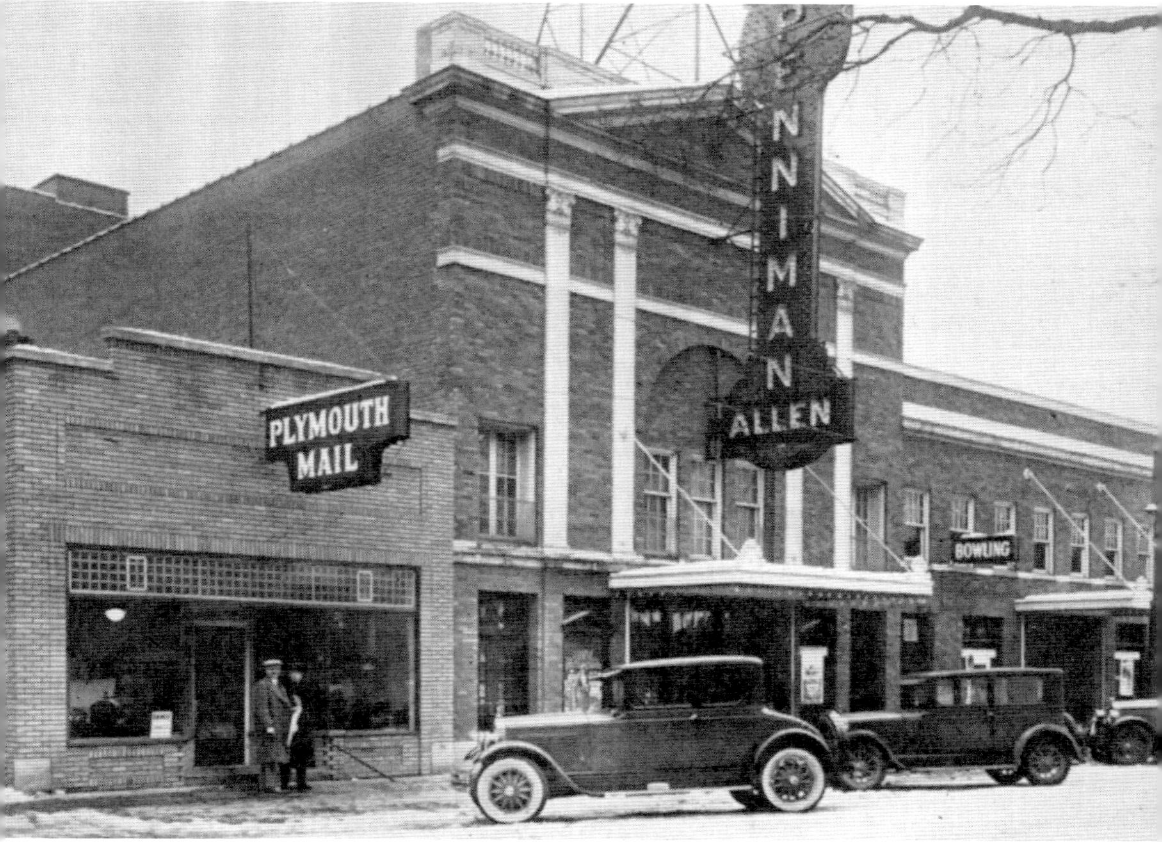

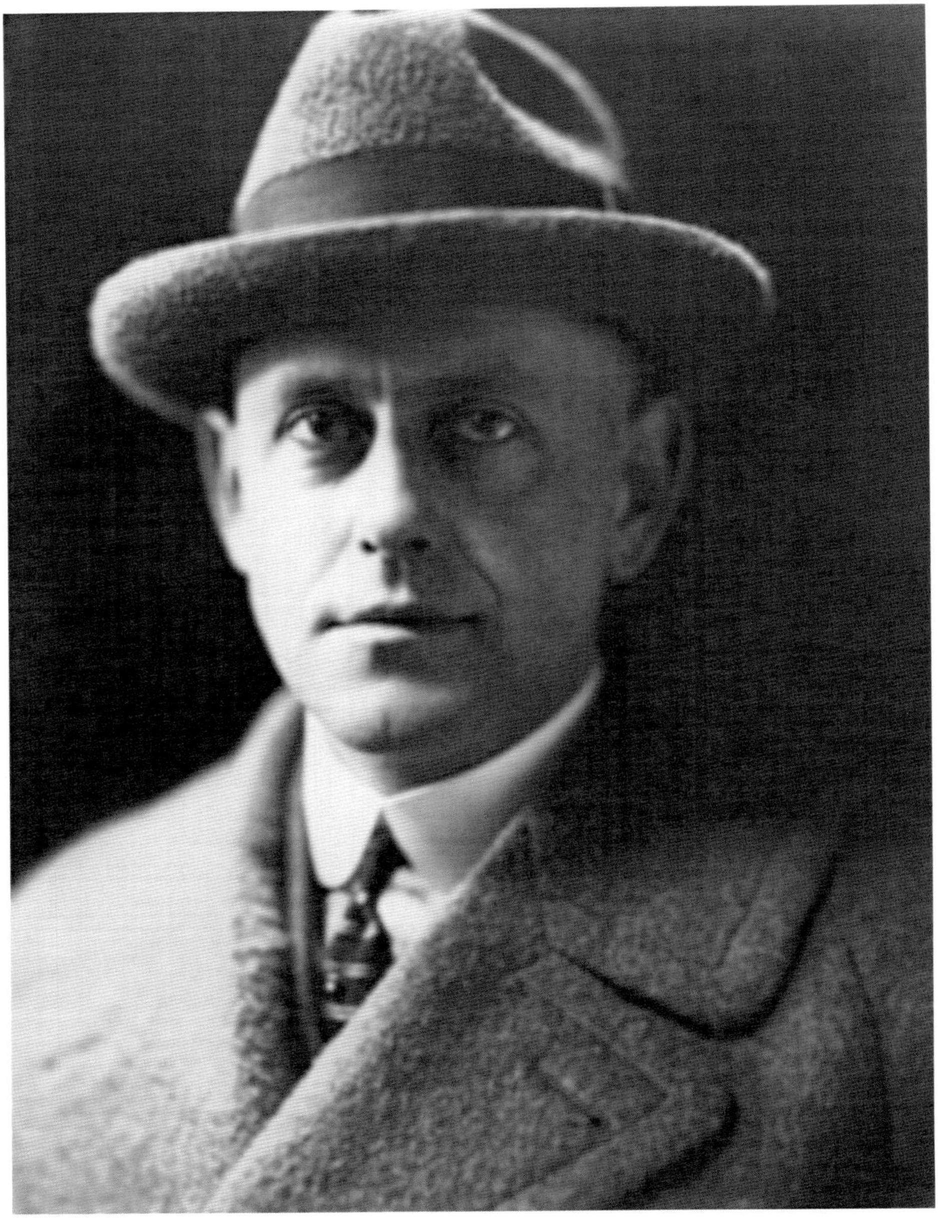

Harry Lush.
In 1941, after working and managing the Penniman Allen Theater, Harry Lush decided to build and open his own theater. The land on which the Penn stands had been purchased from George Wilcox in 1926 by the Woodward Theatre Company. The company had intentions of building a beautiful movie palace, but, when approached by Lush, sold him the property. The Penn Theatre opened on December 4, 1941, showing *Week-End in Havana*, starring John Payne and Carmen Miranda. Lush had a great dislike of popcorn, so the movie treat was not served in the theater until 1950. Lush moved to California that same year, and the theater was then managed by Margaret Wilson. Lush died in La Jolla, California, in 1964 at the age of 69. (Photograph courtesy of Plymouth Historical Museum.)

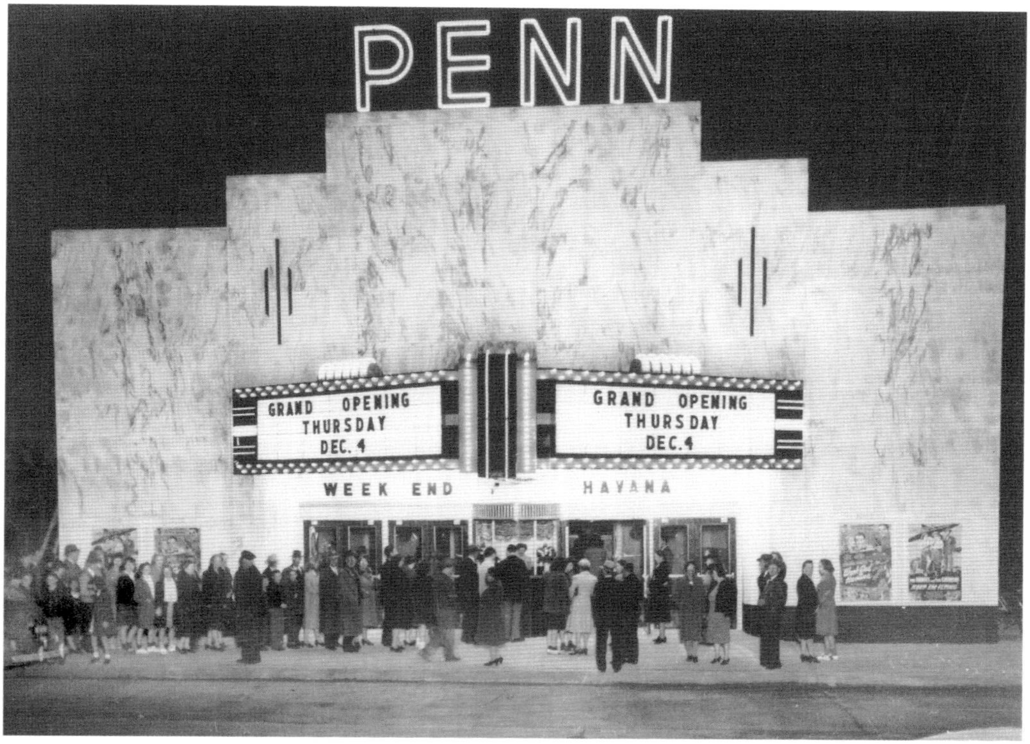

Penn Theatre's Grand Opening, December 1941.
The cost of a movie ticket in 1941 at the Penn Theatre was 30¢. The first movie shown at the Penn was *Week-End in Havana*, starring John Payne, Alice Faye, and Carmen Miranda. (Photograph Courtesy of Plymouth Historical Museum.)

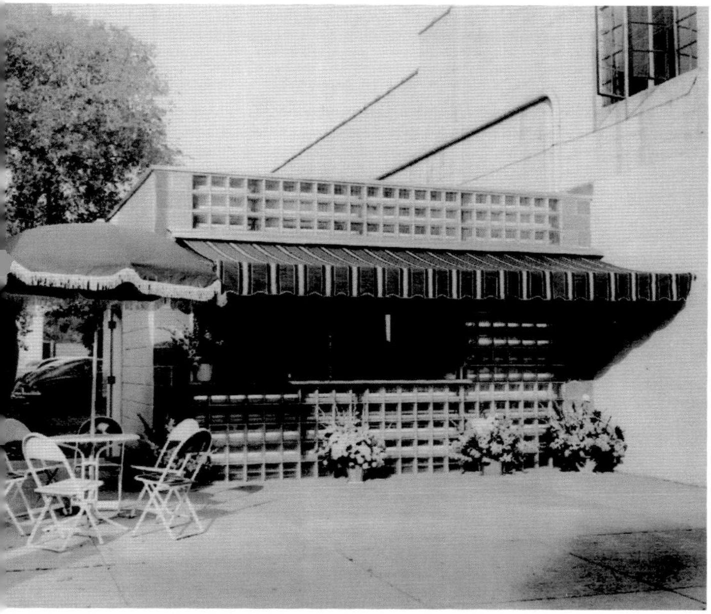

Refreshment Stand, c. 1947.
Next door to the Penn Theatre stood a refreshment and candy stand for patrons of the theater. It was managed by a man named Vincent Simmonetti and operated for a couple of years. The building next to the Penn Theatre has been the location of a number of businesses through the years, but many remember it as a record store. It currently is a Jimmy John's Sandwich Shop. (Photograph courtesy of Plymouth Historical Museum.)

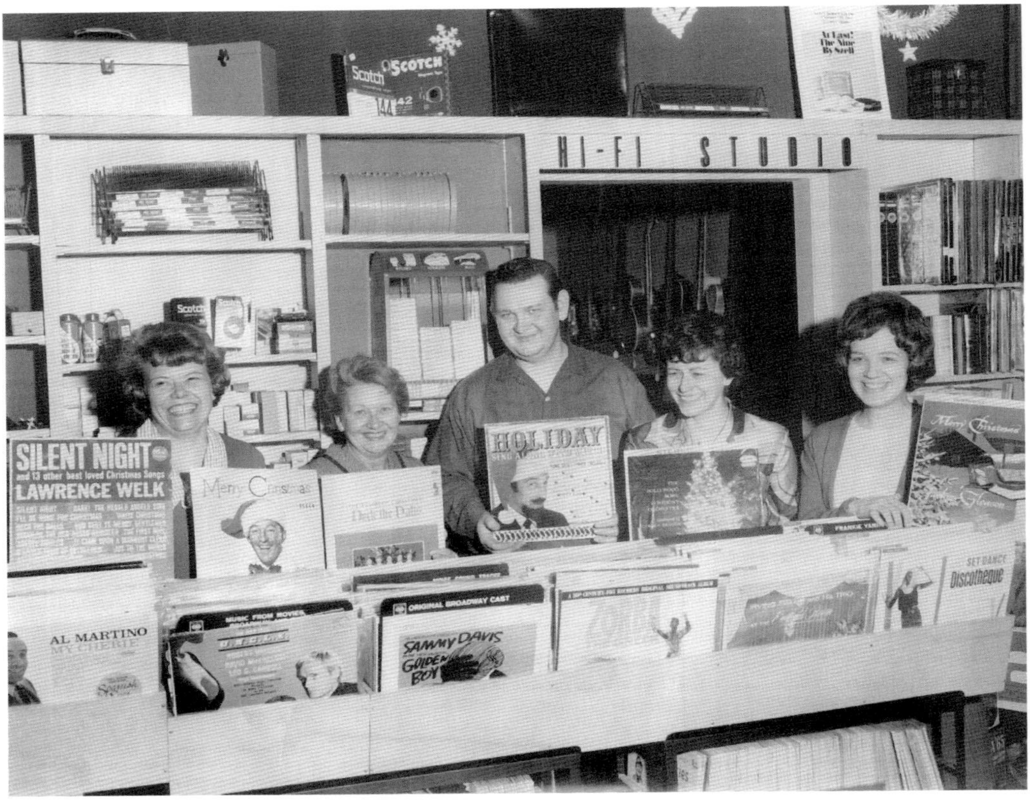

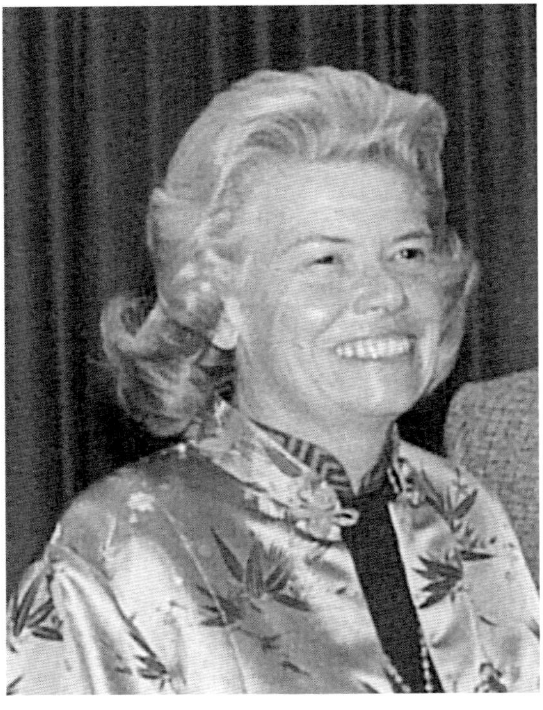

Margaret Wilson.
Margaret Wilson had worked at the theater's cash register. She was a likely candidate to manage the theater when Lush moved to California. Buying it in 1964 for $75,000, she became the second owner of the Penn Theatre. In 1966, Wilson modernized the front entrance and made a new concession area in the lobby. She was a proud owner of the theater and served the community in a number of ways. She was active in the chamber of commerce, serving as the president in 1977–1978; was a Rotary Club member; and worked on the Plymouth Symphony board. She also volunteered her time on the Fall Festival committee. In 1982, Wilson retired and moved to Florida. She sold the theater for $130,000 to Earl and Bonnie Smith. In the photograph above, Wilson (far left) is seen in the record store that at one time was next to the theater. (Photographs courtesy of Plymouth Historical Museum.)

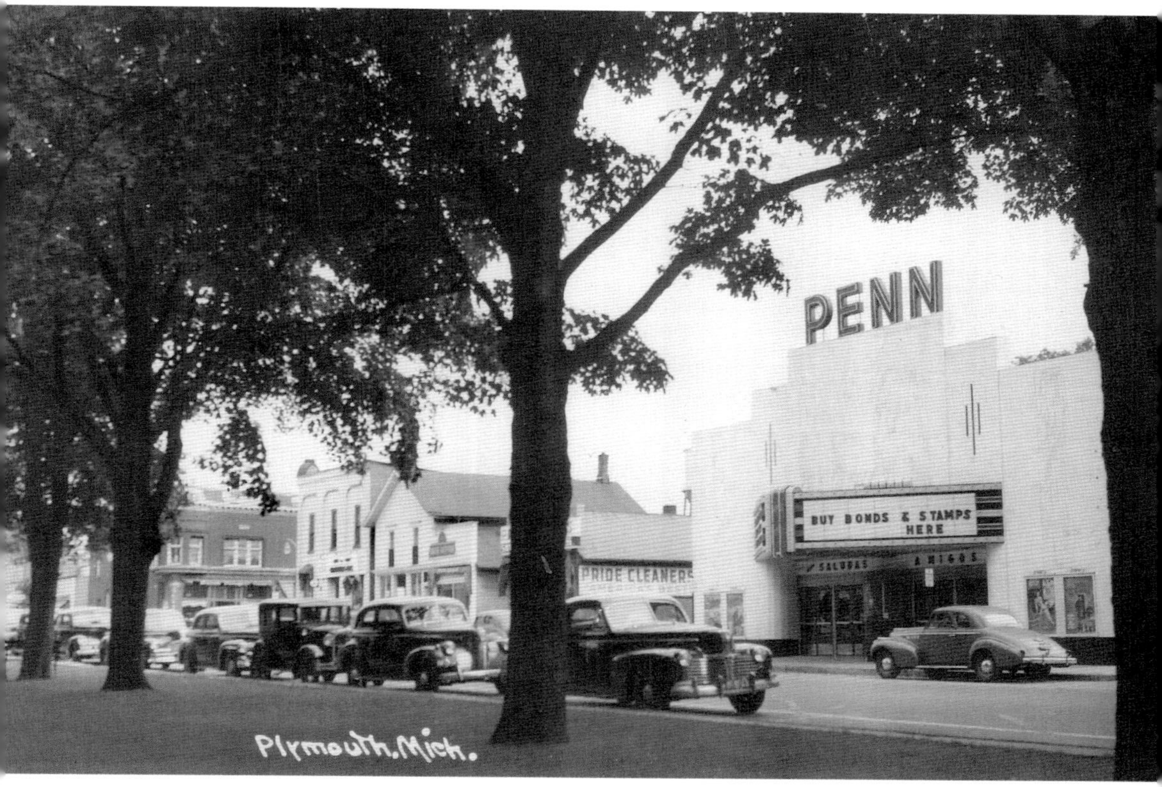

Penn Theatre, 1940s.

The theater has stood the test of time, in large part due to Lush's eye for details. Paying close attention to the seating, he made certain that every seat offered the best viewing experience for his customers. The theater had 676 seats, and they were of varying widths from row to row and seat to seat. The seats that were recently replaced and made handicapped-accessible were made by the same Irwin Seating Company that did the original seats. The Penn now seats 402 patrons. The sound system and projection system were state of the art and have been preserved through the years. The Smiths added draperies to the walls in 1988 to help with the acoustics. In 1988, the Penn Group purchased the theater for $300,000, at which point the Penn's fate became uncertain. (Postcard courtesy of Plymouth Historical Museum.)

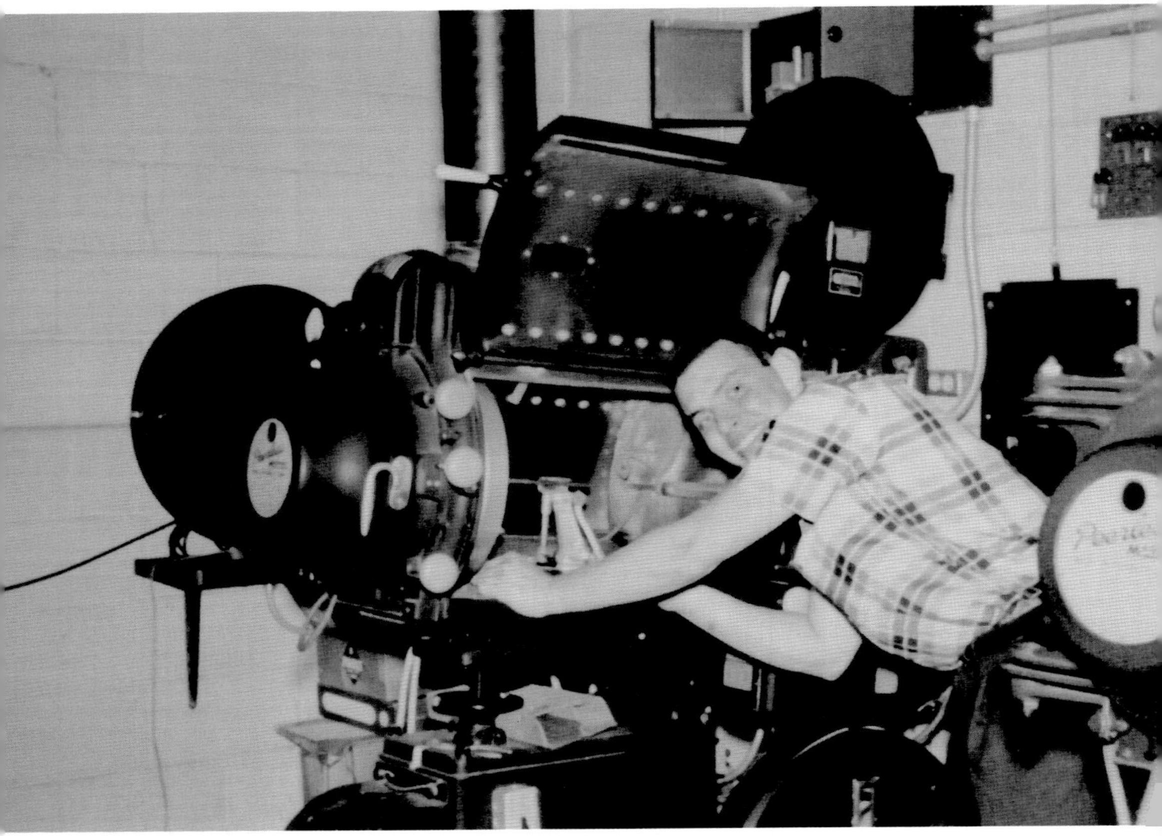

Lloyd Oliver.
Many may not recognize the name Lloyd Oliver. But, for anyone who ever called the Penn Theatre to find out what was showing, he or she would have heard him speak. Known as the "Voice of the Penn," Oliver started every recording with, "This is a recording for the Penn Theatre." His deep, authoritative voice, slow, steady, and clear, would tell what was featured, the showtimes, and the prices. Working as a projectionist from 1958 until his retirement in 2001, Oliver was very faithful to the old theater. In February 2006, Oliver died at the age of 77. Pictured here is an unidentified projectionist at the Penn Theatre in 1957. (Photograph courtesy of Plymouth Historical Museum.)

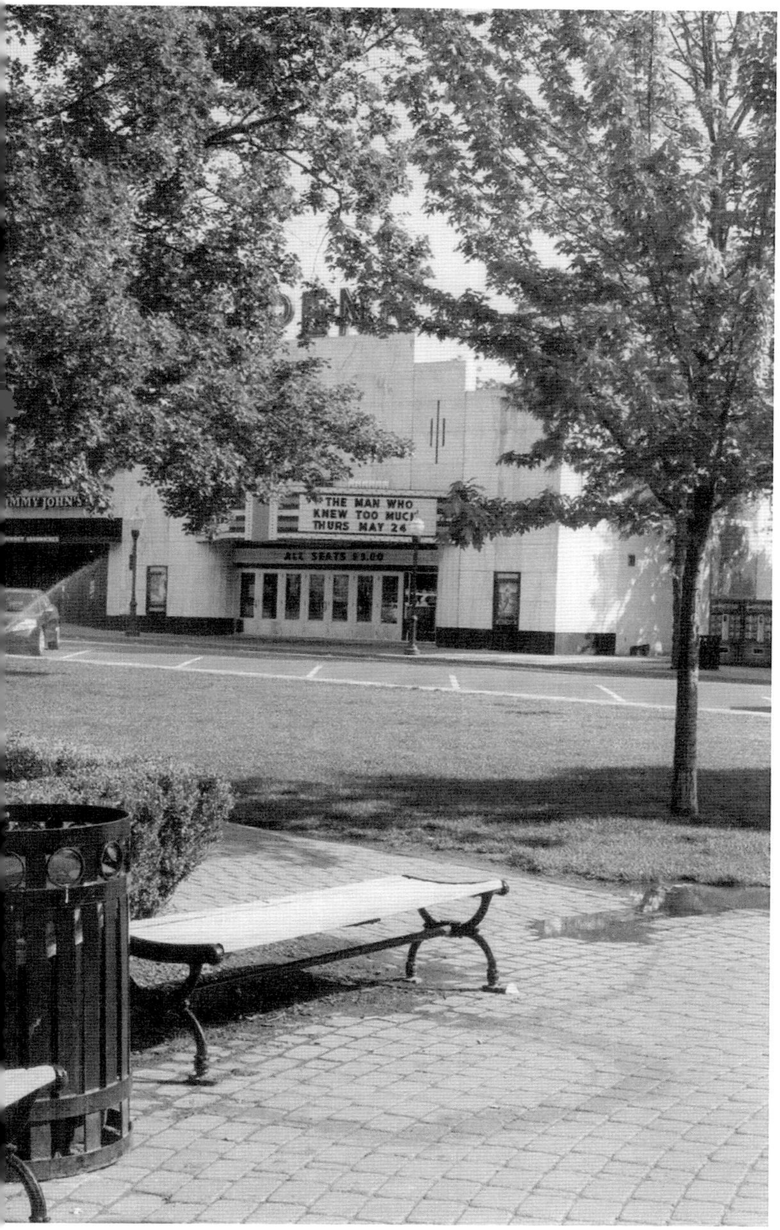

Friends of the Penn. The Penn Theatre is a very expensive building to maintain, and in 1995 it really began to show its years. The Penn Group obtained a liquor license and began to show first-run movies and offer comedy shows, but the theater was not making the money necessary to maintain itself. The Penn Theatre closed its doors in 2003 for remodeling. In 2004, it was sold again, and its marquee failed to light up after 62 years of entertainment. The theater, seen here in 2012, stood empty for one year, and its fate was shaky and uncertain until Friends of the Penn, a nonprofit group formed by concerned citizens in 2005, came to its rescue. The nonprofit group faced a huge obstacle, however: raising money to purchase the building. (Photograph courtesy of author.)

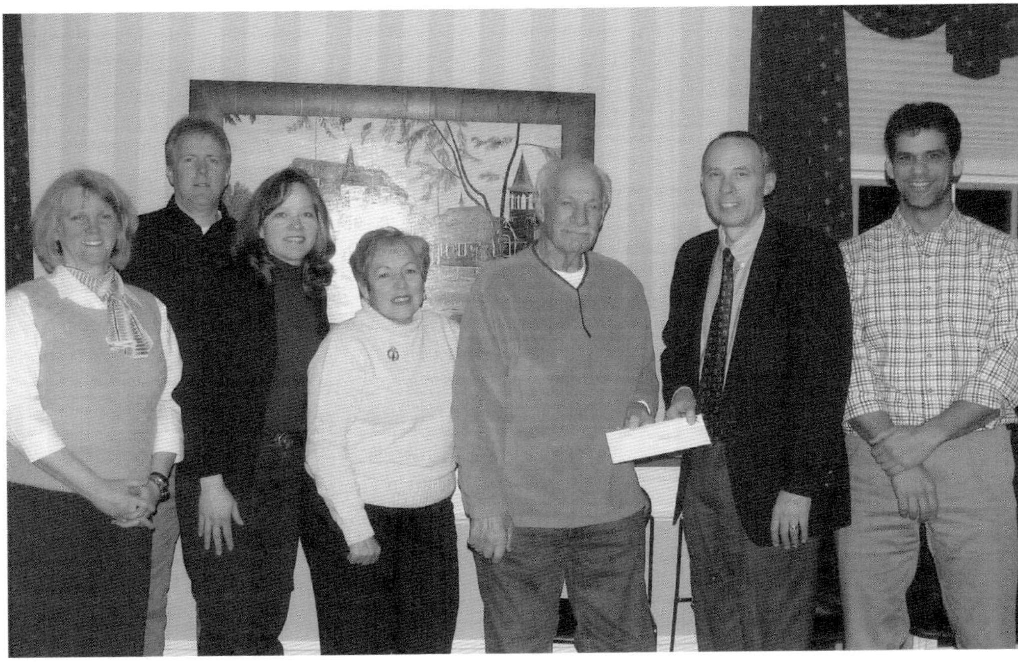

Penn Theatre Today.
Ellen Elliott, named in December 2005 as the executive director of Friends of the Penn, and her husband, Joe Elliott, the renovation manager, are committed to the Penn. Don Soenen, a local businessman (who some may call an "angel"), organized the Penn Theatre Realty Group, LLC and purchased the building for $1.2 million. The building is leased to Friends of the Penn for $1 a year so that money raised and profits made can go into the theater's renovation and maintenance. Here, Friends of the Penn receive a grant award from Jim Jabara of the Community Foundation in January 2011. Pictured here are, from left to right, Susan Stoney, Joe Elliott, Ellen Elliott, Sandy Marulis, Jim Jabara, Gerry Sabatini, and Mike Hatsios. Not shown here is Kevin Simowski. The Penn Theatre reopened in September 2006. In 2011, the theater had over 160 volunteers and welcomed 53,000 patrons. The marquee was beautifully restored in 2009, the auditorium was restored in 2011, and the theater now seats 402 guests. (Photograph courtesy Friends of the Penn.)

CHAPTER SIX

The Plymouth Fife and Drum Corps

This chapter honors a group that is very deserving and has served and represented Plymouth honorably through the years. The Plymouth Fife and Drum Corps, organized in 1971 by Mark and Carol Petty, is the first group of its kind organized in the Midwest. Mark, a percussion instructor for the Plymouth Marching Band at the time, wanted to offer students the opportunity to use their skills more often. Donald Tripp helped develop the corps as its first board president.

The corps strives to preserve the nation's musical history through fifing and drumming. This art form was used during times of war to relay commands to soldiers, help direct movements of units, and lift the mood of soldiers and keep them moving forward. Mark was intent on the group playing music from different periods of history, so that listeners would hear and realize the historical importance of each piece. The corps plays music from the War of 1812, the Revolutionary War, and the Civil War. The tunes' original music is from the Library of Congress. The corps consists of about 50 players, young men and women from the area and surrounding communities, ranging in age from 12 to 18 years old.

The Plymouth Fife and Drum Corps, which is self-supporting, practices year-round for its performance season, which runs from April through October. In addition to fifing and drumming, the group has a color guard. Its biggest hurdle through the years has been obtaining and maintaining uniforms, but the group has been continuously blessed with resources for updates. The members currently wear uniforms that weigh 10 pounds each, replicating what George Washington's foot soldiers would have worn in their day. They are red, white, and blue, have no zippers, and are fitted with real pewter buttons.

This proud group of musicians travels the country and to parts of Canada, performing at various events, historical sites, and parades. In 1996, it was invited to attend the Olympic Torch Ceremony in Dearborn, Michigan. The members have indeed made Plymouth very proud with their hard work, musical excellence, and strong performances. Next time a reader sees this talented group of individuals, he or she should honor them and be reminded of their service and honor to the area and the country.

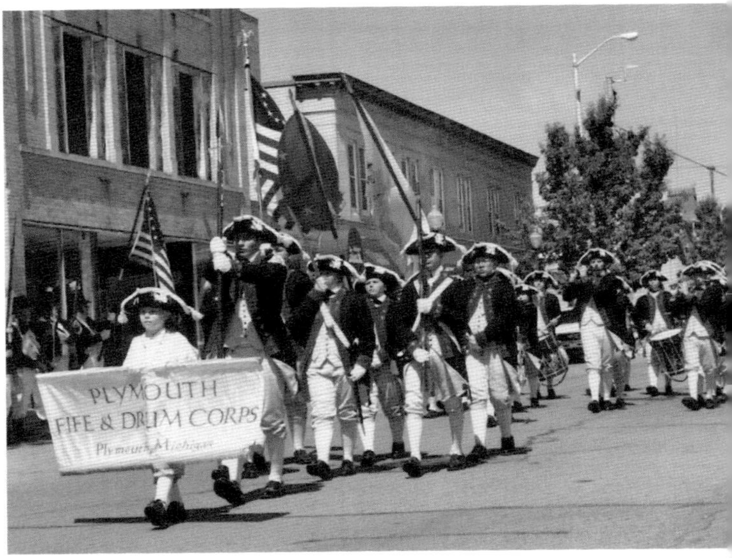

Plymouth Fife and Drum Corps, June 2012.
The Plymouth Fife and Drum Corps performs at the Monroe Muster in Monroe, Michigan, in June 2012. This convention of fife and drum corps drew sixteen corps from seven different states. In wartime, a muster would help assemble troops for battle, display, or discharge. A coming together of soldiers, it was a very important aspect in building teamwork and camaraderie. (Photograph courtesy of Plymouth Fife and Drum Corps.)

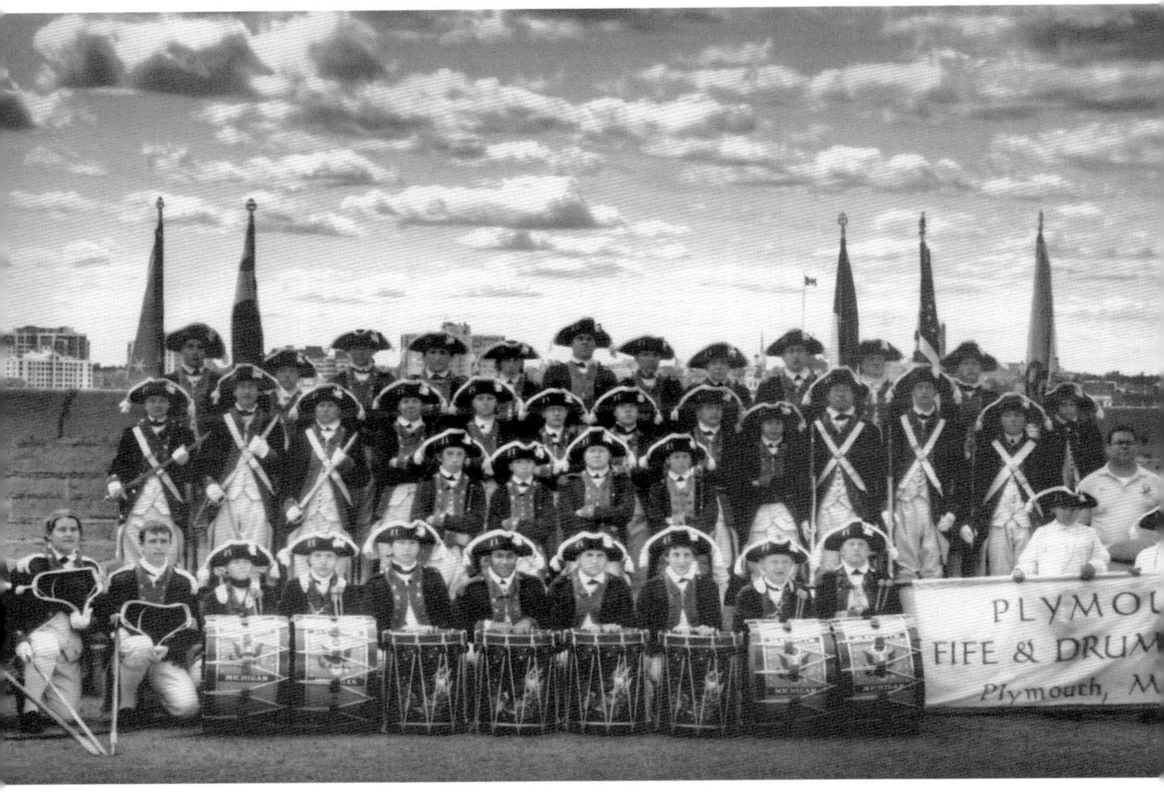

Plymouth Fife and Drum Corps' 2009 Tour.
Looking at the corps' schedule, one quickly realizes that this is a very dedicated group. On the Fourth of July, this group can be seen in a number of parades around the metro area. Throughout its season, the Plymouth Fife and Drum Corps also participates in many festivals and memorials and is often invited to perform at sporting events. (Photograph courtesy of Plymouth Fife and Drum Corps.)

CHAPTER SEVEN

Clubs and Organizations

Throughout this book, events and people are featured that have in some way contributed to the community. In Plymouth, there are over 60 clubs and organizations that one can belong to. If people are interested in sewing, there is a club for them. If drama is a person's thing, there is a group for him or her. If someone would like to welcome people to the area, there is a club for that. If one would like to do community service, there is, of course, a group for him or her. Any number of interests and needs are met in Plymouth.

In this chapter, readers will be introduced to some of these organizations. They will learn about them, about how long they have been around, and what kind of projects or goals they have set for themselves. Again, so many could be recognized, but in these pages, only a few can be shown.

This chapter has been included because this book, in the Legendary Locals series, is about people. People make up the community, and they certainly have an effect on the community. Good deeds, good service, and putting one's self out into the community to give back, has what some might call a cyclical effect. Staying positive and engaged within one's family and within one's community will almost certainly keep a person young at heart. Volunteerism runs strong in Plymouth.

The level of commitment that is shown when people work together is very moving. Driving through Plymouth, a person will see that one individual can indeed make a difference. And, when combined, people can make a big change. They can make life better, richer, and fuller for all. They should never be deterred from helping or giving of themselves; it only makes them better. Mother Teresa once said, "I alone cannot change the world, but I can cast a stone across the waters to create many ripples." The groups in the following pages create rippling effects for good throughout the community and the world. Perhaps, readers will be inspired to cast their own stones.

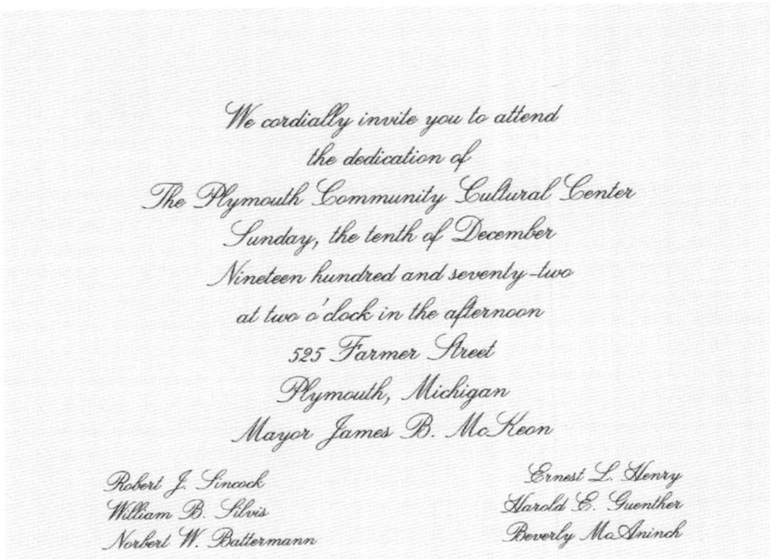

We cordially invite you to attend
the dedication of
The Plymouth Community Cultural Center
Sunday, the tenth of December
Nineteen hundred and seventy-two
at two o'clock in the afternoon
525 Farmer Street
Plymouth, Michigan
Mayor James B. McKeon

Robert J. Sincock
William B. Silvis
Norbert W. Battermann

Ernest L. Henry
Harold E. Guenther
Beverly McAninch

The Plymouth Cultural Center.
The Plymouth Cultural Center was dedicated on December 10, 1972. The center provides meeting room space and an Olympic-sized ice rink, and hosts numerous classes, craft shows, and year-round recreational opportunities. The multipurpose structure was designed by the Nordstrom Samson Architectural Firm and built by the Andrews Construction Company. In the end, the center cost approximately $1.5 million to build. In 1971, the City of Plymouth worked closely with the school district and Mel Blunk, assistant superintendent of business and finance, regarding the leasing agreement between the city and the school district. The cultural center sits on school property, behind Central Middle School. The final agreement was that the land would be leased to the city for 99 years at a cost of $1 per year. (Invitation courtesy of Plymouth Historical Museum.)

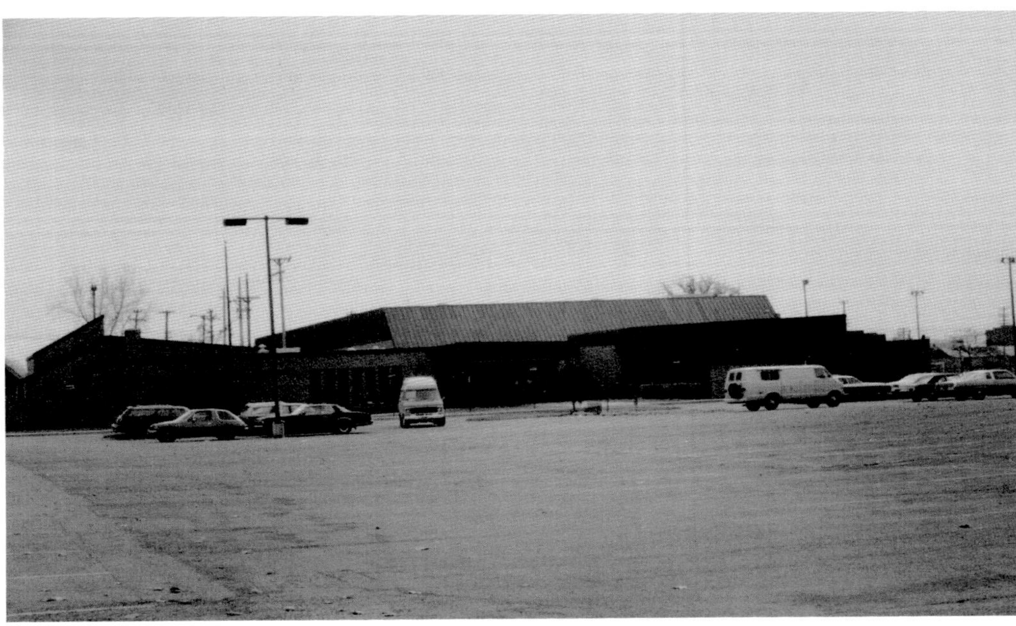

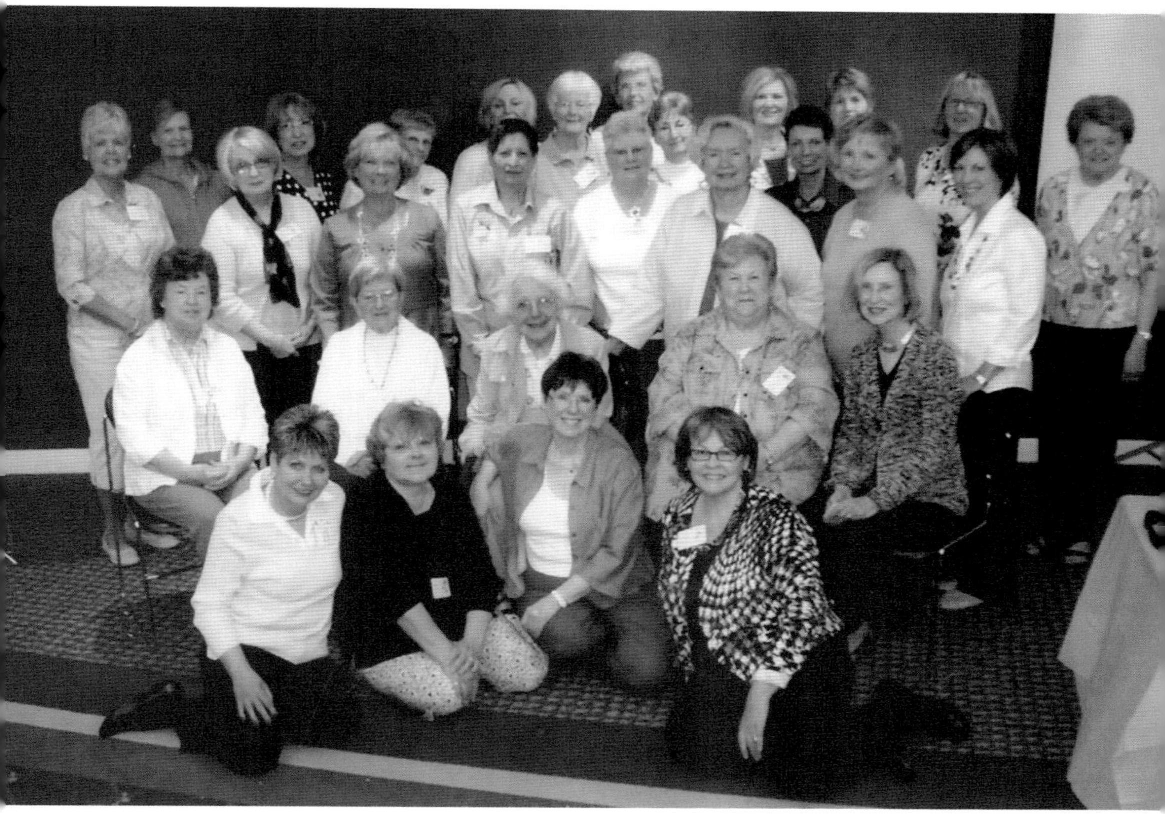

The Women's National Farm and Garden Association.
The Plymouth branch of the Women's National Farm and Garden Association is a busy group of ladies. They have the job of adding color and inspiration to the landscape after long Michigan winters. Throughout Plymouth, one will see this group's work in parks and in raised beds along Main Street. Members also teamed up with the Trailwood Garden Club and the Canton Garden Club to add flowers to the Veterans Memorial Park in front of Central Middle School. Founded in May 1936, the Plymouth Association celebrated its 75th anniversary in May 2011. (Photograph courtesy of Women's Farm and Garden Association–Plymouth.)

Cultural Center, 1972. (OPPOSITE PAGE)
Sam Hudson, author, historian, and a columnist for the *Plymouth Observer and Eccentric,* wrote a column in March 1979 about a man named Russell A. Roe. A local businessman and a huge hockey lover, Roe organized an ice club in the winter of 1928. During their second season, the men built an outdoor ice arena where the cultural center now stands. (Photograph courtesy of Plymouth Historical Museum.)

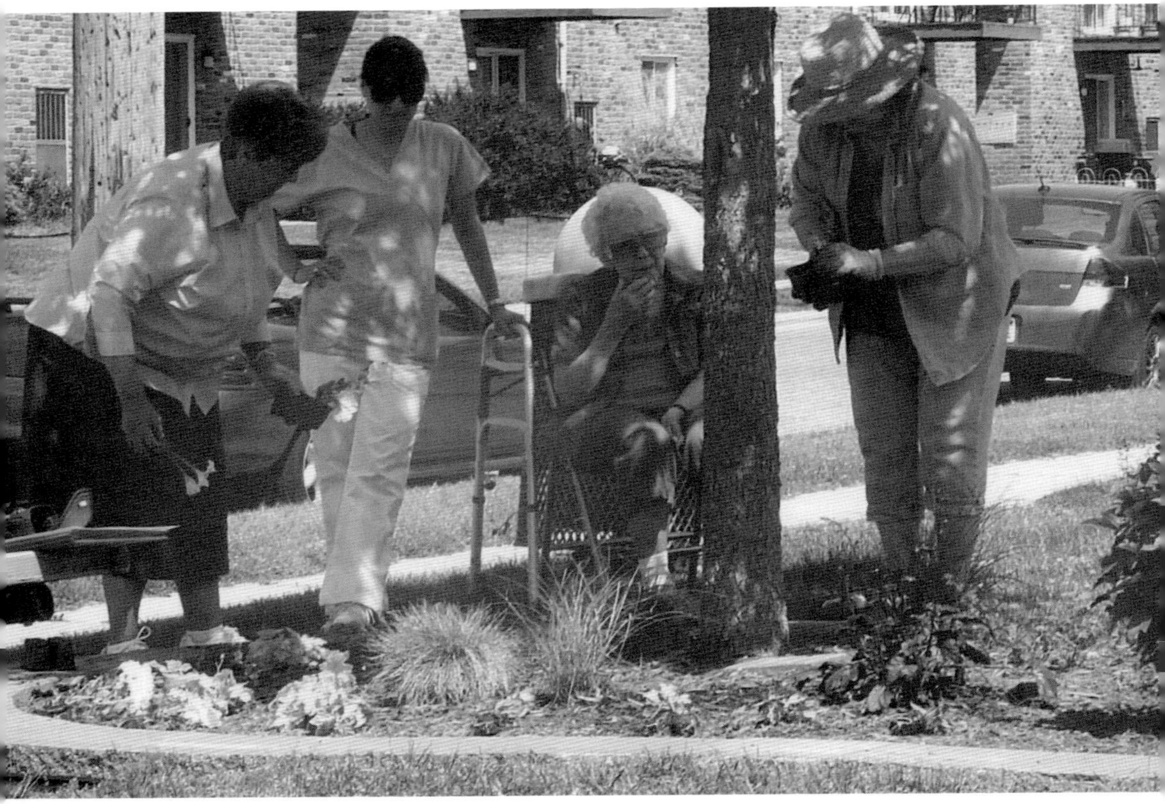

Plymouth Branch of the National Farm and Garden Association at Work.
The Women's National Farm and Garden Association, founded in 1914, seeks to promote agricultural and horticultural awareness and understanding among women in all countries. The Plymouth Garden Association also annually awards three scholarships to deserving students from the Plymouth-Canton high schools. At the DTE Gardens, the group, along with other organizations, take care of the large vegetable gardens that are later harvested and donated to Gleaner's Food Bank. (Photograph courtesy of Women's Farm and Garden Association–Plymouth.)

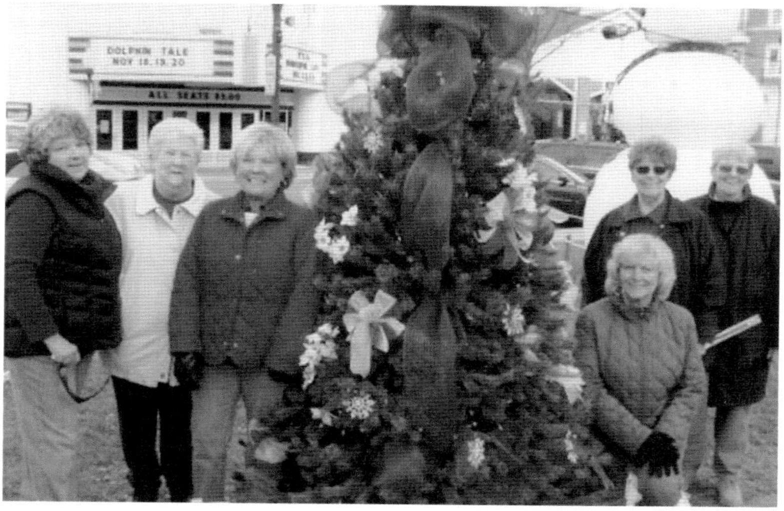

Decorating a Christmas Tree in Kellogg Park, 2011.
Every year, the chamber of commerce places trees in Kellogg Park, and families, businesses, schools, and organizations can decorate their chosen trees with a theme. The Women's National Farm and Garden Association, busy throughout the year, decorates a tree representing the group. This has become a lovely tradition in Plymouth, and many look forward to it every year. Decked out from tinsel to dog bones, feathers to cookies, the trees are original and unique. (Photograph courtesy of Women's Farm and Garden Association–Plymouth.)

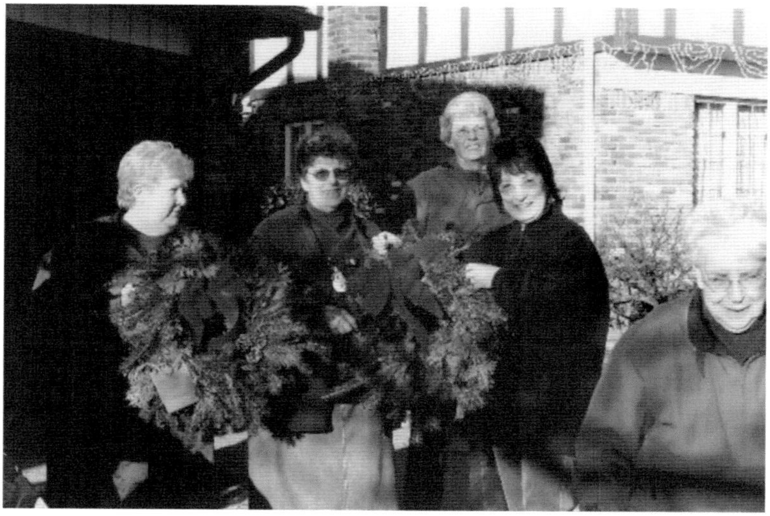

Christmas 2011 Fundraiser.
During the Christmas season, the Plymouth Farm and Garden Association sells wreaths, roping, and swags. The sale of greens is one source of funds the group raises so that it can continue supporting its projects and help students with scholarships. The city is all lit up, trees are decked out in Kellogg Park, local businesses are open late for shopping, and holiday music is playing throughout the city. It is much more relaxed than a mall and is a lovely way to spend some time getting ready for the season. (Photograph courtesy of Plymouth Farm and Garden Association.)

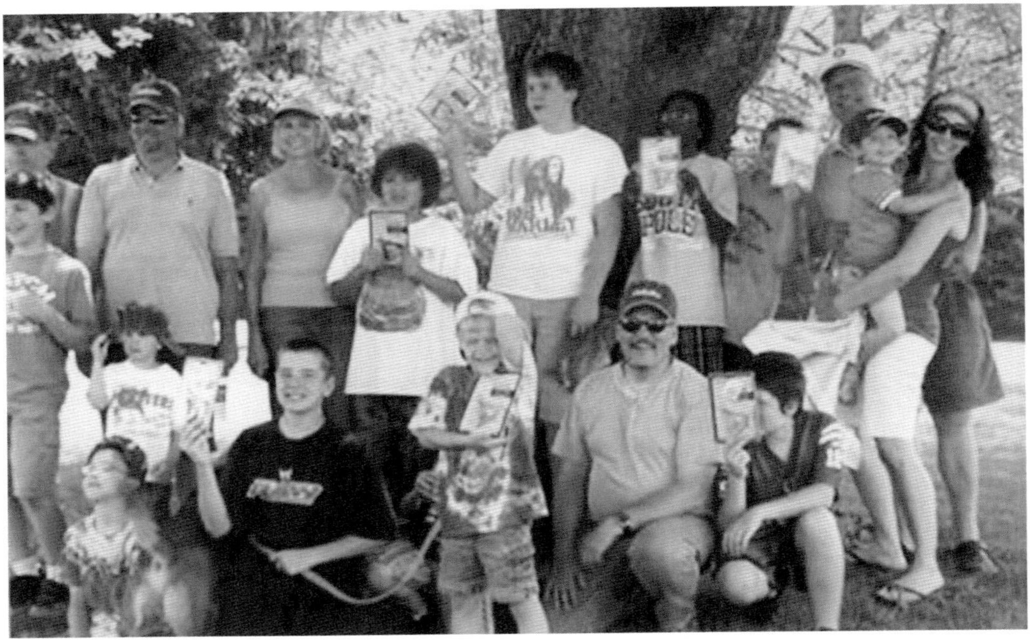

Kiwanis Club of Colonial Plymouth.
The Kiwanis Organization was founded in Detroit in 1915. The Kiwanis Club of Colonial Plymouth started in 1967 and is dedicated to helping children in the area and abroad, actively supporting a number of community services. The group, made up of about 100 members, helps support the international organization called Kids Against Hunger. Receiving assistance in funding, labor, and equipment, the group sends nutritious meals to children around the globe and locally, making a huge impact on many lives. Pictured here is the group's annual fishing derby in the summer of 2011. Held for area children, the day is full of fun, sun, and wonder. (Photograph courtesy of Kiwanis Colonial Club of Plymouth.)

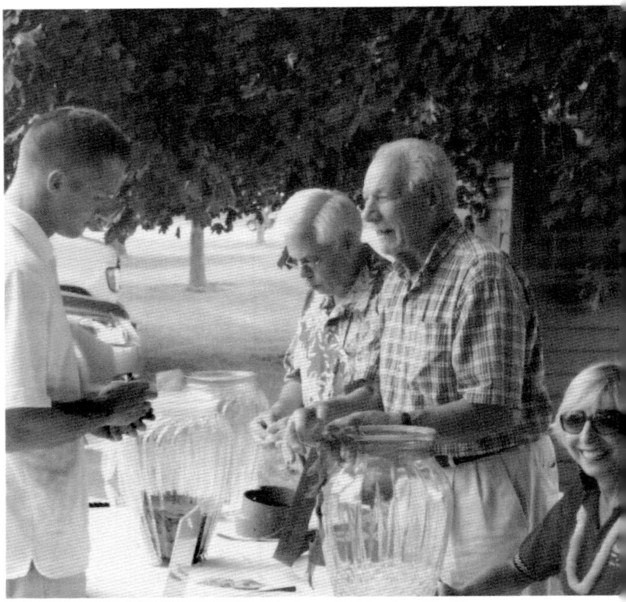

Annual Golf Outing Fundraiser, Summer 2011.
Locally, the Kiwanis Club's activities and projects include the Good Morning USA Parade, held annually on July 4th; the Pancake Breakfast during Fall Festival; a fishing derby for local kids; and bell-ringing during the Christmas season to support the Salvation Army. The club also donates magazines and used cell phones to the Veterans Administration. It also helps with seniors at the nearby Tonquish Creek Manor, and brightens children's holidays at Mott's Children's Hospital in Ann Arbor, Michigan. Pictured at the annual golf outing are, from left to right, unidentified, Jim Eldridge, Jim Jabara, and Shirley Jallad. (Photograph courtesy of Kiwanis Colonial Club of Plymouth.)

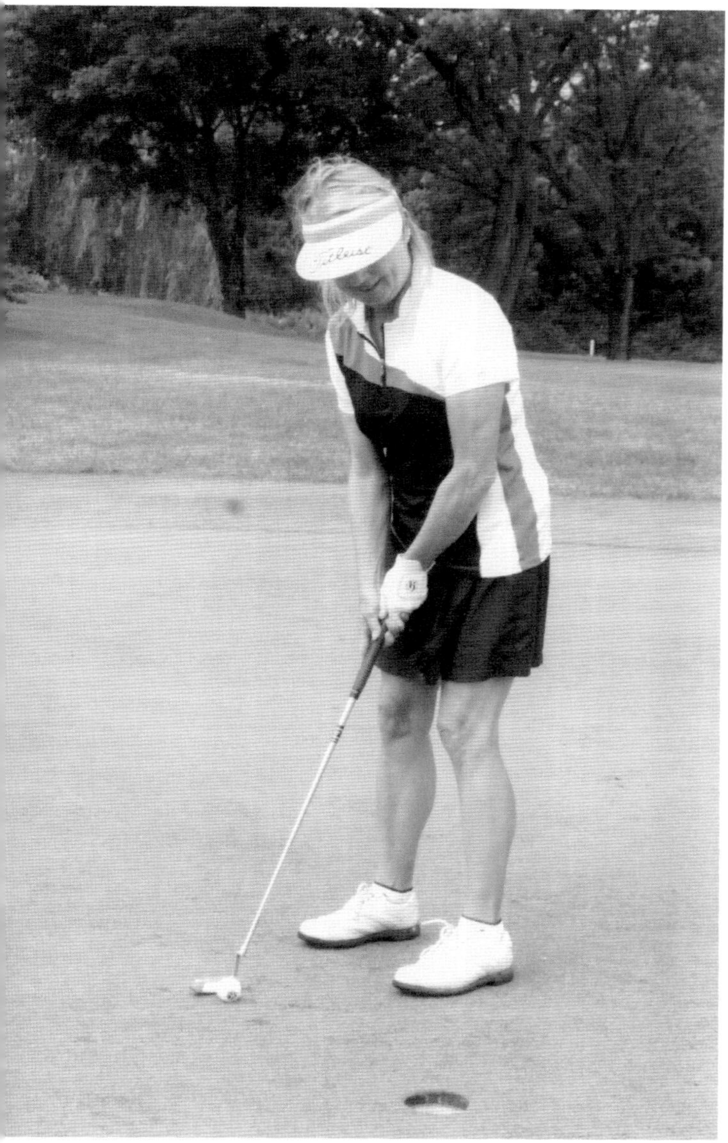

Kiwanis Colonial Club of Plymouth Annual Fundraiser, Summer 2011. The Kiwanis Club of Colonial Plymouth also sponsors the Kiwanis Key Club, for high school students. It currently has over 150 members from the Plymouth-Canton high schools, and the students help out with any number of community service projects. Students learn about the importance of volunteering, camaraderie, teamwork, and leadership skills. Membership in the Plymouth Kiwanis Key Club is the highest in the state. Here, Kiwanis Colonial Club of Plymouth supporter Gail Ryan takes a swing at the annual fundraiser in the summer of 2011. (Photograph courtesy of Kiwanis Colonial Club of Plymouth.)

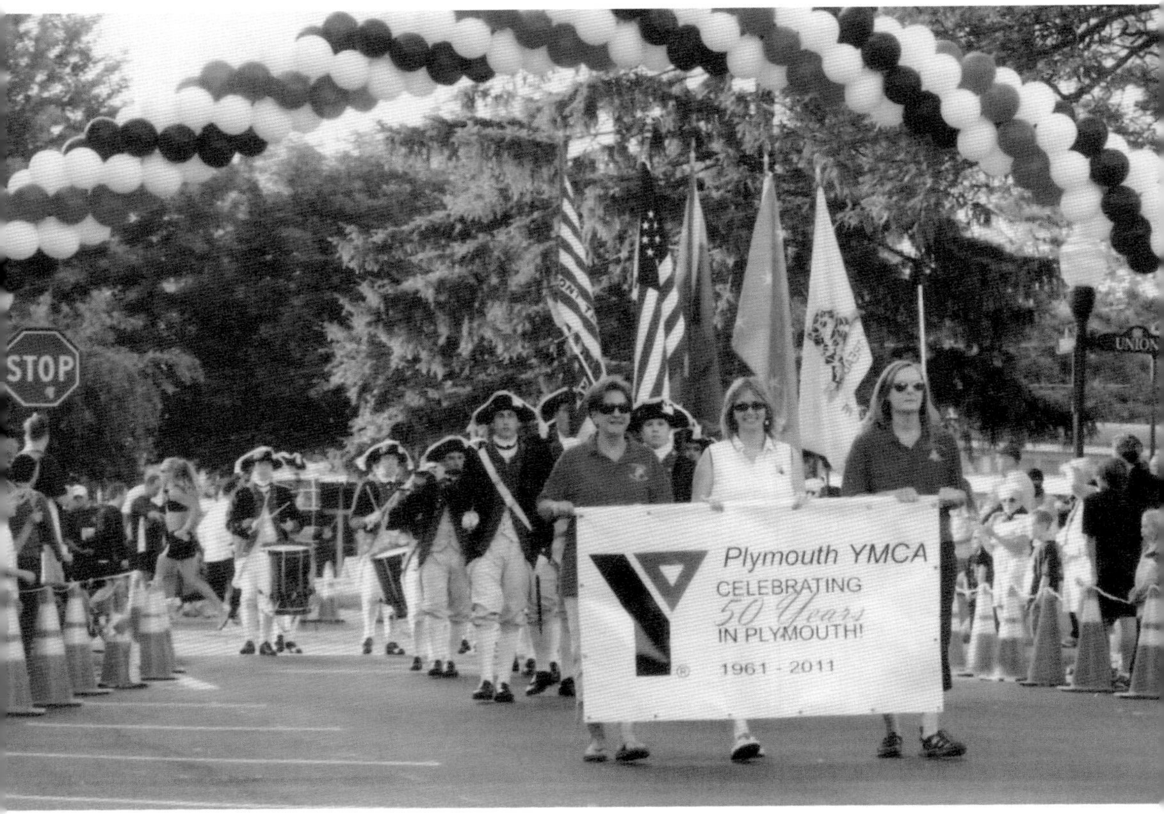

The Plymouth YMCA Celebrates 50 Years.
The Plymouth YMCA has been in the community since May 1961. A group of citizens expressed interest in securing a formal charter and established goals and objectives that would make up the Plymouth YMCA. The YMCA, a nonprofit group, is committed to building strong communities by offering a number of services and programs to families. The YMCA can be found in approximately 10,000 cities across the nation and has been in operation for over 160 years. In the fall of 1961, the Plymouth Community Young Men's Christian Association was incorporated. John Hoben was the director. Here, the Plymouth YMCA celebrates 50 years serving the community at the Plymouth Fourth of July Parade in 2011. (Photograph courtesy of Plymouth YMCA.)

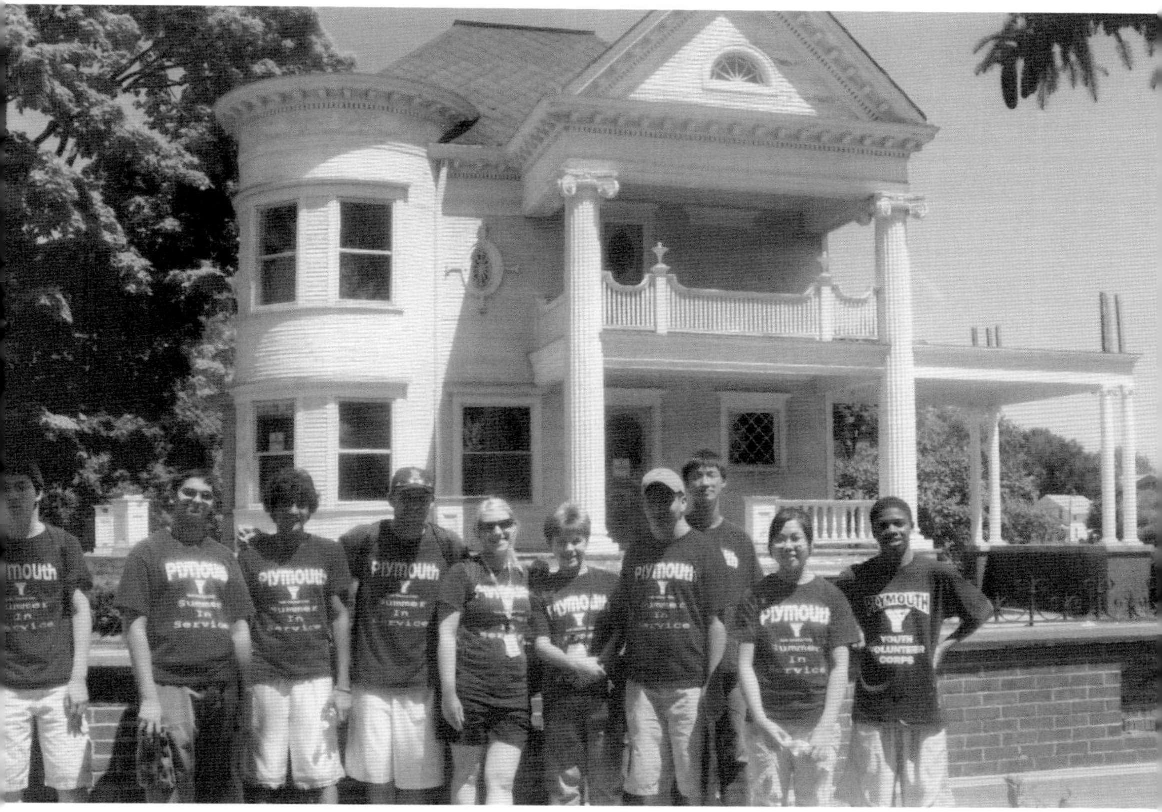

Plymouth YMCA Youth Volunteer Corps in Front of Wilcox House, Summer 2012.
In 1962, YMCA programs started in Plymouth with the initiation of Y-Indian Guides for fathers and sons. From 1963 to 1971, programs were offered through the schools as the Y worked hard to secure funding and a building for their growing programs. During much of the 1970s, the YMCA offered a wide range of programming for children and senior citizens in the community. In 1978, Judge Dunbar Davis generously donated his house and property, located at 185 South Harvey Street, to the Plymouth YMCA. The property was later sold, and the YMCA then purchased its current location at 248 Union Street in 1984. (Photograph courtesy of Plymouth YMCA.)

Plymouth YMCA Annual Father's Day Run, June 2010. In October 1979, the Y's name was formally changed to the Plymouth Community YMCA. From 1980 to 1989, the YMCA in Plymouth experienced a lot of growth in terms of programming. Fundraisers, such as tennis tournaments, golf leagues, and an annual fun run, were added to help grow the YMCA. The first annual Fun Run had 500 runners and was held in September 1980. The annual run was moved from September to Father's Day in June 1985 and now has upwards of 1,500 runners. One of the YMCA's most successful events, the Father's Day Run brings many families to the city of Plymouth. (Photograph courtesy of Plymouth YMCA.)

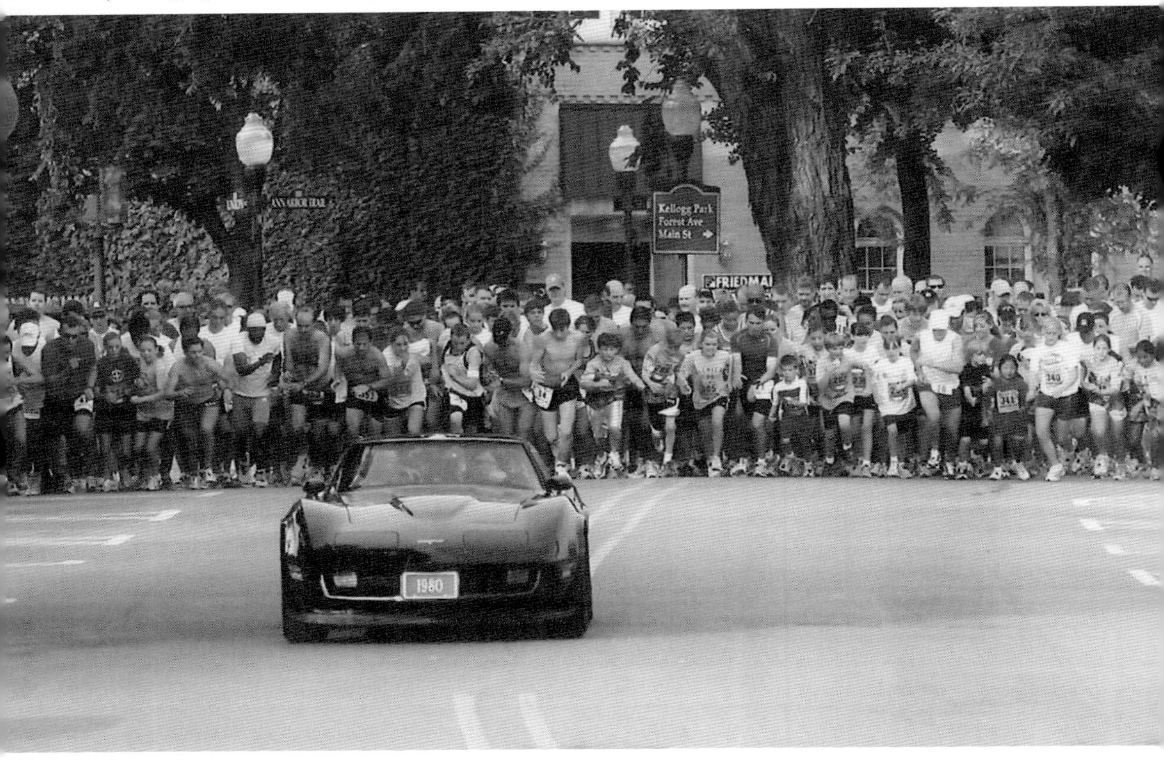

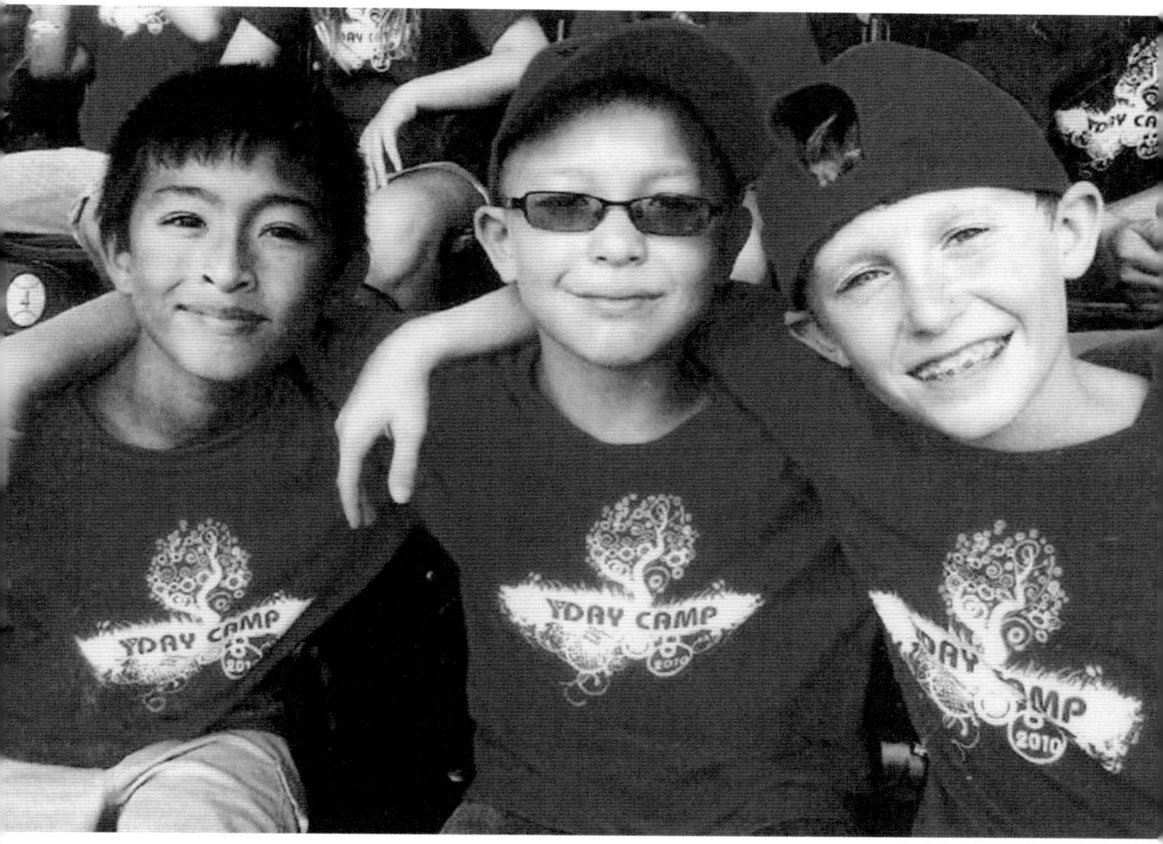

Plymouth YMCA Youth Day Camp Kids, Summer 2010. Each decade, it seems the Plymouth YMCA steadily grows, increasing its programming and offering assistance within the community in a number of ways. Between 2000 and 2005, the Plymouth YMCA launched a Youth Volunteer Corps Program with a grant from the Wilcox Foundation. Over 500 students registered and completed 1,200 hours of community service. In 2005, the Plymouth YMCA partnered with the Plymouth Salvation Army, and a Tiny Tots preschool program was formed. The Plymouth Y also launched a Strong Kids Campaign and reached a goal of increasing awareness for healthy children, raising $58,000 in the process. The Plymouth Community YMCA has a strong commitment to community and family and has added much to the community through its years. (Photograph courtesy of Plymouth YMCA.)

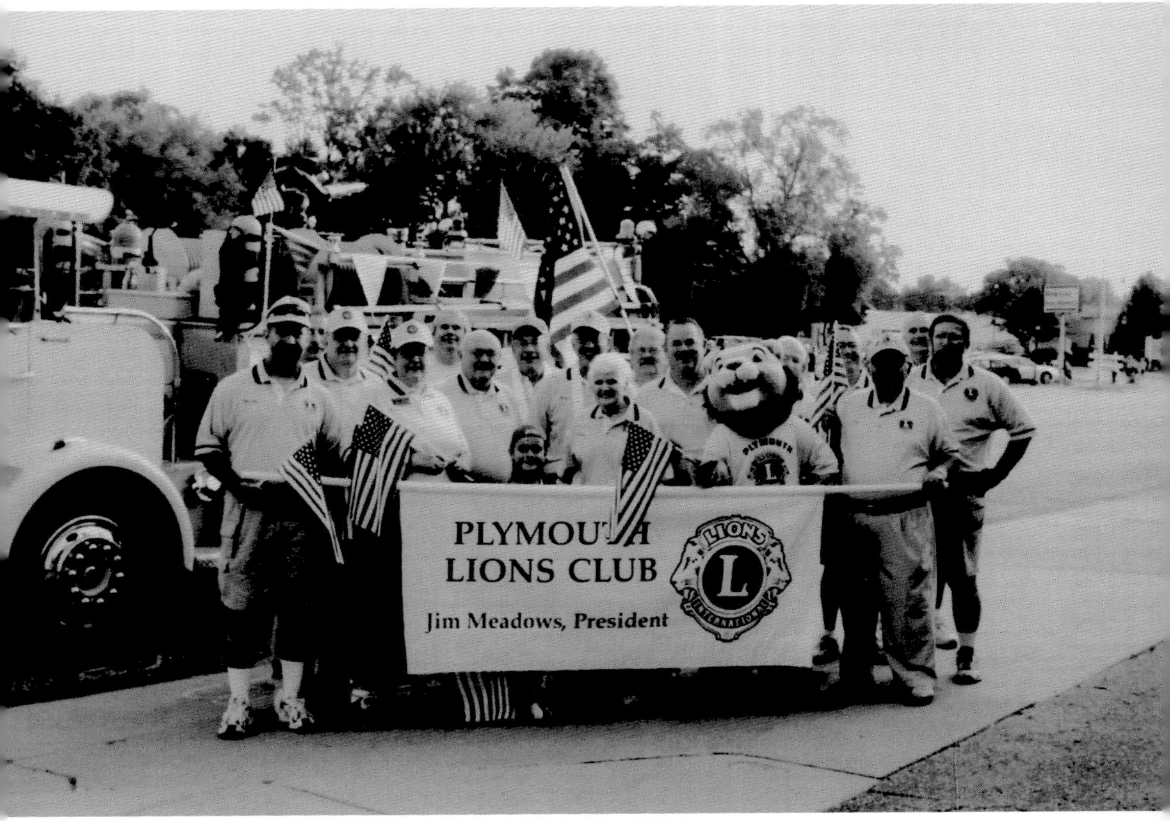

The Plymouth Lions Club.
The Lions Club of Plymouth started in 1948 and is part of an international network of over a million men and women dedicated to meeting the needs that challenge many communities around the world. The club, which organized in 1917, has helped to provide millions of opportunities for people to give back to their communities. One of its annual projects is helping in the prevention of blindness and assisting the blind, inspired in 1925, at an International Lions Club convention, where Helen Keller was the guest speaker. Keller, born blind, deaf, and mute, had been taught by her teacher, Anne Sullivan. Inspired by Keller, the Lions took on the challenge of helping the blind, and to this day sponsor many programs for the blind. Here, the Plymouth Lions Club participates in the annual Fourth of July parade in downtown Plymouth in the summer of 2005. (Photograph courtesy of Plymouth Lions Club.)

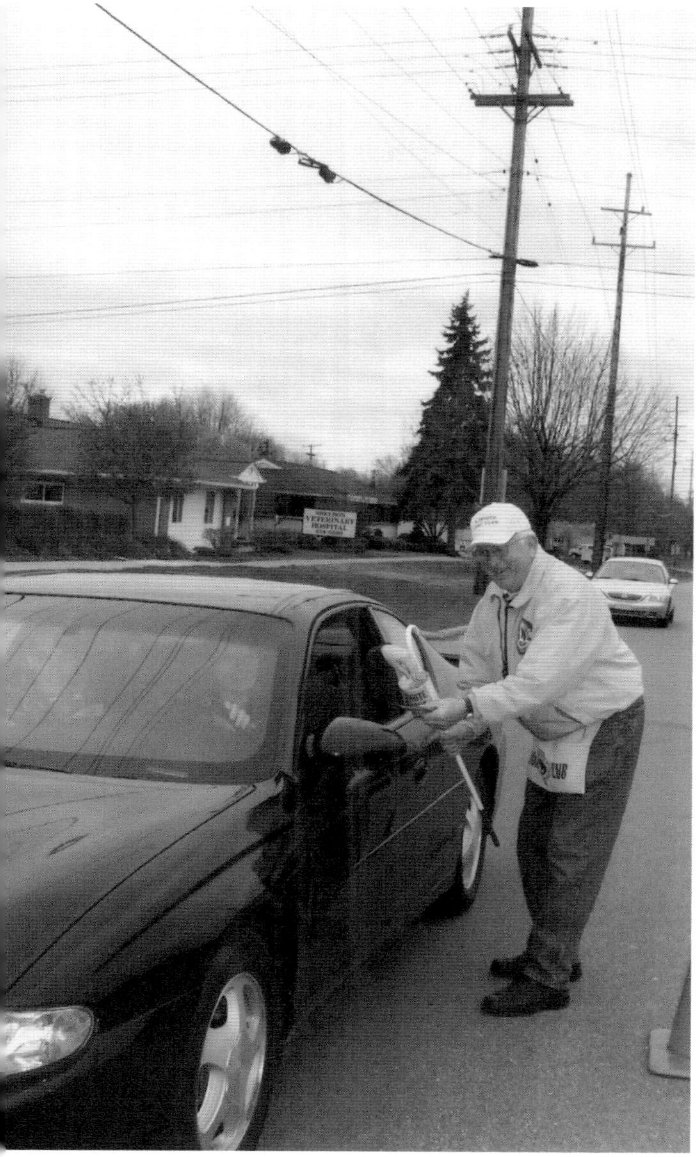

Raising Awareness. The Plymouth Lions Club is consciously increasing its efforts to impact the community with services and projects. The 80-member group has recommitted to improving the quality of life for those in the community—offering assistance for the blind; making eye examinations and glasses available to children in need; donating wheelchairs, canes, and Braille watches; and helping to make available books printed in large type for patrons at the Plymouth District Library. The club also supports the Penrickton Center for Blind Children in Taylor, Michigan, and helps in the funding of eye surgeries and treatments for those in need. The Lions Club of Plymouth also works with Paws for a Cause, which partners and trains dogs to assist people with specific disabilities. Around town, one will see collection bins for used eyeglasses, hearing aids, and cell phones, all of which help the group reach out to those in need. In this 2007 photograph, Plymouth Lions Club member John Roose receives a donation for the Annual White Cane Drive from a Plymouth resident. (Photograph courtesy of Plymouth Lions Club.)

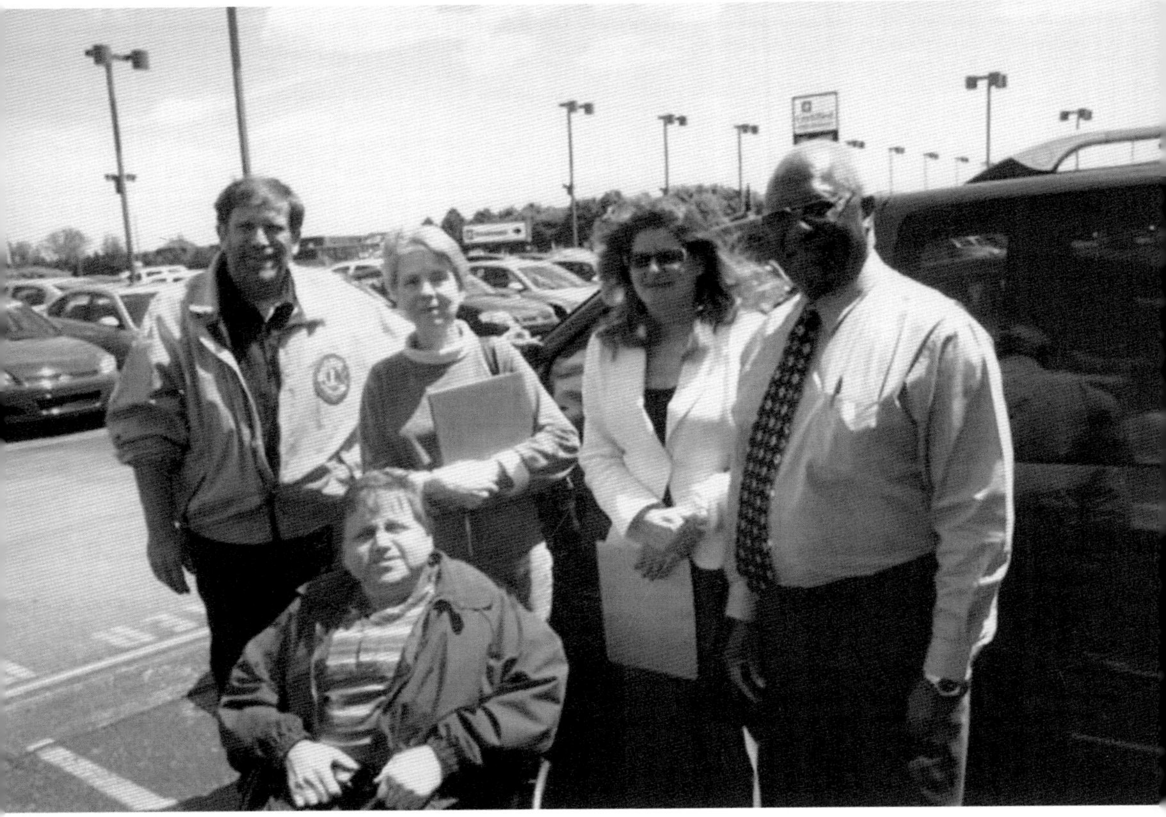

Community Events and Giving.
The Lions Club has also recently put together a support group for those with diabetes that meets at the Plymouth District Library. The Lions Club of Plymouth, never one to shy away from a challenge, has taken on the responsibility of organizing and facilitating the Plymouth Memorial Day Parade and assisting with the Plymouth Township Fireworks and Annual Picnic. The Plymouth Lions Club also helps out with the biannual Kelly Miller Circus that comes to town, assisting with parking and setting up of the circus venue, and the Annual Easter Egg Hunt, held at the Township Park. The Plymouth Lions Club also helped purchase a van equipped with a wheelchair lift for a nearby family in 2008. Here, Lions member Gary Kerstens (at left, in a Lions jacket) presents the vehicle to the family. (Photograph courtesy of Plymouth Lions Club.)

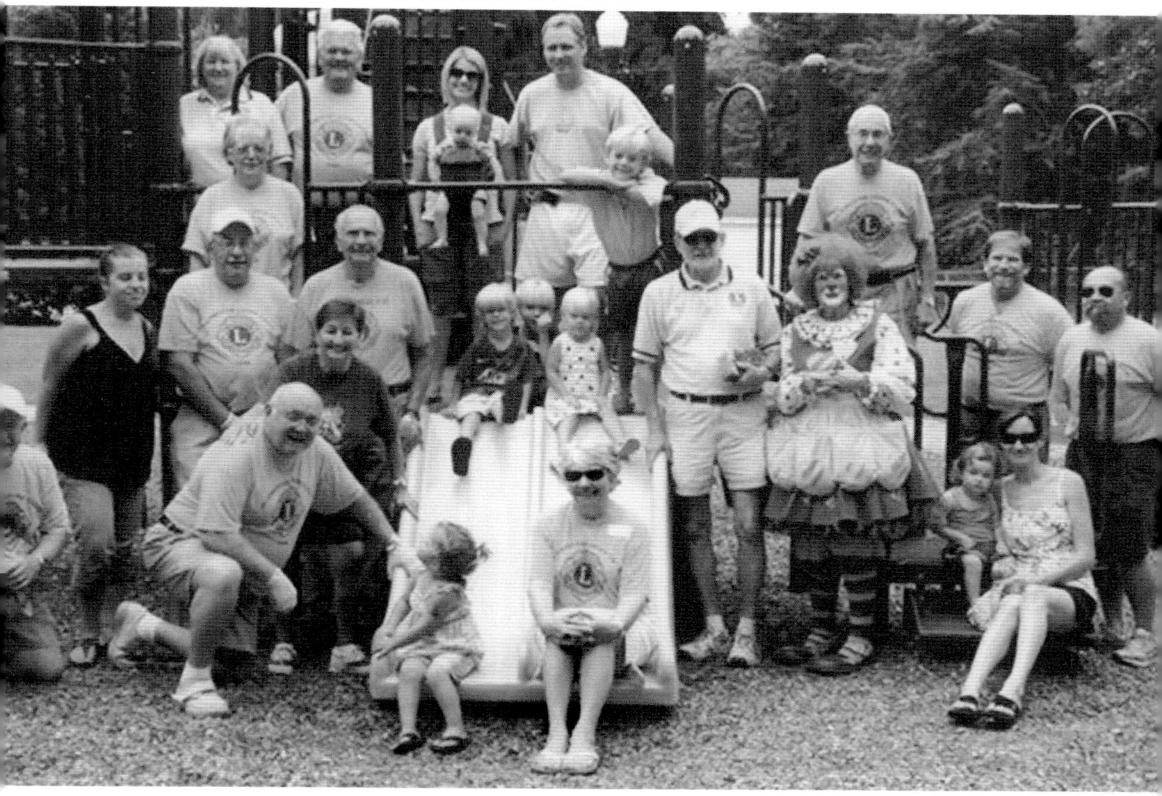

Picnic at Lions Park.

The Lions Club also assisted a local food pantry at Trinity Presbyterian Church in Plymouth, with the purchase of a refrigerator freezer. This has added tremendously to what the church can offer to families in need of assistance. The Lions Club of Plymouth offers a scholarship to one student each year that is given to the recipient for all fours years of college. A very busy organization, the Plymouth Lions Club can be proud as it continually assists in any way it can and offers many citizens the opportunity to give back and help out. Here, the Plymouth Lions Club holds a picnic for residents at Lions Park. (Photograph courtesy of Plymouth Lions Club.)

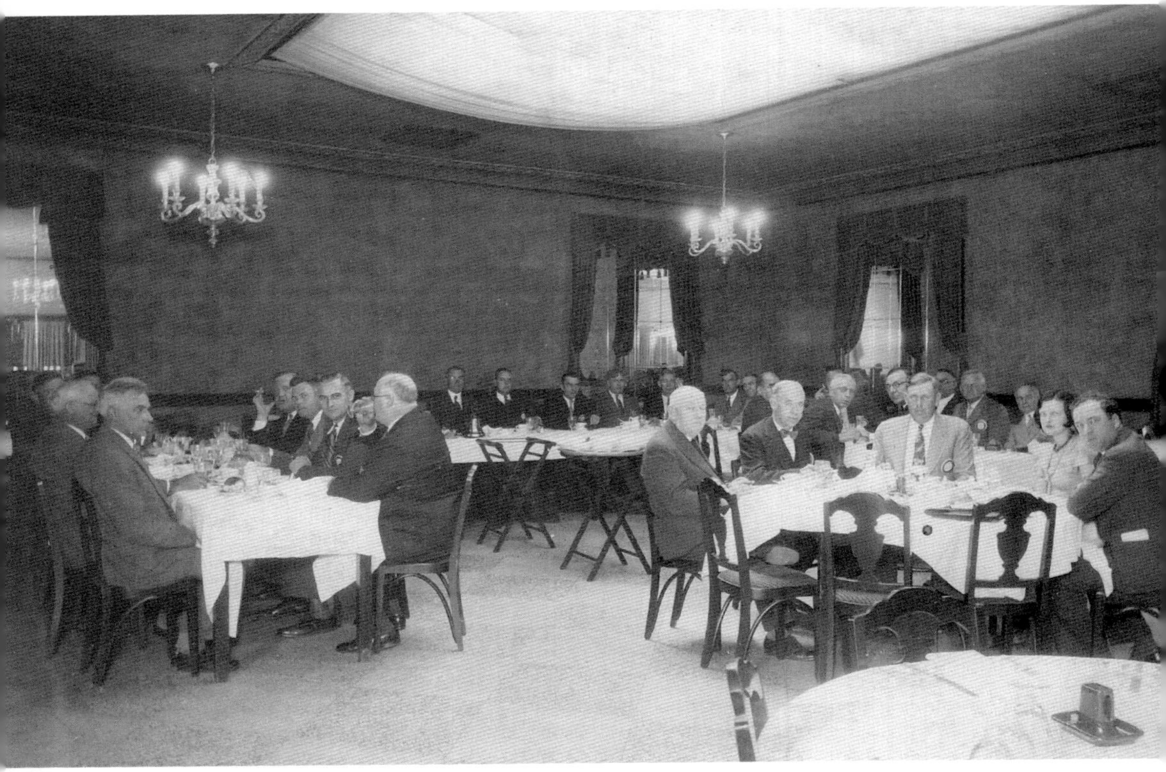

Plymouth Rotary Friday Noon Club.
The Plymouth Rotary Friday Noon Club has a long, rich history in the community. Organized in March 1924, the club was sponsored by the Wayne Rotary Club, which had been established five years earlier. The group, originally known as the Businessmen's Club, quickly committed itself to the community and undertook several service projects. Impressed by the club members' efforts, a Rotarian who was invited to speak at the club suggested they become Rotarians. The Wayne Rotary Club was formed, and it, in turn, sponsored the Plymouth Rotary. For 88 years, the Plymouth Rotary has been very active and instrumental in the community's growth and success. In this photograph, members of the Rotary Club are enjoying lunch at the Mayflower Hotel in the 1930s. (Photograph courtesy of Plymouth Historical Museum.)

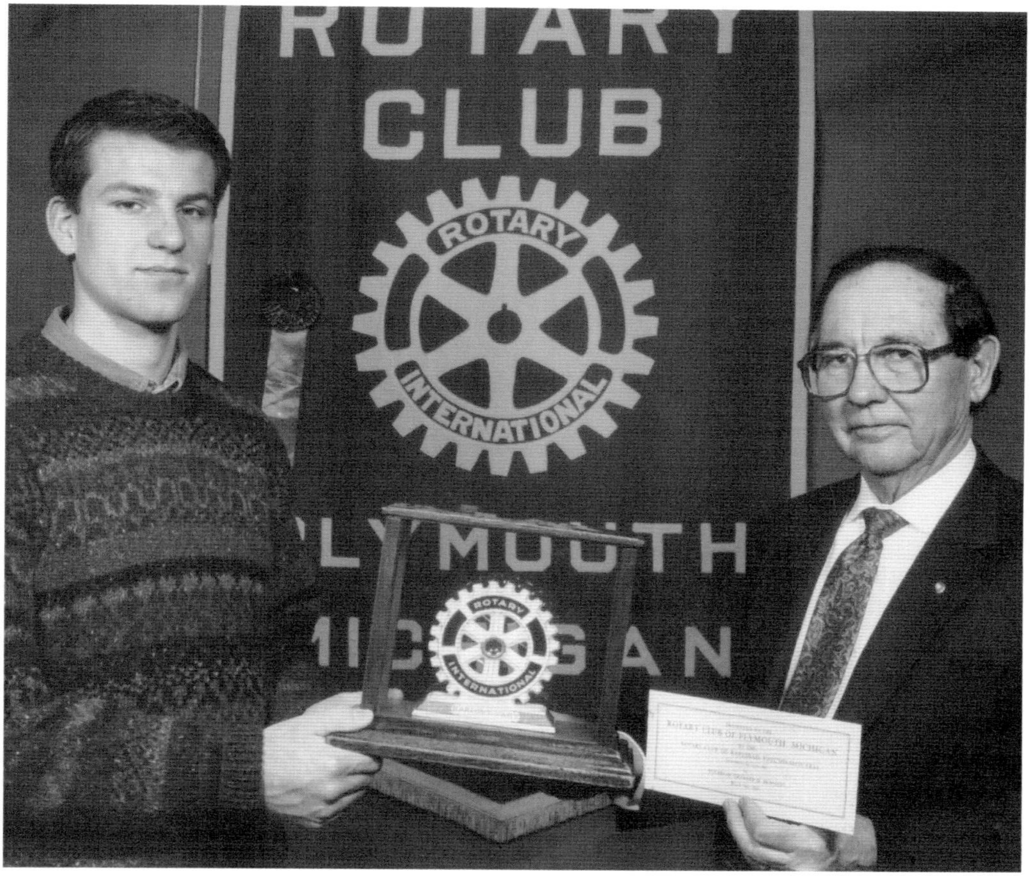

Rotary Wheel, 1980s.
Many of the people written about in these pages have been Rotary members—people such as Ralph Lorenz, George Smith, Harold Guenther, Charles Bennett, and Sidney Davis Strong. Strong received a Silver Beaver Award for his dedication to the Boy Scouts organization and had the Rotary Club sponsor Boy Scout troops so that they could travel, camp, and learn more about Scouting. Strong's interest in youth activities has helped the Rotary Club develop other programming that helps young people, including programs such as the Rotary Youth Exchange Program, and scholarships and loans for those attending college or specialized training. Rotary member E.J. McClendon (right) and exchange student Peter Jandas from Czechoslovakia are pictured with the Rotary Wheel in the 1980s. (Photograph courtesy of Plymouth Historical Museum.)

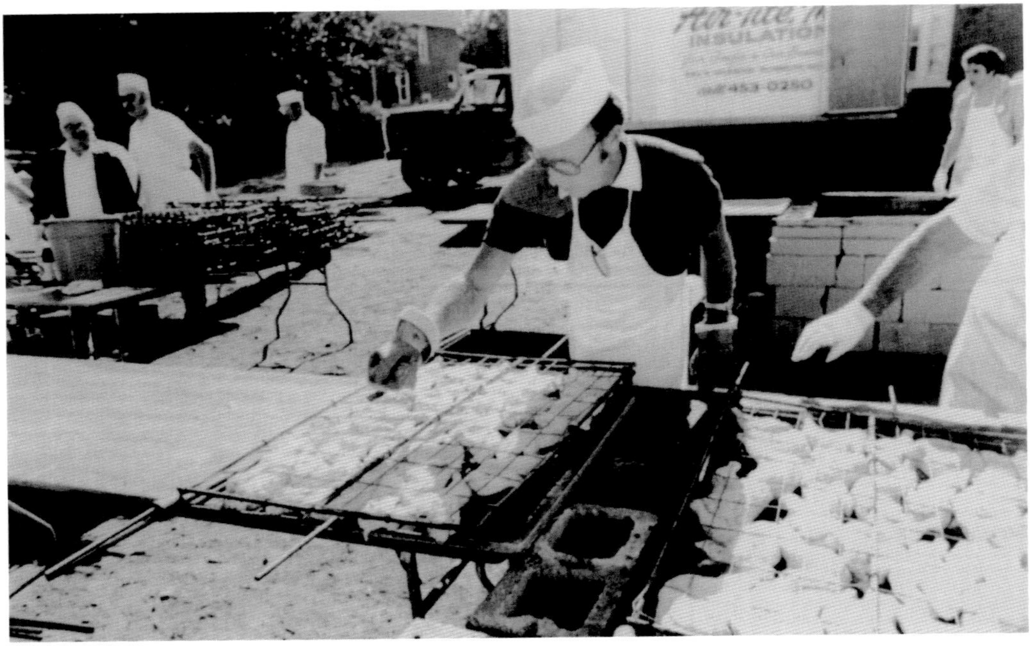

Fall Festival.

It was in the late 1950s when a chicken barbeque dinner/picnic was held for Rotary members. By 1960, that picnic turned into what is now the popular Fall Festival. Held annually on the weekend after Labor Day, the Fall Festival and Chicken Barbeque dinner is the Rotary's largest fundraiser. But, most of all, the annual event gives Rotarians an opportunity to pull together as a team and show the community what being a Rotary member is all about. In 1987, women were allowed to become Rotary members and today make up a large part of the group. In 1977, the Plymouth Rotary sponsored the Canton Rotary, and in 1997, sponsored the Plymouth AM Rotary Club. Both clubs, still strong today, are doing very well and participate in the community in a number of ways. In this photograph, Rotary members are busy preparing chicken dinners at the Fall Festival in the 1970s. (Photograph courtesy of Plymouth Historical Museum.)

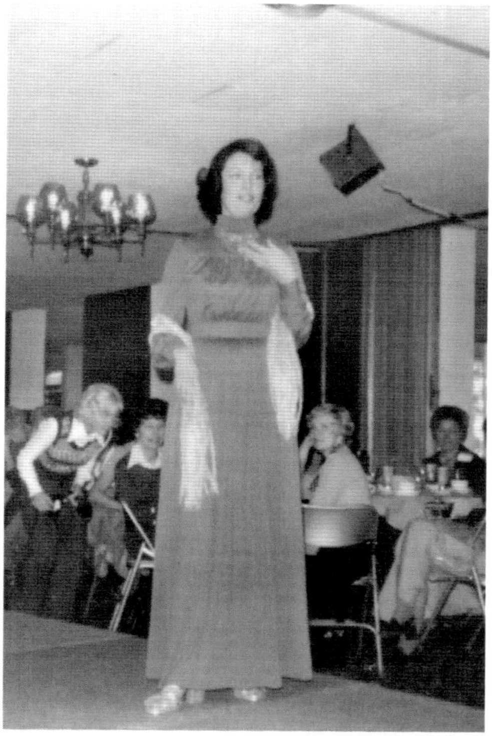

Plymouth Newcomers & Neighbors Club Fashion Show, 1974.
The Plymouth Newcomers & Neighbors Club is a nonprofit social club that started in 1959 and has provided social and service opportunities for those living in Plymouth and its surrounding communities. A fun and diverse group, it offers a wide variety of interests for those new to the area. For those who have lived in Plymouth for a number of years, this group helps to facilitate friendships and networking. The Plymouth Newcomers & Neighbors Club meets regularly from September through May and has a number of interest groups, such as a book club, men's poker, and euchre games. (Photograph courtesy of Plymouth Newcomers & Neighbors Club.)

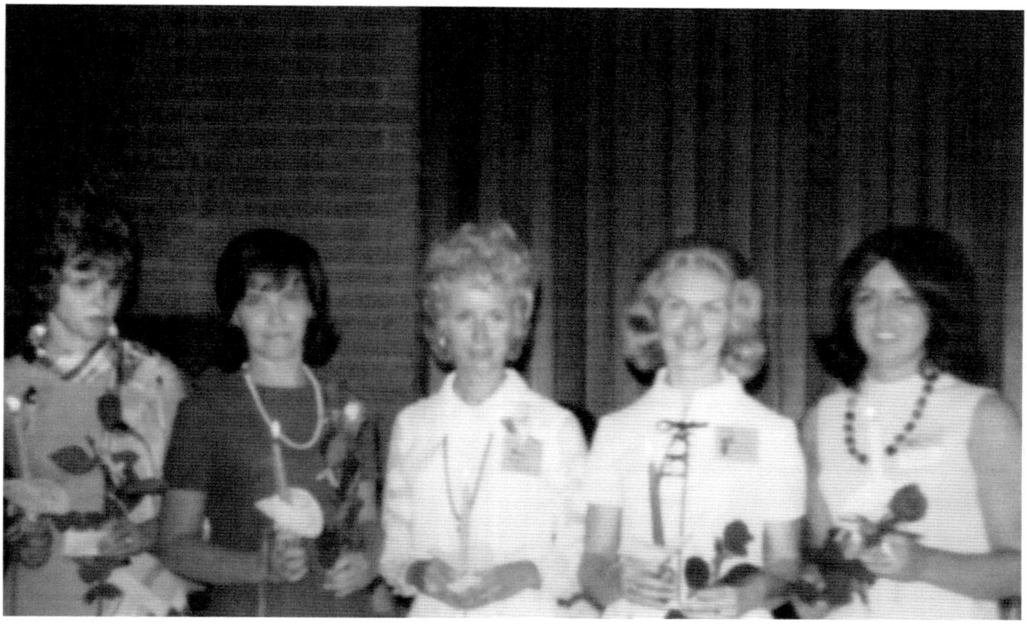

Newly Appointed Officers.
Pictured here are the newly appointed officers of the Plymouth Newcomers & Neighbors Club in 1971. They are, from left to right, Barbara Lynch, Ann Canafax, Elinor Chelian, Jeanne Schwartz, and Vivian Mockett. (Photograph courtesy of Plymouth Newcomers & Neighbors Club.)

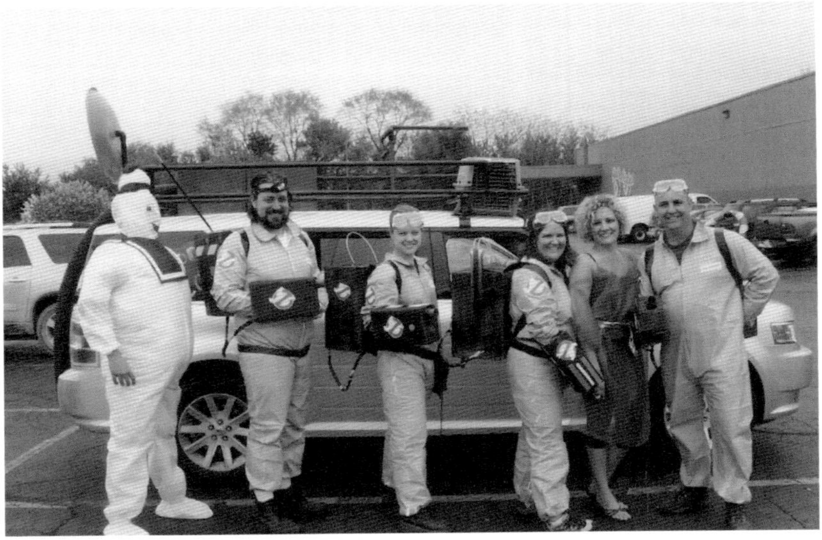

Spring Road Rally 2011, Ghostbusters Team.
Throughout its 50-plus-year history, the Plymouth Newcomers & Neighbors Club, like the other clubs discussed in these pages, has provided assistance to a number of service organizations. Through its annual events—like the Spring Road Rally, Fall Hayride, and Cookies and Cocoa with Santa—the group raises funds, which then benefit local residents and causes. Welcoming people into the community and offering opportunities for residents to be actively involved in the place they call home is what this group has been about from the beginning. Members of the Spring Road Rally's 2011 Ghostbusters team are, from left to right, Paul Branigen, Colin Baker, Sarah Larson, Michele Hill, Tiffany Baker, and Bob Hill. (Photograph courtesy of Plymouth Newcomers & Neighbors Club.)

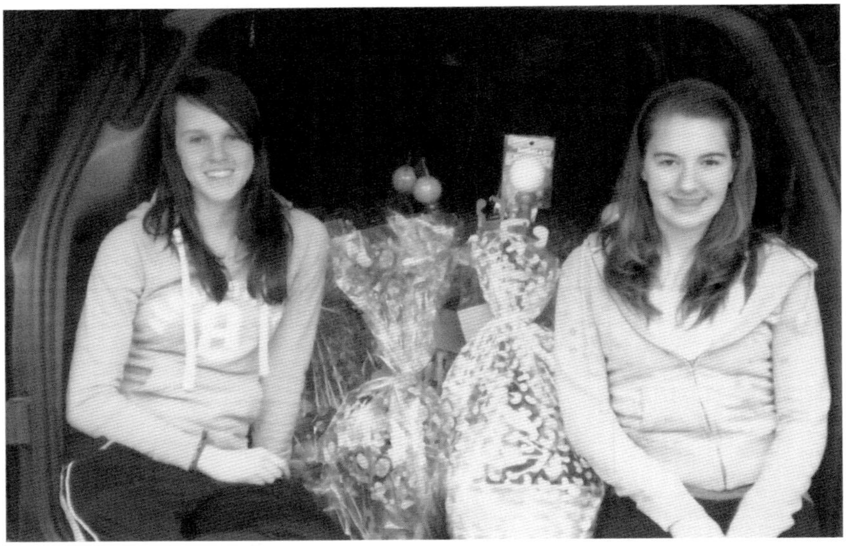

First Step Project, April 2009.
The Plymouth Newcomers & Neighbors Club's First Step Project offers teens from the area a chance to help out and participate in a good cause. Pictured at the 2009 event are Katie Hill (left) and Kayla Ganster. (Photograph courtesy of Plymouth Newcomers & Neighbors Club.)

The Plymouth Historical Society and Museum

The Plymouth Historical Museum, located in downtown Plymouth, is such a treasure that it is hard to know where to start. The 26,000-square-foot building houses items from many of Plymouth's finest moments and its long, rich history. The five-star-quality exhibits include a permanent time line of Plymouth's history, starting with the Indians and early settlers, then highlighting industries, businesses, and life in the early 20th century.

The museum's main level offers a large re-creation of a Main Street and a re-creation of a 19th-century home. The exhibits change periodically throughout the year, offering a look into different time periods of local lives and history. The Abraham Lincoln Exhibit, in a room just off of the Main Street area, houses the largest Lincoln collection in the state of Michigan. All of the exhibits are beautifully displayed and maintained. The museum is staffed by over 100 volunteers. People who have a sincere appreciation for community, service, and history make the museum's continuing operation possible. The museum also includes a gift shop, an archives and research library, and meeting rooms that are available for rent.

The museum offers several additional functions throughout the year, including teas, cemetery walks, and nights at the museum. It is also a great field trip for schools, tying curriculum in with local and state history.

The Plymouth Historical Museum is a special place, and the people who established the historical society should be commended for having such foresight. Their care and provision of history for future generations allow us to know how those before us lived and loved. Such knowledge is crucial as we move forward—as individuals, a community, and a nation.

Much of the information and material used for this book came from the Plymouth Historical Museum. The author gratefully acknowledges the work of all prior historians and archivists, particularly Sam Hudson, who recorded and logged much of Plymouth's history during his life. The author also wishes to thank all of the community members from the schools and clubs who assisted in information and photographs. Their help, kindness, time, and support was greatly appreciated and will always be fondly remembered.

The Plymouth Historical Museum is a great place to learn and spend an afternoon with family and friends. When in town, stop in and pay a visit. The hours are Wednesday, Friday, Saturday, and Sunday, 1:00 to 4:00 p.m.

INDEX

LEGENDARY LOCALS

AN IMPRINT OF ARCADIA PUBLISHING

Find more books like this at
www.legendarylocals.com

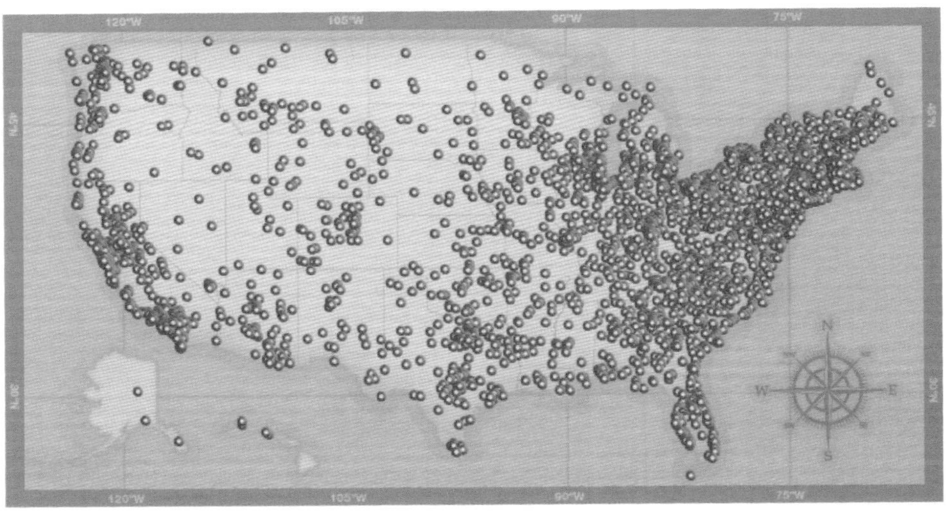

Discover more local and regional history books at
www.arcadiapublishing.com

Consistent with our mission to preserve history on a local level, this book was printed in South Carolina on American-made paper and manufactured entirely in the United States. Products carrying the accredited Forest Stewardship Council (FSC) label are printed on 100 percent FSC-certified paper.

MADE IN THE USA